WORLD WAR I
Day by Day

WORLD WAR I
Day by Day

Ian Westwell

MBI Publishing Company

This edition first published in 2000 by MBI
Publishing Company, 729 Prospect Avenue,
PO Box 1, Osceola, WI 54020-0001 USA

© 2000 Brown Partworks Limited

MBI Publishing Company books are also
available at discounts in bulk quantity for
industrial or sales promotional use. For details
write to Special Sales Manager at Motorbooks
International Wholesalers & Distributors,
729 Prospect Avenue, PO Box 1, Osceola,
WI 54020-0001 USA.

Library of Congress Cataloging-in-Publication
Data Available.

ISBN 0-7603-0938-8

Printed in Singapore

PAGE 1: *French troops man a trench along the summit of Vimy Ridge on the Western Front, December 1915.*

PAGES 2–3: *German stormtroopers drag forward three-inch (77-mm) field guns during Operation Michael, their last offensive on the Western Front, in 1918.*

THESE PAGES: *Heavily-laden Canadian troops advance behind a British tank during the fighting in France, April 1917.*

Editor: Ian Westwell
Art Editor: Duncan Brown
Production: Matt Weyland
Cartographer: William Le Bihan
Indexer: Kay Ollerenshaw

CONTENTS

INTRODUCTION

World War I's origins dated back to the fourth quarter of the nineteenth century when Europe's - and the world's - leading powers embarked on a dangerous game of political brinkmanship. This chiefly involved Austria-Hungary, Britain, France, Germany, and Russia. Their rivalries, motivated by rampant nationalism, centered around economic expansion, the scramble for colonies, and the pursuit of military prestige. Part of this race for power and recognition was Germany's Kaiser Wilhelm II, a militarist who dubbed himself Germany's "First Soldier" but who was also indecisive and easily swayed. He came to power in 1888.

Colonialism, the domination of an area and its people by another state, was fueled by nationalism, the belief than one race is superior to another.

European colonists thought that they were somehow superior, and that they had the right to take the territory of peoples they considered inferior.

VALUABLE COLONIES

To Europe's leading powers, as well as the United States and Japan, colonies had two benefits. Behind the mask of bringing civilization to their indigenous peoples, they knew that colonies guaranteed their industries raw materials and potential markets, and gave their governments prestige among their peers. Colonies were costly to run and were usually exploited by private ventures, but European governments became fixated with keeping up with their rivals, whatever the cost.

Colonial expansion got into its stride in the second half of the nineteenth century. In 1870 some 70 percent of

the globe was controlled by the European powers; by 1914 the figure was 85 percent. In this period colonial interest centered on Africa, which had previously escaped major colonization.

Many early African colonizers had succumbed to rampant diseases; however, advances in medical science conquered or alleviated killers like yellow fever. Technology in the form of modern weapons allowed relatively small numbers of Europeans to crush any local opposition.

By the latter part of the nineteenth century it was clear that new colonies were becoming increasingly difficult to find. The leading powers were coming into conflict - if not outright

▼ Germany's Kaiser Wilhelm II (center, left) attends one of the German Army's annual training exercises.

innovation in military technologies. Weapons were becoming increasingly powerful, more deadly, and available in huge numbers thanks to standardization and mass production.

The naval arms race typified the desire for military parity, if not outright superiority. In the late 1890s Britain, the greatest colonial power, maintained the world's largest navy. However, it was being increasingly challenged by France and Russia.

The British increased their warship production with the intention of

◄ **British troops move forward against the Boer farmers of southern Africa, who were backed by Germany.**

▼ **An armaments factory capable of mass producing the destructive weapons that would come to dominate World War I.**

war – with each other as each attempted to grab areas ripe for colonization. In 1898 Britain and France came close to war when a French expedition marched into Fashoda, a town in British-controlled Sudan. In 1911 Germany sent a gunboat to Agadir, Morocco, which had recently been taken over by the French, to challenge France's right to the country.

Powers were also sometimes willing to intervene indirectly in regions controlled by their rivals. For example, the Boer farmers of gold-rich southern Africa went to war with Britain in 1899 to keep their independence, and received support from Germany during the protracted fighting.

The great European powers also embarked on an arms race that ran in tandem with the scramble for colonies. They needed to protect their far-flung colonies, secure their trade with them, and maintain a balance of military power with their neighbors in Europe. None of the powers was willing to see another gain an unassailable military advantage. The arms race coincided with rapid industrialization and

creating a navy that could take on the combined Russian and French fleets. This, however, was a costly strategy, particularly once Britain became involved in a naval arms race with Germany shortly thereafter. The British answer was to build better warships, a process that reached its apotheosis with the launching of HMS *Dreadnought*, a battleship incorporating several new technologies that was far superior to any vessel afloat, in 1906. Britain's rivals, seeing the

◄ **The British Dreadnought marked a new era in warship design and helped to fuel the ongoing arms race between the world's great powers.**

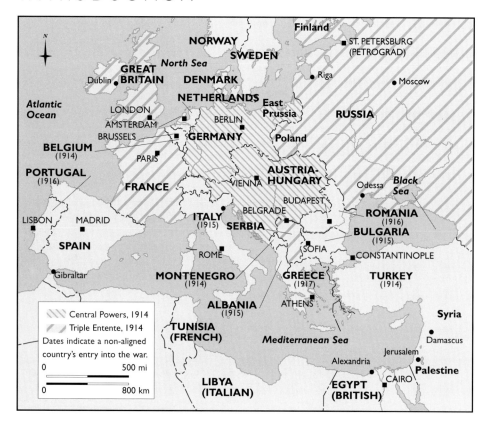

▲ *The geopolitical map of Europe on the eve of World War I, showing the members of the rival power blocs.*

Central Powers, 1914
Triple Entente, 1914
Dates indicate a non-aligned
country's entry into the war.

0   500 mi

0   800 km

sudden vulnerability of their costly fleets, began to build their own dreadnought-type battleships.

Colonial, economic, and military rivalries impacted on the balance of power that regulated the relationships between Europe's leading nations. In the past, if one nation gained an advantage of some type, its chief rival or rivals would act to negate the advantage in some way. The European – and world – balance of power depended on no single nation or nations gaining an unassailable lead.

By the beginning of the twentieth century it was clear that Britain and Germany had clear water between themselves and their rivals. Germany was military superior on land, had a dynamic industrial base, and was intent on extending its power in Europe. Britain was the largest colonial power, had the most powerful navy, and a strong, if declining, industrial base.

In contrast, Russian remained a virtually feudal agricultural society and its armed forces suffered a humiliating defeat during the Russo-Japanese War (1904–05). Austria-Hungary was riven by ethnic tensions, particularly in

those areas it controlled in the Balkans, where its power was being challenged by ardent nationalists in Serbia. France was politically unstable, industrially weak, and full of resentment at its defeat during the Franco-Prussian War (1870–71).

Before the outbreak of World War I Europe's powers had entered into a series of often-shifting alliances with each other, depending on which country was seemingly threatening the balance of power. From the 1890s attention focussed on Germany, whose Kaiser Wilhelm II embarked on a strategy that he intended would make Germany the leading European power. This became increasingly central to Wilhelm's foreign policy as Germany could not embark on any expansion of its overseas possessions as there were few countries left to colonize.

ALLIES AND RIVALS

Germany became allied with Austria-Hungary, the two known as the Central Powers. Arrayed against them were Britain, France, and Russia – the Triple Entente. These networks of alliances, both informal and formal, effectively guaranteed that an attack on one alliance member was considered an attack on all. Kaiser Wilhelm had ambitions to expand German territory into Russian-dominated Eastern Europe, a move that would precipitate war with France, Russia's ally and Germany's old rival in Western Europe. If Germany was to expand into Eastern Europe, it would need a reason to go to war.

All the European powers were aware of the network of alliances, and most developed war plans based on the

▼ *Japanese field artillery in action during the Russo-Japanese War, which was a disaster for the Russian armed forces.*

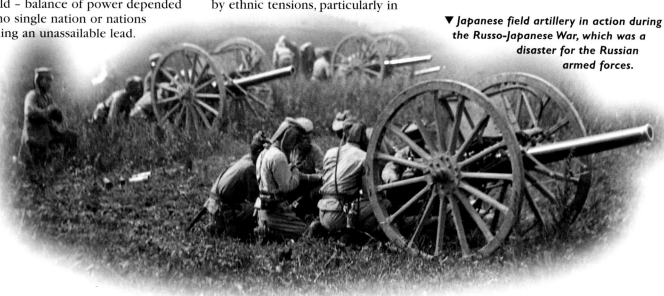

premise that once a war broke out between any two rival alliance members, the others would react immediately. Thus it became necessary to develop plans for the rapid mobilization of armies and their swift movement, usually by rail, to the front.

This need was most acutely felt in Germany, which faced a possible war on two fronts against Triple Entente members France and Russia. Rapid mobilization followed by a pre-emptive strike against France, which was likely to mobilize faster than Russia, became the key element of Germany's war strategy. This also involved an attack through Belgium, whose coal fields would be a valuable addition to Germany's heavy industries. However, Belgium's neutrality was guaranteed by Britain – and all the other major European powers, including Germany.

The flashpoint between the two alliances was the Balkans, a region rent with ethnic divisions and nationalistic aspirations, all overlain with the ambitions of two rival alliance members – Austria-Hungary and Russia, who were both eager to take advantage of Turkey's waning influence in the region. Serbia, whose security was guaranteed by Russia, was an ambitious Balkan power, aiming to curb Austro-Hungarian expansion in the region and establish a "Greater Serbia."

COUNTDOWN TO WAR

The security of Austria-Hungary, the weaker of the Central Powers, was guaranteed by Germany. Indeed, Kaiser Wilhelm II had told his planners to prepare for war in late 1912 to early 1913, when a local conflict in the Balkans saw Serbia gain territory from Turkey and threaten Austro-Hungarian possessions in the northern Adriatic. Austria-Hungary, backed by Germany, stated that it would go to war if Serbia did not give up its gains along the Adriatic. Such a move would have prompted a Russian response, thereby drawing in France. Serbia did back down due to diplomacy. However, the possible route for a local conflict to spark a Europe-wide war, which some were actively seeking, was revealed.

Germany did not have to wait for long to take advantage of a similar political incident. On June 28, 1914, the heir to the Austro-Hungarian throne, Archduke Ferdinand, was assassinated by a Serbian nationalist while touring Sarajevo, the capital of Bosnia, an Austro-Hungarian province.

In 1914 most countries, their civilians and politicians alike, believed that they were going to war for the right reasons. War enthusiasm was rife, but it was destined to die, along with scores of thousands of troops, in the face of machine guns, artillery, and trenches during the first year of war.

▼ *German troops on maneuvers in the years before the outbreak of World War I.*

1914

To many people in Europe the outbreak of war in August 1914 was welcome and seen as an opportunity to right many perceived wrongs, irrespective of either their political or economic validity. The politicians and generals who plunged Europe into this industrial-based war believed it would not last beyond a few months. By December, however, hopes of a swift and decisive victory were dashed against a backdrop of huge casualties, general stalemate, and a widening conflict.

June 28

POLITICS, *BOSNIA*
Archduke Franz Ferdinand, heir to the throne of the Austro-Hungarian Empire, and his wife are assassinated in Sarajevo, the capital of Bosnia, which is a province of the empire. A radical Bosnian-Serb, Gavrilo Princip, is arrested along with other conspirators. Princip is a member of a Serbian nationalist organization, the Black Hand, which is dedicated to the creation of a Serbia-dominated Balkans. Austria-Hungary suspects the direct involvement of Serbia in the plot.

◄ *Austria-Hungary's Archduke Franz Ferdinand is greeted by a Bosnian official shortly before his assassination, June 28.*

July 23

POLITICS, *AUSTRIA-HUNGARY*
Austria-Hungary delivers an ultimatum to Serbia after several meetings with Germany's Kaiser Wilhelm II and his advisers, who back Austria-Hungary's actions. The demands of the ultimatum would, if agreed, destroy Serbia as an independent state. Austria-Hungary demands a reply within 48 hours.

July 25

POLITICS, *SERBIA*
The Serbians, while mobilizing their armed forces, agree to meet all but one of the 10 demands outlined in the Austro-Hungarian ultimatum. The Austro-Hungarians find this unacceptable and Emperor Franz Joseph orders the mobilization of his forces to begin on the following day. Russia's Czar Nicholas II and his minister of war, Grand Duke Nicholas, agree to partly mobilize their forces to protect Serbia from any Austro-Hungarian invasion. Germany, along with Italy one of Austria-Hungary's allies in the Triple

◄ *Germany's Kaiser Wilhelm II. His willingness to back Austro-Hungarian military action against Serbia effectively guaranteed the outbreak of World War I.*

▶ *Austro-Hungarians in Vienna celebrate the opening of hostilities with Serbia.*

Alliance, threatens to begin mobilizing its forces if Britain and France, Russia's allies, do not succeed in curbing Russia's war preparations.

JULY 28

POLITICS, *AUSTRIA-HUNGARY*
Austria-Hungary declares war on Serbia at noon.

POLITICS, *BRITAIN*
The government orders its warships to their various war bases. The main force, the Home Fleet, begins to assemble at its anchorages in Scapa Flow in the Orkneys off the northeast coast of Scotland from where it can dominate the North Sea and block the German fleet's access to the world's oceans.

STRATEGY & TACTICS

WAR PLANS IN THE EAST

The war strategies of both the Austro-Hungarians and Russians were very much shaped to fall in line with Germany's war strategy. Austria-Hungary had two plans. First, there was the strategy known as Plan B to fight in the Balkans, with Serbia as the enemy. Second, there was Plan R to fight on two fronts against Serbia and its ally, Russia.

In the later, more likely, scenario it was planned that the Austro-Hungarian armies would fight in support of their German counterparts, which would be based in East Prussia. The Austro-Hungarian armies were under orders to launch an attack into Russian-controlled Poland in the south to divert Russian troops from East Prussia. Other Austro-Hungarian forces were earmarked to attack Serbia.

Russia also had two war plans. First, if Germany attacked Russia, the Russian armies would fight a defensive war. If, however, Germany chose to attack France first, Russian troops would march into East Prussia as quickly as possible.

Serbia's strategy was defined by the comparatively small size of its armed forces. Its commanders could realistically only fight a defensive war, hoping to delay any attacker for long enough until events on other fronts would force the enemy to pull some of its troops out of Serbia.

JULY 29

POLITICS, *BULGARIA*
The Balkan state declares its neutrality.

POLITICS, *GERMANY*
The navy is ordered to mobilize. This includes the main force, the High Seas Fleet, which begins to assemble along the Jade River. Russia is also informed that its recent partial mobilization will trigger a wider war.

POLITICS, *RUSSIA*
Czar Nicholas II puts his signature to a partial mobilization order, which comes into force on August 4.

BALKANS, *SERBIA*
In the first engagement of what will become World War I, Austro-Hungarian warships on the Danube River bombard Belgrade, the Serbian capital. Serbian artillery replies.

JULY 30

POLITICS, *NETHERLANDS*
The Dutch government declares its neutrality in the war.

JULY 31

POLITICS, *GERMANY*
General Helmuth von Moltke, chief of the General Staff, informs his Austro-Hungarian counterpart, General Franz Conrad von Hötzendorf, that Germany will mobilize its forces. Russia is told that it must cease all war preparations by noon on August 1, and the

French government is requested to explain its political position on any conflict between Germany and Russia.

▼ *Franz Conrad von Hötzendorf, the Austro-Hungarian chief-of-staff, was an advocate of pre-emptive wars to curb Italian and Serbian expansionism.*

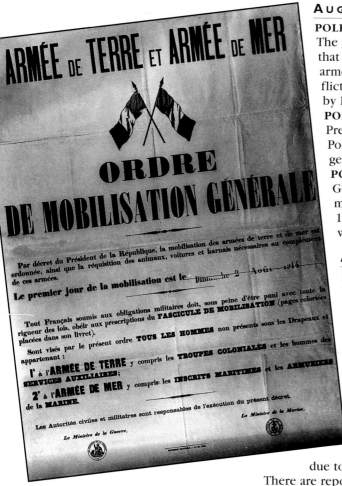

▲ The general mobilization order issued by the French Army and naval authorities on the eve of World War I.

▼ German troops head westward at the opening of their great offensive against Belgium and France, August 1914. They appear confident of a swift victory.

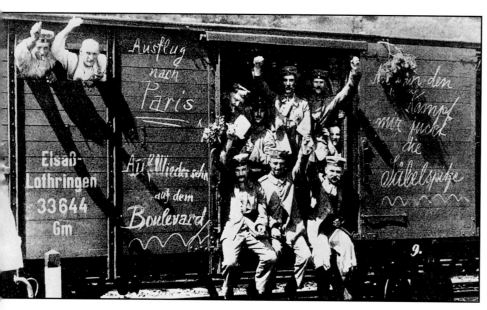

AUGUST 1

POLITICS, *BELGIUM*
The government proclaims that it will maintain its armed neutrality in any conflict, a position guaranteed by Britain and France.

POLITICS, *FRANCE*
President Raymond Poincaré agrees to issue a general mobilization order.

POLITICS, *GERMANY*
Germany begins to mobilize against Russia at 1700 hours and declares war at 1910 hours.

AUGUST 2

POLITICS, *GERMANY*
While German troops occupy neutral Luxembourg, an ultimatum is delivered to Belgium at 1900 hours demanding that German forces be allowed to move through Belgian territory unhindered to pre-empt a French attack on Germany. The ultimatum is due to expire in 12 hours. There are reports of border clashes between French and German troops.

POLITICS, *TURKEY*
War Minister Enver Pasha, an aggressive nationalist eager to restore Turkey's fortunes as a major regional power, arranges a secret military alliance with Germany as a means of protecting his country from possible Russian attack.

AUGUST 3

POLITICS, *BELGIUM*
The Belgian government rejects the German ultimatum demanding that its forces have free passage through Belgian territory and also receives confirmation that Britain and France will provide armed support to combat any German attack.

POLITICS, *BRITAIN*
A general mobilization order is signed.

POLITICS, *GERMANY*
Germany declares war against France.

POLITICS, *ITALY*
Much to the annoyance of its partners in the Triple Alliance – Germany and Austria-Hungary – Italy declares its neutrality. The Italian government argues that Austria-Hungary's attack on Serbia is an act of war not covered in the essentially defensive provisions of the Triple Alliance treaty.

POLITICS, *ROMANIA*
Despite ailing King Karol's wish to join Germany and Austria-Hungary, his government opts for a position of

◀ *Enver Pasha, an ardent expansionist, was made the Turkish Army's deputy commander-in-chief on August 3.*

▶ *The mobilization order published by the British government in the name of King George V.*

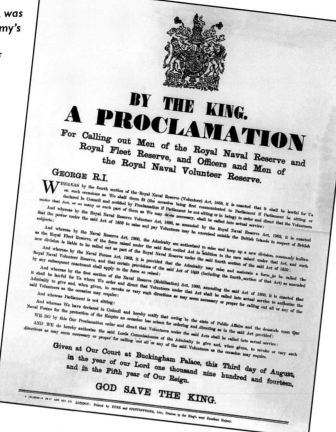

BY THE KING.
A PROCLAMATION

For Calling out Men of the Royal Naval Reserve and Royal Fleet Reserve, and Officers and Men of the Royal Naval Volunteer Reserve.

GEORGE R.I.

[body of proclamation in small print]

Given at Our Court at Buckingham Palace, this Third day of August, in the year of our Lord one thousand nine hundred and fourteen, and in the Fifth year of Our Reign.

GOD SAVE THE KING.

armed neutrality. However, a secret government agreement with Russia made in early October agrees that Romania will gain territory if Russia's armed forces are successful in their war against both Germany and Austria-Hungary. Evidence of Romania's true interests becomes clear on October 23, when it closes its borders to German supplies bound for Turkey.

POLITICS, *TURKEY*
Turkey declares its armed neutrality and mobilizes its forces.

▼ *The German light cruiser* **Breslau**, *a gift for Turkey along with the* **Goeben**.

AUGUST 4

POLITICS, *BRITAIN*
The government declares war at 2300 hours as the Germans reject the British ultimatum requesting that their troops leave Belgian soil.

POLITICS, *GERMANY*
The government declares war on Belgium and its armies invade in force across a narrow front. Leading the main attack are the First Army commanded by General Alexander von Kluck and General Karl von Bülow's Second Army.

STRATEGY & TACTICS

BRITAIN'S COMMITMENT

Uniquely, Britain was the only major European power that did not have some form of conscription at the outbreak of World War I. Its regular army, although much smaller than its European counterparts, was an all-volunteer force. Man for man, however, it was probably the best. Its regular infantry regiments were highly trained, skilled in most aspects of warfare, and renowned for the volume and accuracy of their rifle fire.

One British regular soldier described the impact of accurate rifle fire on a company of Germans at Mons in August 1914: "[They] were simply blasted away to heaven by a volley at 700 yards [680 m], and in their insane formation every bullet was almost sure to find two billets."

The army that Britain sent to France in 1914 was known as the British Expeditionary Force and consisted at the outset of around 100,000 men. It was a generally well-balanced force, but was later found to be lacking trench-busting medium and heavy artillery. It was also short of machine guns — just 120 in total in August 1914. In stark comparison, the German Army, although considerably larger, had 10,500.

At the outset of the war Britain's greatest contribution was its powerful navy of over 500 vessels. In the key area of dreadnought battleships and battlecruisers the British naval forces enjoyed a 28:18 superiority over Germany's High Seas Fleet.

POLITICS, *UNITED STATES*
The government declares its neutrality.

SEA WAR, *MEDITERRANEAN*
Two German warships, the battlecruiser *Goeben* and the light cruiser *Breslau*, under the command of Vice Admiral Wilhelm von Souchon, open

▲ British recruits gather in central London at the outbreak of war. Like thousands of young men across Europe, many saw the conflict as a great adventure.

▼ British troops, part of the force earmarked to protect the neutrality of Belgium, entrain for the Western Front.

fire on Bône and Philippeville, two ports in French Algeria, for 10 minutes. After the attack Souchon heads for Turkey. As he sails east across the Mediterranean, his small squadron runs into two British battlecruisers, the *Indefatigable* and *Indomitable*, sailing west.

The British commander, Vice Admiral Sir A. Berkeley-Milne, refrains from opening fire as the British government's ultimatum demanding that German forces inside Belgium should withdraw or face war does not expire until midnight. Souchon also avoids action and continues on to Turkey.

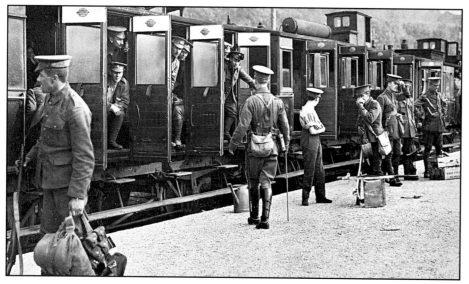

AUGUST 5

POLITICS, *AUSTRIA-HUNGARY*
Austria-Hungary declares war on Russia at 1200 hours.

POLITICS, *MONTENEGRO*
The government of this Balkan state, which has close links with Serbia, declares war on Austria-Hungary.

WESTERN FRONT, *BELGIUM*
German troops launch a night attack on Liège but fail to capture any of the outer ring of 12 powerful forts protecting the city, which is the key border defense in eastern Belgium and a railroad center. It also blocks the route of the German First and Second Armies as they attempt to head for the French border before swinging south toward Paris as part of the Schlieffen Plan, the German war strategy.

AUGUST 6

POLITICS, *SERBIA*
The government declares war on Germany.

WESTERN FRONT, *BELGIUM*
General Erich Ludendorff of the German Second Army wins great fame in his homeland by leading troops through part of Liège's defensive ring of forts to establish a lodgment that threatens the city's Belgian garrison. However, he is cut off until the 10th.

SEA WAR, *EAST AFRICA*
The *Königsberg*, a German light cruiser, attacks and sinks the British light cruiser *Pegasus* off the port of Mombasa. The German warship sailed from Dar-es-Salaam on 31 July; its role

is to interdict British commerce in the Indian Ocean. The British move to deal with the threat posed by this German raider and the *Königsberg* is forced to seek shelter in the Rufiji River, German East Africa, on October 30.

AUGUST 6–7

SEA WAR, *MEDITERRANEAN*
German Vice Admiral Wilhelm von Souchon, pursued by Vice Admiral Sir A. Berkeley-Milne's two British battle-cruisers, continues to lead his two

STRATEGY & TACTICS

THE SCHLIEFFEN PLAN

In 1893 France and Russia signed a military alliance that greatly alarmed Germany's chief of the General Staff, Count Alfred von Schlieffen. Schlieffen was acutely aware of the dangers of Germany fighting a major war on two fronts and saw France as the most immediate threat in any conflict involving the three countries. He then developed a plan (see below) to knock France out of any war in a matter of weeks before Russia could mobilize its vast armies.

Schlieffen realized that France's border defenses with Germany were far too strong to be taken quickly, and that rapid movement through Switzerland's mountainous terrain was impossible. He therefore opted to violate Belgian and Dutch neutrality by sending a massive force, some 90 percent of the total German Army, through these countries and then swing southward to head for Paris. Only five percent of the army would defend Alsace-Lorraine, where Schlieffen, correctly, expected – and wanted – the French forces to attack. The region's strong border fortifications backed by a resolute defense would tie up a large part of the French Army.

The remaining five percent of the army would hold East Prussia. It was expected that these forces would block the Russians

until German forces, fresh from their rapid victory over France, could be rushed east to defeat Russia in turn. Central to the plan were rapid mobilization and the speedy movement of troops by rail.

Schlieffen retired in 1906 and his successor, General Helmuth von Moltke, made modifications to the original plan. Moltke saw that Russia could mobilize more quickly than Schlieffen believed and therefore earmarked 15 percent of the German Army to defend East Prussia. Moltke did not want to give up any of Alsace-Lorraine to France, no matter how temporarily, and therefore increased the forces there to 25 percent. He was also concerned to protect German industry in the adjacent Rhineland. Thus only 60 percent of the German Army was available for the decisive sweep into northern France through Belgium.

Finally, Moltke decided not to attack through the neutral Netherlands, believing that Britain might not go to war to save Belgium if Dutch neutrality was honored. Consequently, the planned attack had to take place on a much narrower front than that envisaged by Schlieffen. It also forced the Germans to contemplate neutralizing the massive defenses of Liège, Belgium, which stood directly in their path.

▼ *A column of German infantry moves through the shell-blasted remains of a Belgian village in early August.*

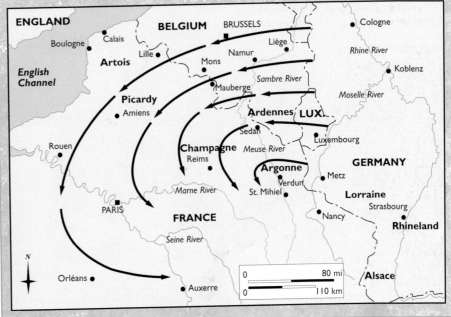

15

AUGUST 7

warships, the *Goeben* and *Breslau*, through the Mediterranean. Southwest of Greece he maneuvers to avoid a squadron of British cruisers led by Rear Admiral E. C. Troubridge, which has been sent to block his route to Constantinople, the Turkish capital.

STRATEGY & TACTICS

FRANCE'S PLAN XVII

France's greatest humiliation following its defeat at the hands of Germany in the Franco-Prussian War (1870–71) was the loss of Alsace-Lorraine on its eastern frontier. France expected to go to war with Germany again at some time in the future and its military leaders developed a war strategy to win back the lost provinces.

Between 1911 and 1914 General Joseph Joffre, the French commander-in-chief, devised Plan XVII. It called for the various French armies to assemble along the key frontier from Switzerland to Belgium, and launch an immediate, devastating attack in strength into Alsace-Lorraine. Joffre did recognize that the Germans might violate Belgium's neutrality in any attack on France, but believed that they could not advance past the Meuse River in northeast France without becoming dangerously overextended. The French also had an informal arrangement with the British that guaranteed that their army would plug any gap on the Franco-Belgian border.

Plan XVII had two key weaknesses. First, Joffre underestimated the quality of the German Army and the speed with which it could mobilize and move. In the event of war this would allow the Germans to have a possibly greater initial front-line strength than the French and permit a movement through Belgium that would not leave them particularly overstretched.

The second weakness of Joffre's war plans was that the French adhered to the doctrine of constant attack. They believed that a resolute attack could fight through any defense. All that was needed was the will power of the ordinary French soldier to carry out what was termed *offense à l'outrance* ("offense at the utmost"). Consequently, French training concentrated on attack and neglected defense. For their part the Germans did train to both attack and defend aggressively – and their infantry units were equipped with a greater proportion of machine guns. As the French learned in 1914, resolute attacks in the face of defensive machine-gun fire could lead to very heavy casualties.

AUGUST 7

WESTERN FRONT, *FRANCE*
The advance guard of the 100,000-strong British Expeditionary Force reaches France. The arrival of this army is completed over the following few weeks and the force takes up a position in the southeast corner of Belgium, around the town of Mons. Field Marshal Sir John French is named as its commander.

AUGUST 8

POLITICS, *BRITAIN*
Field Marshal Sir Herbert Kitchener, the recently appointed secretary of war, calls for 100,000 volunteers to join the British Army. He later poses for a recruitment poster, which depicts him pointing an accusing figure at the viewer and stating "Your Country Needs You." The message first appears on September 5; 175,000 volunteer over the next week.

▼ *French troops with a guard dog keep watch for German troops during their attack into Lorraine, August 1914.*

▶ *Serbian Marshal Radomir Putnik, although severely outnumbered, defeated an Austro-Hungarian invasion in 1914.*

WESTERN FRONT, *FRANCE*
In accordance with a prewar strategic blueprint for war against Germany known as Plan XVII, France's Army of Alsace under General Paul Pau advances against the German-held city of Mulhouse in Alsace, heralding a series of battles along the French and Belgian borders.

AUGUST 10

POLITICS, *FRANCE*
The government declares war on Austria-Hungary.
WESTERN FRONT, *BELGIUM*
The first of Liège's 12 forts falls to the Germans following a pounding by 17-in (42-cm) howitzers brought up by Second Army commander General Karl von Bülow.
SEA WAR, *MEDITERRANEAN*
The German warships *Goeben* and *Breslau* pass through the Dardanelles seaway and their British pursuers call

off the chase. The German ships, along with their crews, become part of Turkey's naval forces operating in the Black Sea. The "gift" of the two warships acts as an encouragement to the Turks to join the war, particularly as two Turkish battleships under construction in British shipyards had been commandeered by the British at the outbreak of the war.

AUGUST 12

POLITICS, *BRITAIN*
The government declares war on Austria-Hungary.

AUGUST 12–21

BALKANS, *SERBIA*
Advancing across the border into Serbia from the north and northwest, some 200,000 Austro-Hungarian troops led by General Oskar Potiorek invade. Although outnumbered, the Serbians forces under Marshal Radomir Putnik put up stout resistance during the Battle of the Jadar River, forcing the invaders to begin withdrawing by August 16.

AUGUST 14

HOME FRONT, *BRITAIN*
Novelist H.G. Wells calls the conflict "The War to End All Wars."

AUGUST 14–22

WESTERN FRONT, *FRANCE*
Southeast of Metz two French armies, the First under General Auguste Dubail and the Second commanded by General Noël de Castelnau, initiate the first of a series of engagements that become known as the "Battle of the Frontiers" by attacking into Lorraine.
   Two German armies make a slow but coordinated withdrawal to give time for reinforcements to arrive. The German counterattack on the 20th forces the French back. A defensive action by General Ferdinand Foch's XX Corps on high ground outside Nancy prevents a major defeat.

AUGUST 15

POLITICS, *JAPAN*
The Japanese demand that the Germans evacuate their colony based at the port of Tsingtao in China.

AUGUST 16

POLITICS, *GERMANY*
Austrian-born Adolf Hitler volunteers to fight with the German Army. He will serve throughout the conflict on the

General Max von Prittwitz's thinly-spread Eighth Army. However, the Russian armies are widely separated, chiefly by the Masurian Lakes, and are lacking in most types of equipment. Prittwitz's troops, although overstretched and outnumbered, act as a delaying force.

On the 17th German forces inflict a defeat on Rennenkampf's advance guard at Stallupönen, causing 3000 casualties and pushing the Russians back to the East Prussian frontier. The German commander at Stallupönen, General Hermann von François, then falls back to Gumbinnen.

AUGUST 18

WESTERN FRONT, *BELGIUM*
King Albert orders the Belgian Army, some 75,000 men, to retreat to the port of Antwerp, which has a garrison of 60,000 men. The move is completed by the 20th and the Germans deploy some 60,000 men to keep Leopold bottled up in the fortified city as the bulk of their forces push toward the Franco-Belgian border.

▲ *Russian troops in a Polish town prepare to march to the front. Although the army had a strength of over four million, it lacked ammunition and equipment.*

Western Front as a messenger, suffer wounds, and receive various medals for valor.

WESTERN FRONT, *BELGIUM*
After days of intense bombardment from the massive German 17-in (42-cm) howitzers, which leave the defenders' forts in ruins, the garrison of Liège surrenders. With the Belgian fortress neutralized, the German First Army commanded by General Alexander von Kluck and the Second Army led by General Karl von Bülow push westward across the Meuse River. The Belgian Army begins to withdraw, destroying bridges as it retreats.

AUGUST 17–19

EASTERN FRONT, *EAST PRUSSIA*
Two Russian forces, the First Army under General Pavel Rennenkampf and General Alexander Samsonov's Second Army, invade East Prussia from the east and southeast, where they are met by

▶ *A German 17-in (42-cm) howitzer is readied for action. It could lob a large shell accurately to a range of 10,000 yards (9140 m) with a flight time of around 60 seconds.*

▶ *German troops subject Belgian citizens to a thorough search. German policy in occupied countries was to use physical force and intimidation to pre-empt any civilian resistance.*

AUGUST 19

WESTERN FRONT, *BELGIUM*
German troops shoot 150 civilians at Aerschot, one of many – often unconfirmed – reports of atrocities committed against non-combatants. It is known that the Germans openly avow the policy of *Shrecklichkeit* ("frightfulness") to cow and intimidate the local population in occupied areas.

AUGUST 20

WESTERN FRONT, *BELGIUM*
German forces occupy Brussels, the Belgian capital.
EASTERN FRONT, *EAST PRUSSIA*
At Gumbinnen, the Germans, who fear encirclement, confront the slowly advancing Russian forces of Rennenkampf. General Hermann von François, who acts decisively, unlike the dithering Prittwitz, drives Rennenkampf back some five miles (8 km) – but other German attacks are unsuccessful. Prittwitz is relieved of his command and is replaced by the elderly General Paul von Hindenburg, who is recalled from retirement. Hindenburg's chief-of-staff is confirmed as the dynamic General

▼ *Belgian civilians look on as a German supply column prepares to move out from Brussels, the recently captured capital.*

Erich Ludendorff, fresh from his role in capturing the crucial Belgian frontier fortress of Liège.
AFRICA, *CAMEROONS*
Some 400 British troops invade German Cameroons from Nigeria.
AIR WAR, *GERMANY*
The German high command is asked to authorize long-range Zeppelin

airship bombing attacks on London, key British ports, and a number of major naval bases.

AUGUST 20–25

WESTERN FRONT, *BELGIUM*
The "Battle of the Frontiers" switches to the wooded Ardennes region to the north of Metz. Two French

armies advancing at all possible speed into Belgium run into two German armies rushing through Luxembourg and southeast Belgium on the 22nd. Three days of bitter, confused fighting follow, with the outnumbered French blunting the German attacks and then launching their own counterattacks.

French losses are severe. Their Third Army (General Pierre Ruffey) is virtually destroyed and General Fernand de Langle de Cary's Fourth Army badly mauled. The French, pursued by the Germans, fall back to positions between the Meuse and Marne Rivers, with their right wing resting on the fortifications of Verdun.

▲ *A French three-inch (75-mm) field gun in action. A lightweight design, it could be moved around the battlefield with ease and thus offer immediate support in both defense and attack. It could also fire up to 20 rounds a minute.*

▼ *German infantry await the order to advance on the Eastern Front.*

AUGUST 22

EASTERN FRONT, *EAST PRUSSIA*
Ludendorff quickly takes charge of the German forces confronting Rennenkampf and Samsonov. He orders the wholesale realignment of the outnumbered German troops facing the Russians, directing the bulk of his units against Samsonov's Second Army in the south of the province by both road and rail. A

▲ *German troops advance during the fighting in the French Argonne sector of the Western Front.*

single cavalry division is directed to delay Rennenkampf in the north. The Germans plan to defeat Samsonov before his forces can link up with Rennenkampf. Unbeknown to Ludendorff and Hindenburg, Lieutenant Colonel Max Hoffmann, Prittwitz's chief of operations, has already begun such a maneuver.

AUGUST 22–23

WESTERN FRONT, *BELGIUM*

North of the Ardennes three German armies are continuing to sweep through western Belgium and are beginning to advance to the south and southwest for France. In the third engagement of the "Battle of the Frontiers" the French commander-in-chief, General Joseph Joffre, orders General Charles Lanrezac's Fifth Army into position between the Sambre and Meuse Rivers to block the unexpected switch in the main axis of the German attack into France.

Again, the French fight stubbornly to halt the German advance, but suffer unacceptably high casualties. Lanrezac seeks and is granted permission by Joffre to withdraw. As this battle is taking place, German troops are using their heavy howitzers to smash the Belgian garrison of Namur. The fortress is finally captured on the 25th.

KEY PERSONALITIES

FIELD MARSHAL PAUL VON HINDENBURG

Hindenburg (1847–1934) actually retired from the German Army in 1911, but was recalled to command the Eighth Army in East Prussia, with General Erich Ludendorff as his subordinate, in August 1914. Together, the two men scored notable victories over the Russians at the Battle of Tannenberg and the Masurian Lakes the same year. Hindenburg was promote to command all German and Austro-Hungarian troops on the Eastern Front and made a field marshal later the same year.

In 1915 Hindenburg won significant victories in Poland, but was later highly critical of the transfer of some of his forces to the Western Front to take part in the Battle of Verdun in 1916. On August 29 Hindenburg replaced Erich von Falkenhayn as chief of the General Staff. Due to the weakness of Kaiser Wilhelm II and the German parliament Hindenburg and Ludendorff effectively took over as military dictators.

Among his key decision during this period was to announce unrestricted submarine warfare (January 1917), and he oversaw the talks at the Treaty of Brest-Litovsk with Russia in the following December. His final role as chief of the General Staff was to back Ludendorff's series of offensives on the Western Front between March and June 1918, which were finally unsuccessful.

In the final days of the war Hindenburg was forced to sue for peace and, although he retired from public life in 1919, he returned to serve two terms as German president. He was made chancellor by Adolf Hitler on January 30, 1933, but was little more than a figurehead until his death on August 2, 1934.

Hindenburg (left) and Ludendorff (right) discuss war strategy with Kaiser Wilhelm II.

KEY PERSONALITIES

FIELD MARSHAL
SIR JOHN FRENCH

Field Marshal Sir John French (1852–1925) commanded the British Expeditionary Force from August 1914 until replaced by General Sir Douglas Haig in September 1915. French had won fame as a cavalry commander during the Second Anglo-Boer War (1899–1902) and risen in seniority.

In 1914 French faced several immediate problems, not least the sweeping early successes of the German Army, which dislocated any Anglo-French war plans, and the need to preserve the British Expeditionary Force. Although he had great charisma and was undoubtedly brave, he was not an easy man to get along with. French quarreled with General Charles Lanrezac, whose French Fifth Army he claimed was offering insufficient support to his own forces. French also got on badly with Lord Kitchener, who was the British secretary of state for war, and relied too heavily on General Henry Wilson, his headstrong deputy chief of the General Staff.

In March 1915, after the Battle of Neuve-Chapelle, French severely criticized the British government (with some justification) for its alleged inability to provide him with sufficient artillery shells, and then dismissed General Sir Horace Smith-Dorrien for failure at the Second Battle of Ypres in April. The crunch came in September, when French failed to commit his reserve corps during the Battle of Loos. Although French had powerful political allies in Britain, he was nevertheless dismissed.

▲ Crowds in Paris turn out to watch the departure of heavy cavalry for the front at the height of the August fighting.

AUGUST 23

POLITICS, JAPAN
The government declares war on Germany and two days later opens hostilities with Austria-Hungary. The Japanese refuse to become involved in the war in Europe and concentrate their efforts against the German colony-port of Tsingtao in China.

WESTERN FRONT, BELGIUM
At Mons, in the final of the encounter of the "Battle of the Frontiers," the British Expeditionary Force meets General Alexander von Kluck's German First Army. Although heavily outnumbered the British repulse the first German attack, inflicting severe casualties with accurate and

▶ A lone German sentry stands guard over the remains of one of Namur's shell-blasted forts, August 25.

▲ German infantrymen move through a French wood. Hot weather and heavy equipment soon tired the troops.

◀ A British cavalry unit falls back after briefly slowing the pace of the German attack at the Battle of Mons.

high-volume rifle fire. Subsequent German attacks force the British back just three miles (5 km). Because of the withdrawal of Lanrezac's French Fifth Army a little to the east, the British are forced to conduct an orderly retreat.

Mons marks the end of the "Battle of the Frontiers." To Helmuth von Moltke, the German chief-of-staff, this sprawling series of battles seems to herald a great victory. French casualties are high (some 300,000 men), and both they and the British are in seemingly disorganized retreat.

On this basis he modifies the Schlieffen Plan further. He orders his forces in northeastern France to continue their wide sweep aimed toward Paris but sends the reinforcements earmarked for them elsewhere – Lorraine – for a new attack. Two corps from the German right wing are also sent to the Eastern Front, where the Russian mobilization has been more rapid than expected. Other German units from the key right wing are to lay siege to Antwerp, where much of the Belgian Army is holding out, and to besiege the French-held fortress-city of Mauberge.

Moltke's evaluation of the strategic situation is false, partly due to his poor communications with his army commanders. In contrast, the French commander-in-chief, General Joseph Joffre, recognizes that, although his

AUGUST 23–24

▶ *A German field forge and smithy on the Eastern Front.*

casualties are heavy, the morale of his forces remains high. Joffre, by now aware of the location of the German armies, prepares a counterattack in northeast France. His forces in contact with the Germans are ordered to continue their orderly withdrawal, while armies around Verdun are to remain in position to act as an anchor for the offensive. Two new armies, the Sixth commanded by General Michel Maunoury, and General Ferdinand Foch's Ninth Army, are created.

Joffre plans to place the Sixth Army to the west of the far right wing of the German forces marching through northeastern France, and the Ninth is moved to bolster the line confronting the German forces advancing a little way to the northeast of Paris. However, the plan is thwarted for the moment by the speed of the German advance, which continues to force the French and British southward.

AUGUST 23–24

EASTERN FRONT, *GALICIA*
While the Germans are preparing to take on the Russians in East Prussia, their Austro-Hungarian allies launch an

▼ *The German victory at Tannenberg cost the Russians 125,000 casualties and 500 guns – against 15,000 German losses.*

offensive from around Lemberg in their province of Galicia into Russian-controlled Poland. The plan, masterminded by the Austro-Hungarian chief-of-staff, General Franz Conrad von Hötzendorf, involves the movement of three armies on a 200-mile (320-km) front. Their objective is to crush the four armies of General Nikolai Ivanov's Russian Southwest Army Group,

which are based southwest of the extensive and barrier-like Pripet Marshes. The main Austro-Hungarian advance begins well, with their First Army pushing back the Russian Fourth Army at the Battle of Krasnik.

AUGUST 24

EASTERN FRONT, *EAST PRUSSIA*
German troops successfully delay

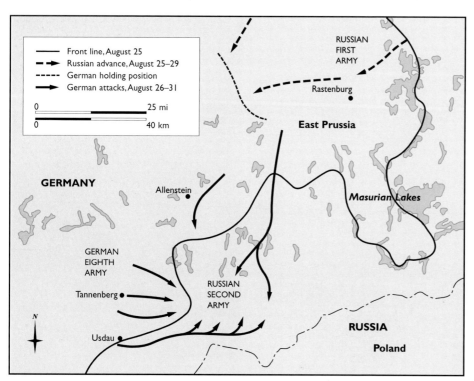

RUSSIAN
FIRST
ARMY

— Front line, August 25
▪▪▶ Russian advance, August 25–29
--- German holding position
▶ German attacks, August 26–31

0   25 mi
0   40 km

East Prussia

Rastenburg

Masurian Lakes

GERMANY

Allenstein

GERMAN
EIGHTH
ARMY

Tannenberg

RUSSIAN
SECOND
ARMY

Usdau

RUSSIA

Poland

N

Samsonov's advance in southern East Prussia in a day-long battle at Orlau-Frankenau, thereby allowing other German units to concentrate at nearby Tannenberg for their forthcoming battle against Samsonov. The Russian high command remains unaware that its uncoded radio traffic is being intercepted by the Germans, who have detailed knowledge of the Russian strength, dispositions, and plans.

AUGUST 25–27

WESTERN FRONT, *FRANCE*

The British Expeditionary Force continues to retreat southward across northeast France, fighting almost continuous rearguard actions against General Alexander von Kluck's First Army. At Le Cateau the British II Corps, some 40,000 men, fights for its life as the Germans attempt to surround it. The German attacks are beaten off but at terrible cost to the corps, which suffers 7800 casualties.

AUGUST 26

AFRICA, *TOGOLAND*

An Anglo-French expedition operating inside the German colony of Togoland in West Africa wins a decisive victory at Kamina, which effectively destroys the German presence.

AUGUST 26–31

EASTERN FRONT, *EAST PRUSSIA*

The Germans strike at Samsonov's Second Army outside Tannenberg from the north and south, and also in the center. By nightfall on the 29th Samsonov has been surrounded and he is believed to have committed suicide. Attempts by Rennenkampf in the north to come to the aid of Samsonov's beleaguered forces come to nothing. Tannenberg is a major German victory. Russian losses are enormous, their invasion of East Prussia is decisively rebuffed, and France and Britain's faith in their ally on the Eastern Front is severely shaken by the crushing defeat.

AUGUST 26–SEPTEMBER 1

EASTERN FRONT, *GALICIA*

The Austro-Hungarian broad-front offensive against the four armies of General Nikolai Ivanov's Russian Southwest Army Group in Poland continues with mixed results. At the Battle of Zamosc-Komarów the Austro-Hungarian Fourth Army pushes back the Russians. However, two Russian armies, the Third and Eighth, strike against the Austro-Hungarian Third Army at the Battle of Gnila Lipa, forcing it back to Lemberg, the base for the Austro-Hungarian attack.

▼ *Lines of Russian prisoners, some of the more than 90,000 captured by the Germans during the Battle of Tannenberg in East Prussia, queue for field rations in early September.*

KEY PERSONALITIES

MARSHAL JOSEPH JOFFRE

Marshal Joseph Joffre (1852–1931) was the commander-in-chief of the French Army between 1911 and December 1916, when he was replaced by General Robert Nivelle and took no further part in the war. Joffre (above, left) was a methodical officer and can claim credit for holding the Germans in 1914, chiefly through the rapid transfer of forces from his right flank to the threatened left flank along the Marne River.

Renowned for his calm manner, he was also held in great affection by the French troops and was known as "Papa Joffre." His stock reached its zenith during the fluid campaign of 1914, but he was less suited to the demands of static trench warfare, despite his background as a military engineer.

Joffre failed to adapt to the realities of trench warfare and was blamed by some for choosing the wrong places to launch attacks, chiefly at Loos in September 1914 and the Somme in 1916. Both were costly British failures, which soured his relationship with his main ally.

Also in 1916 he was blamed for the parlous state of Verdun's defenses when it was attacked by the Germans, although he displayed considerable skills in the early stage of the battle. Nevertheless, the credit went to General Henri-Philippe Pétain and Nivelle, Joffre's successor.

AUGUST 27

POLITICS, *TURKEY*
German General Liman von Sanders is made commander of the Turkish First Army.

AUGUST 28

SEA WAR, *NORTH SEA*
British cruisers launch a foray into German waters as part of a plan to lure elements of the German High Seas Fleet into an unequal fight, and also prevent German warships from attacking convoys transporting follow-on units of the British Expeditionary Force across the English Channel to France. The engagement, known as the Battle of Heligoland Bight, begins at 0700 hours. British light cruisers and destroyers under Commodore Tyrwhitt catch the Germans by surprise and enjoy success against German torpedo-boats.

However, the Germans recover from their surprise and their more powerful warships get up steam and sail out from their anchorage in the Jade River to attack the

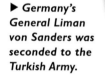

▶ *Germany's General Liman von Sanders was seconded to the Turkish Army.*

▲ *French cavalry on the move during the build-up to the decisive Battle of the Marne, late August 1914.*

British. The German warships threaten to inflict severe losses, but the sudden arrival of reinforcements, chiefly five battlecruisers under Admiral Sir David Beatty, cover the withdrawal of the initial British force. No British ships are sunk during the battle, while four German vessels are sent to the bottom. The battle is seen as a clear-cut success by the British, but

their euphoria serves to mask severe shortcomings, particularly in the planning and conduct of complex multi-force naval operations. However, the British raid has a profound impact on the morale of the German high command. Kaiser Wilhelm II warns his

naval commanders that the High Seas Fleet, already outnumbered by the British navy, cannot afford such losses. Plans to use the High Seas Fleet in large-scale offensive operations in the North Sea are shelved.

AUGUST 29–SEPTEMBER 2

WESTERN FRONT, *FRANCE*

General Joseph Joffre, the French commander-in-chief, orders the French Fifth Army to launch a flank attack against the German First Army around Guise to take some of the pressure of the withdrawing British Expeditionary Force to the west. The attack makes little progress, but the Fifth Army's I Corps under General Louis Franchet d'Esperey temporarily stops the advance of the German Second Army under General Karl von Bülow in a supporting attack.

Bülow now calls on the commander of the German First Army, Alexander von Kluck, to come to his aid. Kluck is under orders to advance to the west of Paris but any support for Bülow would take his forces to the east of the capital. However, Kluck believes the British are effectively defeated and that there are no sizeable enemy forces menacing his exposed right flank. (He is unaware of the newly-created

▲ *A horse-drawn German field artillery battery on the move.*

French Sixth Army assembling a little to the north of Paris.) Kluck cannot reach Moltke, the chief of the German General Staff, for clarification, so moves to support Bülow on his own initiative. By September 2 his army is stretched out from the Marne River at Château-Thierry to the Oise River.

▼ *German troops maintain the pace of their drive through northern France.*

▼ *The advance of the German Army through Belgium and northern France, August–September 1914. The bold sweeping movement was finally halted at the Battle of the Marne.*

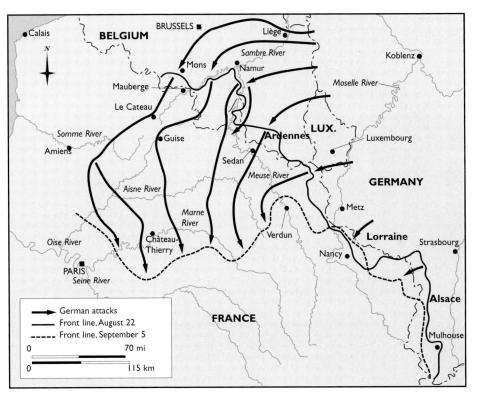

DECISIVE WEAPONS

THE FRENCH "75"

The three-inch (75-mm) Field Gun Model 1897 was a revolutionary design. The key to its success was axial recoil, which made firing more accurate and faster. To fire the weapon, the loader simply opened the breech and threw in the round, then closed the breech with a swift flick of the wrist.

Once the gun was fired, the recoil did not roll the carriage backward as in older designs. The 75's carriage remained perfectly still, but the gun barrel itself flew backward in its holding cradle to a distance of some four feet (1.2 m) and then slid back to its original position due to the hydraulic recoil system. As the barrel returned, the loader could simply flick open the breech, which automatically ejected the spent cartridge, and then throw in another round.

The military benefits of this firing system were obvious. The crew did not have to jump clear when the gun was fired as they would have had to do if the carriage moved. Consequently, they were in position to reload quickly. Second, the gun remained in position and therefore did not need re-laying on its target after each round was fired. The "75" was capable of delivering six or so rounds a minute with accuracy up to ranges of 7500 yards (6900 m). However, in extreme circumstances up to 20 rounds a minute could be fired.

A French 75-mm field gun captured at the moment of the barrel's maximum recoil. The crew is poised to reload the weapon immediately.

▲ *Austro-Hungarian prisoners of war are marched into captivity by the Russians after their defeat in Poland.*

Thanks to air reconnaissance General Joseph Joffre, the French commander-in-chief, is aware of Kluck's change of direction and has set his plans for a massive counteroffensive along the line of the Marne River by French and British forces accordingly.

AUGUST 30

AIR WAR, *FRANCE*
Paris becomes the first capital city to suffer aerial bombardment when a German Taube monoplane drops four small bombs and propaganda leaflets.

SEPTEMBER 3–11

EASTERN FRONT, *GALICIA*
The Austro-Hungarian offensive into Poland meets with further disaster. The Russian Fifth Army is able to drive a wedge between the Austro-Hungarian First and Fourth Armies at the Battle of Rava Ruska. The attack forces the Austro-Hungarians to abandon their main base at Lemberg and retreat 100 miles (160 km) back to the Carpathian Mountains. With the exception of the fortress of Przemysl, the Russians now control all of Galicia.

The faith of the Germans in their Austro-Hungarian ally, whose forces have suffered 350,000 men killed, wounded, or taken prisoner in the Galician campaign, is severely shaken. The Austro-Hungarian armed forces are clearly not able to fight a modern industrial war. It also becomes clear that the Russians are preparing further attacks and that the Austro-Hungarians can only survive with extensive German military assistance.

SEPTEMBER 4

WESTERN FRONT, *FRANCE*
General Joseph Joffre orders a major attack against the overextended German armies holding the line south of the Marne River to the east of Paris. It begins the next day.

SEPTEMBER 5

WESTERN FRONT, *FRANCE*
The French and British launch their counterattack against the German forces along the Marne River between Paris and Verdun. The key to the plan is for the French Sixth Army to strike at the exposed western flank of General Alexander von Kluck's First Army to the east of Paris, around Château-Thierry, with the British Expeditionary Force advancing into the gap between Kluck's force and General Karl von Bülow's Second Army. This offensive, known as the Battle of the Marne, has six main phases.

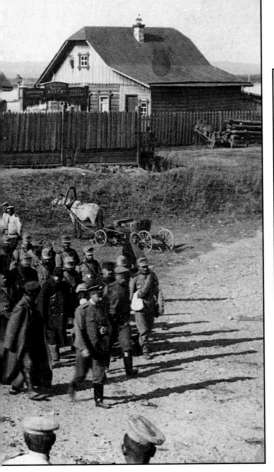

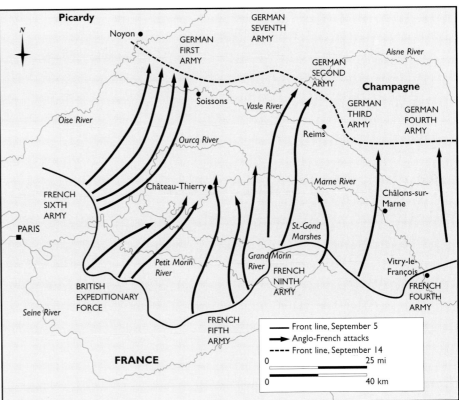

▼ French General Joseph Galliéni commanded the Sixth Army during the opening phase of the Battle of the Marne.

▲ The successful French and British attack along the Marne exploited the gap between two German armies.

SEPTEMBER 5–9

WESTERN FRONT, *FRANCE*

The first phase of the Marne offensive, known as the Battle of the Ourcq, involves the French Sixth Army under the temporary command of General Joseph Galliéni, the military governor of Paris, striking against the exposed right flank of Kluck's First Army to the east of Paris. Kluck's right flank is just able to avoid being surrounded, mainly due to the aggressive response of the local commander, General Hans von Gronau, to the French onslaught.

Kluck, however, believes that the French attack is only a diversion and sends few reinforcements to the aid of the hard-pressed Gronau. The remainder of the First Army continues to push to the south, chasing the British Expeditionary Force until Kluck realizes on the 7th that the French attack is crucial.

The German commander immediately pulls his army back over the Marne River and heads westward to confront the French Sixth Army, now back under the command of General Michel Maunoury. The Germans launch powerful attacks that come close to breaking Maunoury, but the tide is stemmed by Galliéni, who rushes some of the much-needed reinforcements from Paris to the front in taxicabs.

SEPTEMBER 6–10

WESTERN FRONT, *FRANCE*

While the Battle of the Ourcq is raging, the British Expeditionary Force to the southeast moves slowly into the widening gap that has opened up between Kluck's First Army and von Bülow's Second Army. The French Fifth Army, now commanded by General Louis Franchet d'Esperey, also exploits the gap and then swings eastward to launch its greater strength against the right flank of the German Second

29

Army in what becomes known as the Battle of the Two Morins. After hard fighting von Bülow withdraws his right flank some six miles (9 km) and realigns it to face westward, thus further opening the gap between himself and Kluck's First Army. The British, meanwhile, are pushing northward, crossing the Marne River on September 9, and thereby drawing ever closer to the rear of Kluck's First Army.

As the Battle of the Two Morins rages, the French Ninth Army under General Ferdinand Foch attacks the left flank of von Bülow's Second Army. At the same time elements of the German Third Army run into Foch's right wing.

Foch's forces meet great resistance and fall back, pursued by the Germans. Despite repeated assaults, the Germans are unable to achieve a decisive breakthrough of Foch's front and the French hold. Foch telegraphs his situation to Joffre, his superior: "My center is falling back. My right retreats. Situation excellent. I attack!" This engagement, the Battle of St.-Gond, ends on the 8th.

To the east of Foch, the fifth engagement of the Marne offensive, the Battle of Vitry-le-François, is taking place between General Langle de Cary's French Fourth Army and Duke Albrecht of Württemburg's German

Fourth Army, which is supported by elements of the German Third Army. The French attack on the 6th but are quickly counterattacked. For three days the Germans batter unsuccessfully against the front of the French.

The final component of Joffre's Marne offensive is the attack of the French Third Army led by a new commander, General Maurice Sarrail. Sarrail attacks the Crown Prince's German Fifth Army from around Revigny in the Argonne Forest to

▲ A French priest looks on as a column of soldiers advances to the front during the opening stages of the successful Marne counterattack.

the north of Verdun. The French attack on the 6th begins just as the Germans open their own. There is fierce fighting and, although the Germans almost break through to Sarrail's rear, the French hold firm.

Although not strictly part of the Marne offensive, there is also fighting between the

◄ *British officers look on as a French field gun, with its ammunition caisson close by, is readied for action.*

the chief of the German General Staff, sends a subordinate, Lieutenant Colonel Richard Hentsch, to von Bülow's embattled Second Army to assess the situation. Hentsch arrives on the 8th to find von Bülow under great pressure from the French Fifth Army, which is threatening to turn his right flank, and planning to withdraw. Hentsch is also made aware that the British Expeditionary Force is advancing on the rear of von Kluck's First Army.

French First and Second Armies and the German Six and Seventh Armies in Alsace-Lorraine to the southeast of Verdun. The Germans lead the way with powerful attacks, which begin on the 4th, but the French just manage to stem the tide. The Germans call off their onslaught on the 10th.

SEPTEMBER 7–17

BALKANS, *SERBIA*

Austro-Hungarian troops under General Oskar Potiorek launch a second invasion of Serbia. They establish a number of positions across the Drina River, which are repeatedly attacked by the Serbians under Marshal Radomir Putnik. After 10 days of intense combat Putnik pulls his exhausted troops, who are short of supplies, back to positions around Belgrade, the Serbian capital, thus ending the Battle of the Drina River.

SEPTEMBER 8

WESTERN FRONT, *FRANCE*

While the Battle of the Marne is raging, General Helmuth von Moltke,

▲ *French troops escort German prisoners to the rear – some of the 29,000 captured during the fighting along the Marne.*

▼ *British troops come under accurate German artillery fire during the Battle of the Marne.*

SEPTEMBER 9

WESTERN FRONT, *FRANCE*

Lieutenant Colonel Hentsch concurs with von Bülow that the German Second Army should withdraw and later orders von Kluck's First Army to fall back from the east of Paris. These movements are confirmed by von Moltke, who also orders his armies to undertake a general withdrawal to a line stretching from Noyon on the Oise River to Verdun. The move is completed in five days.

The German withdrawal ends the Battle of the Marne. Although the Germans are far from crushed, they have suffered a decisive strategic defeat of profound consequence. The original Schlieffen Plan had called for a single sweeping victory over France in the first few weeks of the war. The Battle of the Marne makes this an

impossibility. Von Moltke's watered-down Schlieffen Plan has been unsuccessful and its failure bring about the nightmare scenario that it is meant to avoid – Germany facing a war on two fronts.

WESTERN FRONT, *BELGIUM*

King Albert launches an attack against the German forces outside Antwerp. The Belgian sortie so worries Kaiser Wilhelm II that he orders the immediate capture of the port. Over the next few weeks German reinforcements and large-caliber

▶ General Erich von Falkenhayn was made chief of the German General Staff on September 14.

howitzers threaten to overwhelm the garrison, despite the arrival of some British naval infantry.

SEPTEMBER 9–14

EASTERN FRONT, *EAST PRUSSIA*

Swift to capitalize on their recent victory against the Russian Army outside Tannenberg, the Germans strike against Rennenkampf's First Army at the Masurian Lakes. The Germans again attempt to surround the

▲ Cooks of a small field kitchen prepare food for German troops in East Prussia on the Eastern Front.

▼ British infantry take cover by a French roadside during the series of battles that became known as the "Race to the Sea."

Russians, but Rennenkampf launches a limited but successful counterattack, which allows his battered forces to escape. Nevertheless, the action at the Masurian Lakes is a major German success. In addition to losing 150 artillery pieces and 50 percent of their transport, the Russians have 125,000 men killed, wounded, or captured. The German casualties total 40,000 men.

SEPTEMBER 14

POLITICS, *GERMANY*
General Helmuth von Moltke pays the price for the failure of the Schlieffen Plan and strategic defeat in the Battle of the Marne. He is sacked and replaced as chief of the General Staff by General Erich von Falkenhayn.

SEPTEMBER 15–18

WESTERN FRONT, *FRANCE*
Planning to exploit his success at the Battle of the Marne, Joffre orders the French and British armies to attack the withdrawing German armies in what becomes known as the Battle of the Aisne. The main effort is by the British against the Chemin des Dames Ridge between Soissons and Craonne in the direction of Laon. The attack meets stubborn resistance. Joffre calls off the British and French offensive.

▲ *A German transport column moves into Galicia, a province of Austria-Hungary, during the successful attempt to prevent a Russian attack into Silesia, one of Germany's key industrial areas.*

Both sides now attempt to outflank each other – the Germans by attacking the French and British left flank, while they in turn strike against the opposing German right flank. What follows is a succession of similar turning actions that gradually take the rival forces ever closer to the North Sea as the year draws to a close. These indecisive encounters become known as the "Race to the Sea."

SEPTEMBER 17

POLITICS, *AUSTRALIA*
Prime Minister Andrew Fisher states that Australia will support Britain "to the last man and the last shilling" during an election campaign speech.

SEPTEMBER 17–27

EASTERN FRONT, *GALICIA*
Having roundly defeated the Russian forces menacing East Prussia, Generals Paul von Hindenburg and Erich Ludendorff rush troops by rail to support the badly-mauled Austro-Hungarians in Galicia.

They believe, correctly, that the Russians are preparing to strike into Silesia, one of Germany's key mining and industrial centers. The rail transfer is speedy, allowing the creation of the new German Ninth Army under Hindenburg's personal command in the vicinity of Cracow.

SEPTEMBER 22

SEA WAR, *NORTH SEA*

In a severe blow to British morale, the German submarine *U-9* sinks three British cruisers, the *Aboukir*, *Hogue*, and *Cressy*, in rapid succession off the Dutch coast. The loss of life totals over 1400 men.

SEA WAR, *INDIAN OCEAN*

A German light cruiser, the *Emden* under Captain Karl von Müller,

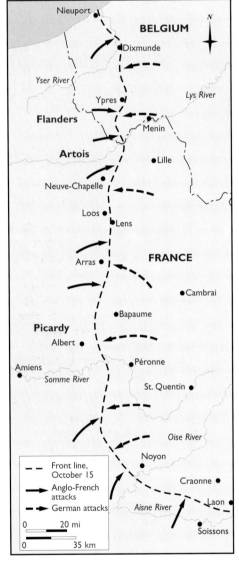

Front line, October 15

Anglo-French attacks

German attacks

0   20 mi

0   35 km

bombards British oil facilities at Madras, India. The *Emden*, which has been in action since August 22, continues to operate in the Indian and Pacific Oceans until it is sunk by the Australian cruiser *Sydney* off the Cocos Islands on November 9.

AIR WAR, *GERMANY*

The British launch their first air raid on Germany. Four Royal Navy Air Service Tabloids drop bombs on Zeppelin airship facilities at Cologne and Düsseldorf.

◄ *The "Race to the Sea" across northern France and Flanders took place between September and October. Neither side gained any advantage.*

▼ *British infantry move north in the attempt to attack the open right flank of the German forces on the Western Front.*

SEPTEMBER 22–24

WESTERN FRONT, *FRANCE*
German attacks against the fortress-city of Verdun are repulsed, but the French are forced to withdraw from the St. Mihiel salient, which the Germans will hold until 1918.

SEPTEMBER 22–26

WESTERN FRONT, *FRANCE*
The Battle of Picardy involves flank attacks by the French and Germans. The fighting is hotly contested and losses on both sides are severe. Neither gains an advantage and the offensives, part of the

"Race to the Sea," succeed only in extending the front northward across the Somme River in the direction of the French towns of Péronne and Albert.

SEPTEMBER 27–OCTOBER 10

WESTERN FRONT, *FRANCE*
The "Race to the Sea" continues with the Battle of Artois. It opens with Falkenhayn directing his commanders, who have received substantial reinforcements, to attack around the French and British left flank. However,

◀ *French cavalry and infantry officers study the progress of the fighting during the engagement along the Aisne River during September.*

▶ *Belgian troops oversee the destruction of a rail bridge to slow the German advance through their country.*

▼ *German infantry, in open order to reduce casualties from enemy fire, await the order to advance.*

Joffre is equal to the threat and rushes troops from the far right of his line and elsewhere in France to block the German attacks. Again, there is no decision beyond stretching the front line farther north to the Lys River in the area of the Franco-Belgian border. Over the following days the British Expeditionary Force moves into Belgium to prepare for the climax of the "Race to the Sea."

SEPTEMBER 28–NOVEMBER 1

EASTERN FRONT, *GALICIA*
Although Hindenburg's 19 German divisions are outnumbered by 60 Russian divisions, his Ninth Army strikes against the Russians west of the Vistula, reaching the river to the south of Warsaw, the Polish capital, on October 9. The German offensive runs out of steam three days later in the face of stiffer Russian resistance.

▲ Australian infantry at Melbourne embark on the transports that will take them to the Western Front.

◀ Austro-Hungarian troops, supported by heavy machine guns, advance against the Russians in Galicia during October.

Hindenburg, who has disrupted the Russian plans for their offensive into Silesia, now executes a careful, coordinated withdrawal, which begins on October 17. His units lay waste to the countryside as they retreat. Austro-Hungarian armies to the south of Hindenburg also make some progress against the Russians before being forced to withdraw.

▶ *German prisoners trudge to the rear watched over by their British escorts. As 1914 drew to a close, exhaustion, heavy losses, and bad weather ended the fighting on the Western Front.*

On November 1 Hindenburg is promoted to commander-in-chief of the Eastern Front, but is told he can expect to receive no reinforcements because of German commitments on the Western Front. Nevertheless, he plans a pre-emptive strike against the Russians in the area of Lódz.

OCTOBER 6

WESTERN FRONT, *BELGIUM*
The Belgian defenders of the port of Antwerp are close to being totally cut off. It is agreed that what remains of the Belgian field army should be evacuated. The evacuation is completed by the 8th and those troops who escape are landed between Zeebrugge and Ostend. Antwerp surrenders on the 10th.

OCTOBER 11

MIDDLE EAST, *TURKEY*
The commander of the Turkish Third Army reports that ethnic Armenians are deserting and that arms are being supplied to the Armenians by Russia.

OCTOBER 13

HOME FRONT, *BRITAIN*
The first Canadian troops in Europe land at Plymouth.

OCTOBER 16

HOME FRONT, *NEW ZEALAND*
The New Zealand Expeditionary Force sails for Europe from Wellington, after the arrival of a stronger naval escort.

OCTOBER 17

HOME FRONT, *AUSTRALIA*
Around 20,000 troops embark to fight on the Western Front in France.

OCTOBER 18–28

WESTERN FRONT,
FRANCE/BELGIUM
Field Marshal Sir John French orders the British Expeditionary Force to advance toward Menin, Belgium, and Lille, France, on the 18th in the opening stage of the Battle of the Yser. However, this move is pre-empted by

▼ *The Belgian countryside was flooded to slow the German advance on the Channel ports used by the British.*

the Germans, who had begun a slow advance a few days earlier aiming to capture the Channel ports used by the British. Falkenhayn has rushed massive reinforcements to the sector.

The British, with the aid of the French, are able to hold the German attack but at great cost. However, to the north, Belgian forces with limited French support struggle to contain the enemy advance. Eventually, King Albert of Belgium orders the opening of canal and sea-defense sluice gates. This

OCTOBER 20

desperate act floods a key area in the path of the German advance along the low-lying Belgian coast and brings it to a standstill.

On the 19th the newly-arrived British I Corps under General Sir Douglas Haig counterattacks the Germans from its positions around the Belgian city of Ypres. Haig's move effectively ends the German offensive and the British launch their own counterstroke.

This, however, fails due to the heavy rains that have turned the low-lying fields of Flanders into a morass and the stubborn German defense of the low-lying hills that circle around the north, east, and south of Ypres. French and British losses are heavy in what is the preliminary round of what becomes known as the First Battle of Ypres. The fighting around Ypres continues into late November.

OCTOBER 20

SEA WAR, *NORTH SEA*
The British *Glitra* becomes the first merchant ship to be sunk by a submarine. It is intercepted, boarded, and scuttled by the German *U-17* a few miles off the Norwegian coast.

OCTOBER 23

MIDDLE EAST, *MESOPOTAMIA*
British Indian Army forces land in Turkish-controlled Mesopotamia from their base on the island of Bahrain in the Persian Gulf, where they have been defending the British protectorate's oil installations. The limited British attacks are sufficient to evict the Turkish garrisons in southern Mesopotamia. The region's main port, Basra, located

close to the confluence of the Tigris and Euphrates Rivers, falls to the British on November 23.

OCTOBER 29

POLITICS, *TURKEY*
The government declares war. The decision to go to war is announced by the Turkish fleet bombarding the Russian Black Sea ports of Odessa, Sevastopol, and Theodosia. The fleet is commanded by German Vice Admiral Wilhelm von Souchon and includes the former German *Goeben* and *Breslau*.

Turkey's siding with the Central Powers closes the Dardanelles, the vital seaway linking the Mediterranean to the Black Sea. Crucially, the closure of this major route by Turkey prevents France and Britain sending military equipment to Russia and also cuts off the return trade in foodstuffs from the Russian Ukraine.

▼ *British forces, part of an artillery battery, move through the deserted streets of a Belgian village during the First Battle of Ypres.*

▲ Soldiers of the British Indian Army occupy a roadside embankment during the fighting around Ypres in late October.

◄ Turkish troops drill outside the walls of Constantinople, their capital.

OCTOBER 29–NOVEMBER 24

WESTERN FRONT, *BELGIUM*

General Erich von Falkenhayn, the chief of the General Staff, has steadily been building up the strength of the German Fourth and Sixth Armies around British-held Ypres to break through to the ports of Calais and Boulogne. Locally, the Germans enjoy an advantage of six-to-one and are superior in medium and heavy artillery. The offensive opens well and, despite French and British reserves being rushed to the sector, German units come close to breaking through southeast of Ypres on the 31st. Desperate fighting by the French and British stems the tide.

In early November the Germans renew their attempts to break through. Some progress is made and they take Dixmunde, to the north of Ypres, from the Belgians on the 11th. However, the British, who are bearing the brunt of the onslaught, finally halt the major German attacks on the same day.

Despite several German pushes over the following days, the worst of the fighting is over. The first snows fall on

▶ A German six-inch (15-cm) howitzer goes into action during the opening phase of the main attack against Ypres in October. This stalemated battle ended with both sides digging trench systems.

the 12th, heralding an end to the campaigning season. This, the First Battle of Ypres, is a success for the French and British, but it has been won at high cost. Half of the British Expeditionary Force are casualties. All sides now begin digging in earnest the trenches that will soon stretch from the North Sea to the Swiss border.

NOVEMBER 1

SEA WAR, *PACIFIC*

A powerful squadron of German warships commanded by Admiral Maximilian von Spee inflicts a major defeat on Vice Admiral Sir Christopher Cradock's British squadron off Coronel, Chile.

Spee, whose warships have been taking on coal from German colliers in Chilean waters, leads his two heavy cruisers, the *Gneisenau* and *Scharnhorst*, and three light cruisers, the *Dresden*, *Leipzig*, and *Nürnberg*, into battle in the late afternoon and in heavy seas.

NOVEMBER 2

Cradock's force, which has been hurriedly assembled to deal with Spee, consists of two old heavy cruisers, the *Good Hope* and *Monmouth*, the light cruiser *Glasgow*, and an armed former ocean liner, the *Otranto*. A fifth vessel, the aging battleship *Canopus*, has been left behind in the Falklands, a British coaling station in the South Atlantic, because it could not keep up with the rest of Cradock's squadron.

Spee's two heavy cruisers use the longer range of their main guns to smash Cradock's cruisers and frustrate the maneuvers of the British, who try to get to close range to use their smaller guns. Both the *Good Hope* and *Monmouth* go down with all hands, including Cradock, in the early evening. The *Glasgow* and *Otranto* escape under cover of darkness. The British are fearful that Spee's squadron will move into the Atlantic to disrupt their commerce and quickly send a squadron of warships under Vice Admiral Sir F. D. Sturdee to intercept Spee's warships.

▶ *A German mine has destroyed the bow of this British vessel. German surface vessels and submarines laid scores of mines in British waters during the campaign to starve Britain into surrender.*

▼ *Admiral Maximilian von Spee, the victor of the Battle of Coronel (far left).*

AIR WAR, *GERMANY*
Grand Admiral Alfred von Tirpitz, commander-in-chief of the Imperial Germany Navy, demands mass firebomb raids on London.

NOVEMBER 2

POLITICS, *SERBIA/RUSSIA*
Both countries declare war on Turkey. The Russian I Caucasian Corps invades

▶ *The German heavy cruiser* Gneisenau *was one of Admiral Maximilian von Spee's warships at the Battle of Coronel.*

▶ *Damage caused by the German naval bombardment of British ports.*

Turkish-governed Armenia at five points, but is repulsed by a Turkish counterattack on the 11th.

NOVEMBER 3

SEA WAR, *NORTH SEA*
German warships begin to bombard and lay mines off a number of towns along Britain's east coast. The raids reach their peak on December 16, when German heavy cruisers led by Admiral Franz von Hipper attack the ports of Whitby and Hartlepool and cause over 700 casualties.

Although the brief raids have little military impact, the dead toll of civilians and damage to property sends shockwaves through the British establishment. Of more military value are German mine-laying operations in British inshore waters.

NOVEMBER 3–4

AFRICA, *GERMAN EAST AFRICA*
A British amphibious assault directed against Tanga, a German-held port, is decisively defeated by General Paul von Lettow-Vorbeck.

▶ *German-officered local troops – known as askaris – drill in East Africa.*

Lettow-Vorbeck's force consists of a few German companies and local troops – askaris. Tanga marks the beginning of a four-year-long guerrilla war by Lettow-Vorbeck, which will see him operate at will throughout East Africa, tying down increasingly large British and Commonwealth forces with little aid from Germany. His campaign is a model of guerrilla warfare.

NOVEMBER 5–30

BALKANS, *SERBIA*
In the face of a renewed Austro-Hungarian offensive directed toward Belgrade and desperately short of ammunition, Marshal Radomir Putnik's Serbian troops holding positions outside the capital city withdraw slowly and in good order. However, Austro-Hungarian troops cannot be prevented from occupying Belgrade on December 2.

NOVEMBER 7

POLITICS, *TURKEY*
The government declares war on Belgium.

NOVEMBER 8

ESPIONAGE, *BRITAIN*
The naval high command forms the decoding unit known as Room 40, which becomes the hub of Britain's intelligence-gathering operations.

NOVEMBER 10

FAR EAST AND PACIFIC, *JAPAN*
After a siege that began in late August, the Japanese secure the formal surrender of the German base at Tsingtao, China.

NOVEMBER 11–25

EASTERN FRONT, GALICIA
The German Ninth Army, which has been commanded by General August von Mackensen since Hindenburg's recent promotion, is launched against the Russians. Mackensen's main aim is to drive a wedge between the Russian First and Second Armies and defeat each in turn. General Pavel Rennenkampf's First Army is overwhelmed by Mackensen and the Russian Second Army is virtually surrounded near Lódz.

However, a unusually swift Russian counterattack turns the tables on the Germans, and one of Mackensen's spearhead units, General Reinhard von Scheffer-Boyadel's XXV Reserve Corps, is surrounded. However, Scheffer-Boyadel displays exemplary powers of leadership, breaking out of the Russian encirclement and taking 16,000 Russian prisoners and more than 60

▶ Japanese siege artillery bombards the German colony of Tsingtao in China prior to an infantry assault on the defenses.

▼ Serbian forces launch an attack against the larger Austro-Hungarian forces that are menacing their capital Belgrade in late November.

December 1

artillery pieces with him in a running fight that lasts nine days in atrocious winter weather.

Although the Russians have rebuffed the German offensive directed against Lódz, the strategic initiative remains with Hindenburg, who, although still outnumbered, has thwarted the Russian plan to invade the German industrial heartland of Silesia. German casualties in the battle total 35,000 men killed or wounded; Russian casualties are at least three times as many.

December 1

MIDDLE EAST, *CAUCASUS*
Renewed fighting sees the Russians capture Sarai and Batumi.

▶ *Survivors from the German heavy cruiser* **Gneisenau** *make for the British battleship* **Inflexible** *following the Battle of the Falklands.*

▼ *Russian soldiers captured by the Germans during the fighting around Lódz await the arrival of transportation to take them to their prison camps.*

him. Spee had intended to destroy the British coaling and communication facilities at Port Stanley in the Falkland Islands, but unknown to him a British squadron commanded by Vice Admiral Sir F. D. Sturdee, which arrived two days earlier, is waiting for him.

On sighting the British, Spee orders his warships to withdraw. However, Sturdee's two dreadnought battleships, the *Inflexible* and *Invincible*, give chase supported by a number of armored cruisers commanded by Rear Admiral Stoddart. As the two dreadnoughts emerge from Port Stanley harbor, the aging battleship *Canopus*, which escaped the British defeat at Coronel, opens fire on Spee's ships from the harbor, where the vessel has been beached to create a steady gun platform.

Spee's position is hopeless: the British warships are faster and carry heavier armaments. The *Scharnhorst*,

▼ Damage caused to the British cruiser Kent by a German shell during the Battle of the Falklands.

DECEMBER 3-9

BALKANS, *SERBIA*

Serbian forces under Marshal Radomir Putnik, now supplied with ammunition by France, launch a major attack on the Austro-Hungarian forces inside Serbia. The Battle of Kolubra is a major Serbian victory. The Austro-Hungarian armies collapse under the Serbian assaults and are thrown out of Serbia.

The Austro-Hungarian commander, General Oskar Potiorek, is sacked for this humiliating defeat and replaced by Archduke Eugene. Austro-Hungarian casualties in the campaign, which began in September, are enormous – roughly 50 percent, some 230,000 men. The Serbian casualty list in the campaign totals 170,000 men out of 400,000 engaged.

DECEMBER 4

MIDDLE EAST, *MESOPOTAMIA*

At the First Battle of Qurna, an initial British landing party is blocked by Turkish forces, but the town is captured on the 9th.

DECEMBER 8

SEA WAR, *ATLANTIC*

German Admiral Maximilian von Spee, fresh from his victory at Coronel, Chile, in early November is surprised by a British squadron sent to intercept

December 14

Spee's flagship, is the first of the two German armored cruisers to be sunk and is followed by the other, the *Gneisenau.* Two of Spee's other three vessels are also sunk. The light cruisers *Nürnberg* and *Leipzig* are sent to the bottom by the armored cruisers *Kent* and *Cornwall* respectively.

Spee's last warship, the light cruiser *Dresden,* escapes from the Falklands. However, the *Dresden* is cornered three months later in Chilean territorial waters by the *Glasgow* and

Kent. Unable to evade its British pursuers, the last of Spee's squadron is scuttled by its crew.

December 14
WESTERN FRONT, FRANCE/BELGIUM
Despite the worsening weather and the growing strength of the German

▶ *Turkish artillery in action during Enver Pasha's large offensive into the Russian-occupied areas of Armenia.*

defenses, the French and British undertake a general offensive along the Western Front, from the North Sea to Verdun. They believe, correctly, that they outnumber the Germans, who have rushed large numbers of men to the Eastern Front. However, they underestimate the strength of the German trench system or the excellent qualities of the German soldiers.

Most of the attacks end by December 24 and little progress is made. Only in Champagne, where the French have made moderate gains at the expense of huge casualties, does the fighting go

◀ *British artillerymen prime shells and prepare to fire a light field gun from behind rudimentary defenses in the Ypres sector.*

▼ *The German cruiser Dresden settles on the seabed after being scuttled by its crew off Chile.*

on over the winter months. The First Battle of Champagne continues into 1915, but elsewhere the fighting dies down as both sides come to recognize that their belief in a swift victory is totally misplaced.

World War I is just six months old and the casualty lists are unparalleled in the history of warfare. On the Western Front alone the French, British, and Belgians have suffered more than one million casualties, of which the vast majority are French. The Germans have had around 675,000 troops killed, wounded, or missing in action.

Equally, losses on the Eastern Front are unprecedented. Some 275,000 Germans have

been killed, wounded, or taken prisoner, while the equivalent figures for Austria-Hungary are up to one million and for Russia some 1.8 million.

In the Balkans the Austro-Hungarians have suffered 225,000 men killed, wounded, or taken prisoner, while Serbia acknowledges casualties totaling around 170,000 men.

DECEMBER 18

POLITICS, *BRITAIN*

To secure their strategic position in the Mediterranean and Middle East, the British declare a protectorate over Egypt and begin to move troops to defend the Suez Canal, the strategic waterway that connects the British with the oil-producing regions around the Persian Gulf and their key colonial possession, India.

MIDDLE EAST, *ARMENIA*

Despite the onset of winter, Enver Pasha prepares to launch a complex offensive against the Russian forces in Armenia and the Caucasus. This begins on the 21st and has forced three Russian divisions to retreat by the end of the year.

DECEMBER 29

MIDDLE EAST, *CAUCASUS*

The Russian commander General Vorontsov thwarts the Turkish advance toward Kars in the Caucasus at the Battle of Sarikamish, but the fighting continues. Neither side is able to gain a victory.

KEY MOMENTS

CHRISTMAS TRUCE

By Christmas 1914 the soldiers on the Western Front were exhausted and shocked by the scale of the losses they had suffered since August. At dawn on the 25th the British holding trenches around the Belgian city of Ypres heard carols ringing out from the opposing German positions and then spied Christmas trees being placed along the front of the German trenches. Slowly, lines of German soldiers climbed out of their trenches and advanced to the halfway point of no-man's land, where they called on the British to join them. The two sides met in the middle of the shell-blasted wasteland, exchanged gifts, talked, and played games of football.

Such events were common all along the line where British and German troops sat in opposition to each other and the fraternization continued for up to a week in some places until the military authorities ordered it to be stamped out. There were, however, no such truces in the sectors where French and German forces opposed each other.

British and German soldiers fraternize in the middle of no-man's land around Ypres in Belgium during the 1914 Christmas truce.

1915

In 1915 the war became much more global – Italy sided with Britain and France and the Bulgarians threw in their lot with the Central Powers. Both sides were confronted by strategic dilemmas over where they could best exploit their military might to advantage. Equally, the list of casualties was growing ever longer as the stalemate of the trench fighting intensified. Neutral powers, particularly the United States, were also feeling the war's impact.

JANUARY 1–3

MIDDLE EAST, *CAUCASUS*
The Battle of Sarikamish, which began in late December 1914, continues. Some 100,000 Russian troops are opposing a Turkish advance toward the city of Kars. The Turkish attack is badly managed by Enver Pasha, whose 95,000-strong army is suffering severely from the bitter cold. A sudden Russian counterattack forces the Turks to retreat to Erzerum. Some 30,000 Turks are killed in the battle and around only 19,000 of those who escape to Erzerum are fit for further service. Enver Pasha renounces his command. The Russian commander, General Vorontsov, shows little drive in pursuing the Turks and is replaced by General Nikolai Yudenich.

JANUARY 11

POLITICS, *BRITAIN*
An offer of Turkish territory in return for Greek military support of Serbia is rejected by the Greek government. It is made by the British foreign secretary, Sir Edward Grey. Similar offers are rebuffed over the following weeks, chiefly because the Greeks demand Anglo-French forces to protect their sovereignty.

JANUARY 13

POLITICS, *AUSTRIA-HUNGARY*
Foreign Minister Count Leopold von Berchtold resigns and is replaced by Hungarian Baron Burian.
POLITICS, *BRITAIN*
A council of war decides upon a naval attack against Turkey with the aim of opening the Dardanelles seaway to the

◀ *Turkish cavalrymen operating against the Russians in the Caucasus pictured at their field camp.*

▼ *German destroyers move cautiously while rescuing survivors from the Blücher, a battlecruiser sunk at the Dogger Bank.*

 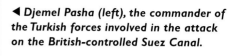

◄ *Djemel Pasha (left), the commander of the Turkish forces involved in the attack on the British-controlled Suez Canal.*

any German incursion into the North Sea. The interception of German radio traffic means that the British are informed of Hipper's raid.

On the 24th Beatty and Hipper meet at the Dogger Bank shoals roughly in the center of the North Sea. Hipper, surprised by the British, orders a withdrawal but is soon caught by Beatty's faster and better-armed warships. The first of Hipper's ships to suffer from British fire is the *Blücher*, which sinks shortly after midday. However, Beatty's flagship, the *Lion*, suffers extensive damage from one of *Derfflinger*'s shells and falls out of the battle line. Helped by the confusion caused by Beatty's need to transfer his flag to the *Princess Royal*, Hipper is able to make his escape.

▼ *Admiral Franz von Hipper led the German battlecruiser squadron at the Battle of the Dogger Bank. He was able to outrun a larger British force.*

flow of supplies between Russia and France and Britain. The British seek French approval, which is given on the 26th. First Lord of the Admiralty Sir Winston Churchill is the chief advocate of the operation.

JANUARY 14

MIDDLE EAST, *PALESTINE*
Some 25,000 Turkish troops backed by more than 50 artillery pieces begin an advance from Beersheba in Palestine against the British troops defending the Suez Canal in Egypt. Their commander is Djemal Pasha, the Turkish minister of marine.

JANUARY 19–20

AIR WAR, *BRITAIN*
The Germans launch their first Zeppelin airship raid. Two Zeppelins, the *L3* and *L4*, bomb eastern England, causing 20 casualties among civilians.

JANUARY 24

SEA WAR, *NORTH SEA*
A clash between elements of the British Home Fleet and Germany's High Seas Fleet is partly brought about by public disquiet at the seeming ease with which German warships are bombarding ports on the east coast of England. On the 23rd Admiral Franz von Hipper's German battlecruiser squadron of four ships (*Blücher*, *Derfflinger*, *Moltke*, and *Seydlitz*) with destroyer, light cruiser, and airship cover sails to attack ports and the British fishing fleet. However, the British have already moved a force of warships under Admiral Sir David Beatty from distant Scapa Flow in the Orkneys to Rosyth in southern Scotland, from where it can more easily intercept

▲ *The engine room of a German U-boat. These submarines bore the brunt of efforts to strangle the flow of supplies to Germany's enemies.*

▼ *General August von Mackensen (left) was one of Germany's most successful commanders on the Eastern Front.*

The Battle of the Dogger Bank curtails German naval raids on Britain, but also highlights certain weaknesses in British naval procedures. The gunnery of Beatty's warships has been extremely poor – just 73 hits out of 958 shells fired. Equally, the orders between the various British vessels has been slow and ambiguous. Neither shortcoming is properly addressed.

On the plus side Hipper has been forced to withdraw after losing one vessel. Although the British do not know it, he has also suffered damage to the *Seydlitz*; a severe fire in one of its turrets has killed 159 sailors. The Germans study the causes of the fire and introduce new safety regulations.

JANUARY 29

POLITICS, *BRITAIN*
Government minister David Lloyd George suggests to the British War Council that Anglo-French forces be sent to Salonika, Greece, to encourage various Balkan states to declare war on Austria-Hungary. However, the Greeks reject the offer.

JANUARY 30

SEA WAR, *ENGLISH CHANNEL*
Two British ships are torpedoed without warning by the German submarine *U-20*, marking an escalation in the naval war. Previously, submarines have stopped suspect vessels and allowed their crews to abandon their ships before sending them to the bottom.

JANUARY 31

POLITICS, *AUSTRIA-HUNGARY*
As relations between erstwhile Triple Alliance allies Austria-Hungary and Italy deteriorate, the Austro-Hungarians

complete the transfer of 30 battalions to protect their long and mountainous border with the Italians.

POLITICS, *SOUTH AFRICA*
The authorities introduce adult male conscription.

EASTERN FRONT, *RUSSIA*
The German Ninth Army under General August von Mackensen attacks toward Warsaw. The advance, known as the Battle of Bolimov, is opened by 600

DECISIVE WEAPONS

GAS WARFARE

Gas was first used in 1915, initially by Germany and then Britain and France. Some of the early gas attacks were launched from cylinders sited in forward trenches and required a favorable prevailing wind for the clouds to drift toward the enemy. This method of discharge was unsatisfactory, so gas shells were developed. Germany used gas shells to little affect on the Eastern Front in January 1915, but France developed the most practical device. This consisted of a shell largely filled with gas and only a small explosive device to crack the casing and allow the gas to escape.

There were also a number of different gas types used. The first was xylyl bromide, a type of tear gas. This was followed by chlorine. However, lethal gas types were soon developed, chiefly phosgene and mustard gas. The latter was the most feared: not only did it attack the body through the lungs, it also burned the skin and damaged the bloodstream, and could cause permanent blindness. It was also a persistent agent and would usually lie on the ground for three days or so after an attack.

The British Livens gas projector was a simple steel tube sunk into the ground. A gas shell and propellant were placed in the tube and fired by electric charge.

▲ *German artillerymen prepare to fire a Krupp-manufactured six-inch (15-cm) howitzer in Galicia. The howitzer, however, has yet to be elevated.*

artillery pieces bombarding the Russian positions with 18,000 poison gas shells – the first time poison gas has been used in the war. However, the intense cold and adverse winds minimize the impact of the poison gas to such an extent that the Russians hardly notice its use and fail to notify their allies. Russian counterattacks on February 6 recapture ground lost to the Ninth Army at a cost of 40,000 casualties. German losses total 20,000.

Bolimov is, in fact, a diversionary attack designed to mislead the Russians as to the true nature of the forthcoming German and Austro-Hungarian offensive. Directed by Field Marshal Paul von Hindenburg, the forthcoming offensive, scheduled to begin on February 7, has been planned as a massive pincer attack. In the north two German armies, the Eighth and Tenth, are poised to strike eastward into Russia from around the Masurian Lakes in East Prussia.

▲ *Russian troops receive supplies of ammunition. Although numerically strong, the Russian Army was short of many basic military necessities.*

▼ *German troops move forward rapidly during their attempted breakthrough to the besieged fortress of Przemysl.*

From their positions along the Carpathian Mountains to the south, three other armies are poised to strike northward into the Austro-Hungarian province of Galicia, much of which was captured by the Russians in 1914. The Austro-Hungarian and German army commanded by German General Alexander von Linsingen is under orders to drive toward the fortress of Lemberg, which was lost to the Russians on September 3, 1914.

This attack is supported by General Karl von Pflanzer-Baltin's Austro-Hungarian Seventh Army. General Svetozan Borojevic von Bojna's Austro-Hungarian Third Army is tasked with breaking through the Russian forces outside Przemysl, whose Austro-Hungarian garrison has been besieged on and off since September 1914.

FEBRUARY 1

POLITICS, *GERMANY*
The government agrees to permit an unrestricted submarine campaign – ships, even those of neutral countries, can now be sunk without warning.
HOME FRONT, *GERMANY*
The authorities introduce bread and flour rationing in the capital, Berlin.

FEBRUARY 3

MIDDLE EAST, *EGYPT*
Turkish forces attempt to cross the Suez Canal, but the attack is repulsed by British-officered Indian troops. The Turks fall back to Beersheba, Palestine, after suffering close to 2000 casualties.

▲ The sweeping successes enjoyed by German and Austro-Hungarian armies on the Eastern Front in 1915.

▼ British-officered Indian troops occupy shallow trenches during their defense of the Suez Canal against the Turks.

▲ German troops continue their advance into northern Russia following the Second Battle of the Masurian Lakes.

FEBRUARY 4

POLITICS, *GERMANY*
The authorities announce that submarines will blockade Britain from the 18th. All vessels, whether sailing under combatant flags or not, are deemed legitimate targets.

FEBRUARY 7–22

EASTERN FRONT, *EAST PRUSSIA*
Field Marshal Paul von Hindenburg begins his pincer offensive against the Russians by sending his German Eighth and Tenth Armies against the Russian Tenth Army. The Eighth Army attacks first in the face of a blizzard. It nevertheless strikes hard against the left flank of the Russian Tenth Army. On the 8th, General Hermann von Eichhorn's German Tenth Army attacks the Russian Tenth Army's right.
The Russians fight back hard but are forced back into the Augustow Forest, where only the heroic action of the Russian XX Corps prevents a complete disaster. The corps is

forced to surrender on the 21st, but its action has allowed the Russian Tenth Army's other three corps to escape encirclement. Nevertheless, the Russian front line has been pushed back some 70 miles (112 km). The Germans capture some 90,000 Russians during this action, which is known as the Second Battle of the Masurian Lakes.
After their defeat at the Masurian Lakes, the Russians hastily form the Twelfth Army under General Wenzel von Plehve, who launches a counter-attack against the German right flank with some success on the 22nd.

FEBRUARY 12

POLITICS, *GERMANY*
Kaiser Wilhelm II issues an order regarding the prosecution of the air war against Britain. The list of key

53

General Svetozan Borojevic von Bojna's Austro-Hungarian Third Army fails to make any significant progress in the attempt to relieve the besieged garrison of Przemysl.

FEBRUARY 19

SEA WAR, *MEDITERRANEAN*
Several French and British warships commanded by Vice Admiral Sackville Carden bombard Turkish forts protecting the Dardanelles seaway between the Mediterranean and Black Sea. Operations against the forts intensify over the following weeks.

FEBRUARY 20

MIDDLE EAST, *EGYPT*
Australian and New Zealand troops training in Egypt are earmarked to take part in operations against the Turkish-controlled Dardanelles.

FEBRUARY 22

AFRICA, *SOUTHWEST AFRICA*
General Louis Botha, the prime minister of the Union of South Africa, leads a reconnaissance into German Southwest Africa. Over the following weeks

▲ German cavalrymen escort Russian prisoners to the rear – some of the 60,000 taken at the fall of the town of Czernowitz in Galicia.

targets includes fuel stores, dockyard facilities, and military bases – but it specifically excludes raids on urban residential areas and royal palaces.

FEBRUARY 14

POLITICS, *TURKEY*
The three-man Committee of Union and Progress agrees to launch a genocidal war against the Armenians, who occupy the country's northern border with Russia and are suspected of having close links with the Russians.

FEBRUARY 17

EASTERN FRONT, *GALICIA*
General Karl von Pflanzer-Baltin's Austro-Hungarian Seventh Army captures the Russian-held town of Czernowitz as part of the joint German and Austro-Hungarian drive into Galicia from their positions along the line of the Carpathian Mountains. However, progress elsewhere is limited due to the awful weather, Austro-Hungarian incompetence, and Russian resistance. General Alexander von Linsingen's army fails to reach Lemberg and

▲ Russian troops march through a town in the Austro-Hungarian province of Galicia in an attempt to block advancing enemy forces.

▼ Austro-Hungarian troops man the firestep of a trench in Galicia.

an invasion force of some 43,000 South Africans is massed at four points. German troops total 9000. The invasion begins on March 7.

FEBRUARY 24

HOME FRONT, *AUSTRIA-HUNGARY*
The government takes over the direct distribution of both grain and flour supplies.

MARCH 1

POLITICS, *BRITAIN*
The government, with French backing, announces that it "would prevent commodities of any kind entering or leaving Germany," thus marking the

beginning of a naval-led economic blockade. There are protests from, among others, the United States.

AIR WAR, *FRANCE*
The first ever specialized fighter unit is established by Commandant Baron de Tricornet. Its pilots fly Parasol two-seater aircraft.

MARCH 6

POLITICS, *AUSTRIA-HUNGARY*
The Austro-Hungarian chief-of-staff, General Conrad von Hötzendorf, informs General Erich von Falkenhayn, the chief of the German General Staff, that war with Italy is inevitable.

MARCH 10

POLITICS, *BRITAIN*
Secretary of War Lord Kitchener tells General Sir Ian Hamilton that he will command the ground forces earmarked for the attack on the Gallipoli Peninsula in Turkey. The first landings are scheduled for April.

AIR WAR, *WESTERN FRONT*
The British Royal Flying Corps develops five innovations to support the Neuve-Chapelle offensive: a "clock system" whereby observers can plot the fall of an artillery shot on a celluloid disk; the coordination of bombing attacks with the ground offensive;

▼ South African mounted troops prepare to advance into German Southwest Africa. Some South Africans opposed supporting the British and launched a short but unsuccessful rebellion.

▲ *Camouflaged British howitzers begin the 35-minute bombardment that heralded the opening of the attack at Neuve-Chapelle on March 10.*

patrols to identify counterattacking German troops; photo-mosaic mapping of the German trench system; and protective patrols over British troops moving up to the battlefield.

MARCH 10–13

WESTERN FRONT, *FRANCE*
Field Marshal Sir John French's British Expeditionary Force launches a limited offensive at Neuve-Chapelle in Artois, northeastern France. Following a short bombardment by some 350 artillery pieces, four British and Indian divisions attack along a 4000-yard (3660-m) front. Early progress is comparatively good – Neuve-Chapelle falls, as do several lines of German trenches. However, ammunition shortages and rapid German counterattacks blunt the advance. The British dig in on the captured ground and beat off subsequent German attacks. British casualties total 11,500 men by the end of the offensive on the 13th. The British conclude that artillery fire is the key to success in trench warfare.

▼ *British troops man a fairly basic front-line trench. As the war progressed, they would be dug deeper and strengthened. Men would be protected by dug-outs and their trenches fronted by barbed wire.*

◄ *A Russian 11-inch (280-mm) howitzer outside the Austro-Hungarian fortress of Przemysl, which fell on March 22.*

▲ *A French six-inch (155-mm) gun is readied for action. An obsolete design, it was in service due to artillery shortages.*

MARCH 18

AFRICA,
SOUTHWEST AFRICA
General Louis Botha leads 21,000 troops in the main invasion of German Southwest Africa.
SEA WAR, *MEDITERRANEAN*
The final Anglo-French attempt to force a way through the Dardanelles by naval power alone fails. Three warships from the fleet commanded by Rear Admiral John de Robeck are sunk by Turkish mines and three badly damaged. De Robeck orders his surviving warships to withdraw from the Dardanelles.

▶ *Rear Admiral John de Robeck failed to break through the Dardanelles with naval power.*

Unbeknown to de Robeck, the Turks are in fact on the point of collapse – they are short of ammunition and many of their batteries are inoperable. However, the British and French begin to push ahead with their planning for an overland attack aimed at Constantinople via the Gallipoli Peninsula. French and British troops are already gathering for the landings. However, problems with loading men and equipment push back the operation to late April. The Turks, who are aware of the invasion, begin to strengthen

their defenses. German General Liman von Sanders is placed in charge of the 60,000 Turkish troops in the area.

MARCH 22

EASTERN FRONT, *GALICIA*
The 110,000-strong Austro-Hungarian garrison of Przemysl surrenders to the Russians following the recent unsuccessful attempts to relieve it by the Austro-Hungarian Third Army. It has been under almost constant bombardment since early February.

MARCH 27

HOME FRONT, *BRITAIN*
The press begin a campaign criticizing the shortage of artillery shells following the publication of Field Marshal Sir John French's letter concerning the same issue in *The Times* newspaper. French's superiors are outraged.

APRIL 5

WESTERN FRONT, *FRANCE*
The French launch their First and Third Armies in an attack against the German-held St. Mihiel salient in the Meuse–Argonne region. Progress is limited due to a combination of poor

weather, thick mud, and the extensive German defenses. The attack peters out within a few weeks, but small-scale skirmishing continues over the following months.

APRIL 8

POLITICS, *TURKEY*
Turkish troops begin to crush any support for the Russians in Armenia and Armenian desires for independence. A systematic campaign of great brutality follows: men are murdered, while women and children are deported to other Turkish provinces.

▲ *Turkish cavalrymen advance through an Armenian village. The Armenians, a Christian minority in a Muslim country, were ruthlessly persecuted by the Turks.*

By September some estimates suggest that one million Armenians have been killed outright or died through neglect or starvation. A further 200,000 Armenians have been forced to convert to Islam from Christianity. The surviving Armenians revolt against the Turks.

APRIL 12

MIDDLE EAST, *MESOPOTAMIA*
A Turkish advance on the British base at Basra is defeated at Shaiba. Although outnumbered two-to-one by 12,000 Turks, the British troops inflict some 3200 casualties.

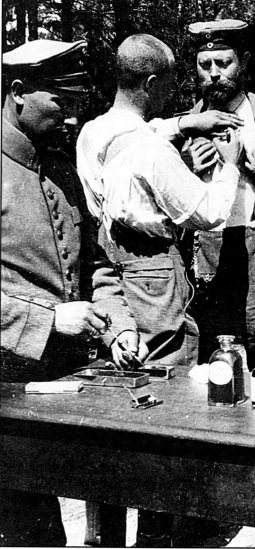

▲ German troops are vaccinated against cholera on the Eastern Front.

◄ Germany's commitment to the Eastern Front grew in 1915 due to the increasing military weakness of Austria-Hungary and a belief that Russia could be knocked out of the war quickly.

STRATEGY & TACTICS

EAST VERSUS WEST

Both Germany's military planners and their enemies faced a strategic dilemma in 1915: where was the war to be won? On the Western Front the Germans held French and Belgian territory and had no immediate need to attack. They could extend their defense lines, launch counterattacks, and give up unimportant ground if necessary. Matters were different on the Eastern Front, where the fighting was more fluid and more suitable to the sweeping flanking attacks the Germans favored. Germany had already won several spectacular victories on the Eastern Front, but also had to lend extensive support to the less competent Austro-Hungarian Army.

If Russia was comprehensively defeated then the German forces on the Eastern Front could be sent west to deliver a knock-out blow against the British and French. Hindenburg and Ludendorff favored an all-out onslaught to smash Russia, while Falkenhayn believed that the war could only be won on the Western Front and that victories against Russia would have only a limited overall impact. Hindenburg and Ludendorff, backed by Kaiser Wilhelm II, won the argument.

The British faced a similar dilemma. Some, mainly politicians, believed that the Western Front was a slogging match that offered little more than a growing casualty bill for negligible gain. They argued that action on other fronts, in the Middle East and the Balkans, might achieve more by knocking out of the war one or both of the two weaker Central Powers – Turkey and Austria-Hungary. Their opponents, chiefly senior military figures, argued that victory could only be achieved by defeating Germany on the Western Front. In 1915, at least, the politicians had their way.

APRIL 13

POLITICS, *GERMANY*

Kaiser Wilhelm II accedes to the demands of his military planners that German military efforts must focus on the Eastern Front, particularly in the light of recent Austro-Hungarian offensive shortcomings. Eight divisions are to be transferred by rail from the Western Front to the south of Cracow and a new German Eleventh Army under General August von Mackensen is formed on the 16th. General Erich von Falkenhayn travels east to take overall command of the forthcoming attack, although he believes that victory can only be truly won on the Western Front.

The offensive involves Field Marshal Paul von Hindenburg's forces north of Warsaw launching limited attacks to occupy the Russian forces opposite them. The key attack will, however, take place to the south and be led by Mackensen's Eleventh Army. Mackensen's army will launch a broad-front offensive directed toward the towns of Gorlice and Tarnow. Austro-Hungarian troops will also take part in the attack.

APRIL 14

▶ *Dutch aviation engineer Anthony Fokker developed a device allowing machine guns to fire through propellers.*

APRIL 14

POLITICS, *GREECE*
The government rejects an offer of Turkish territory if it joins the war against the Central Powers.

APRIL 17

SEA WAR, *MEDITERRANEAN*
The British *E17* becomes the first submarine to break through the Turkish defenses (forts, mines, and nets) guarding the Dardanelles in 1915. Others will follow in the wake of the *E17* and score many successes against German and Turkish shipping operating in the Black Sea.

APRIL 19

TECHNOLOGY, *GERMANY*
Aviation engineers working for Dutch-born Anthony Fokker develop the mechanical interrupter gear, which allows machine-gun bullets to be fired through the blades of a rotating aircraft propeller. This greatly facilitates the development of dedicated single-seater fighters.

APRIL 20

MIDDLE EAST, *ARMENIA*
Some 1300 armed Armenian rebels and 30,000 non-combatants are besieged in the city of Van by Turkish forces. They successfully hold out until the siege is broken by Russian forces on May 19.

APRIL 22

WESTERN FRONT, *BELGIUM*
The Second Battle of Ypres begins with the first use of poison chlorine gas on the Western Front. The Germans have amassed 4000 gas cylinders,

▶ *The Second Battle of Ypres, fought in April and May, saw the Germans reduce the size of the British-held salient around the Belgian town.*

▼ *A British submarine, the E11, is cheered home after a successful sortie against enemy shipping in the Black Sea.*

BELGIUM

Langemarck •   • Passchendaele
   • Pilckem
     • St. Julien

BELGIUM
     • Frenzenberg

Ypres •   • Bellewaarde

—— Front, April 22
- - - Front, May 24

0   3 mi
0   4 km

Wytschaete •

▲ German troops in a reserve trench on the Western Front wear an early form of gas-mask consisting of a gauze pad tied around the mouth and nose.

▶ German machine-gunners begin to move their Maxims into the front line.

which they use to open an attack by their Fourth Army. Having no protection against the gas, several units holding the northern flank of the salient panic and run away, opening a gap in the front line some five miles (8 km) wide. A second gas attack takes place the next day.

APRIL 23

MEDITERRANEAN, *SKYROS*
British poet Rupert Brooke dies of blood poisoning on a hospital ship lying off the Greek island.

APRIL 24

WESTERN FRONT, *BELGIUM*
The Germans use gas in their offensive against the Ypres salient. Their attack concentrates on St. Julien, which is held by the 1st Canadian Division. The Canadians improvise gas protection by

MUSTAFA KEMAL

Later known as Ataturk and regarded as the founding father of modern Turkey, Mustafa Kemal (1881–1938) remains a national hero to many modern Turks. A professional soldier, he served in the Turco-Italian War (1911–12) and the Balkan Wars (1912–13). He rose to public prominence for his role in defeating the Anglo-French landing at Gallipoli in 1915, where his energy and drive prevented the invaders from capitalizing on their surprise attack.

After Gallipoli Kemal served in the Caucasus and Syria, where his radical proposal for the abandonment of many provinces of the Turkish Empire in the Middle East offended his superiors. He was sent on indefinite sick leave (December 1917), but was recalled to active service in the later summer of 1918, just in time to witness Turkey's defeat.

After World War I Kemal became head of an alternative government to that in Constantinople and fought to prevent the dismemberment of Turkey. In 1922 he advanced on the capital from his base around Ankara, securing the withdrawal of the occupying World War I victors.

He was proclaimed president of the new secular Republic of Turkey in October 1923 and established a new capital at Ankara. He also instituted wide-ranging reforms to modernize the country. Held in great popular esteem, he was given the name Ataturk, meaning "Father of Turks," in 1934.

using handkerchiefs soaked in water or urine, and prevent a major German breakthrough.

APRIL 25

MIDDLE EAST, *TURKEY*

The Anglo-French invasion of the Gallipoli Peninsula begins. The plan calls for three initial landings, totaling 30,000 men. The first involves British troops landing at Cape Helles on the very tip of the peninsula. The second involves the Australian and New Zealand Army Corps (ANZAC) forces coming ashore to the north of Cape Helles at Ari Burna. The third is designed as a diversionary attack and involves French troops landing at Kumkale on the opposite side of the Dardanelles.

Naval gunfire is used to support each attack and there is a demonstration by warships against Bulair, some 50 miles (80 km) north of Cape Helles to distract the attention of the local commander, German General Liman von Sanders.

The landings on the peninsula do not go smoothly. At Cape Helles the British 29th Division comes ashore at five beaches in the face of intense fire from the local Turkish defenders. Despite heavy casualties, elements of the division almost reach their chief objective – the commanding heights

▲ *A British field hospital in Belgium during the fighting around Ypres. Medical orderlies attend the lightly wounded.*

▼ *German troops enjoy a break before the opening of the attack toward the towns of Gorlice and Tarnow, both of which capitulated in early May.*

of Achi Baba and the town of Krithia – on the 28th. However, confusion reigns and some of the troops stop to make tea. The Turks rush troops forward and occupy both positions, from where they can shoot down on the British landing beaches.

The ANZACs at Ari Burna are also tasked with capturing high ground – the ridge of Chunuk Bair. The area is relatively lightly defended and the ANZACs come very close to capturing it. However, the prompt action of a Turkish officer, Mustafa Kemal, who rushes reserves to the sector just in time, prevents the ANZACs from taking their primary objective.

APRIL 26

POLITICS, *ITALY*

The government agrees to become in-volved in the war against its former ally Austria-Hungary and has been promised substantial territorial gains in the event of victory. The Austro-Hungarians rapidly move reinforce-ments to their border with Italy from the Eastern Front and Serbia to strengthen their defenses.

APRIL 28

MIDDLE EAST, *TURKEY*

The British launch an attack to capture the Turkish positions around the town of Krithia on the Gallipoli Peninsula. They advance just two miles

▲ *A Turkish shell explodes close to one of the piers used by the British to land troops and supplies at Cape Helles on the tip of the Gallipoli Peninsula.*

▼ *The Anglo-French landings at Gallipoli were a costly failure.*

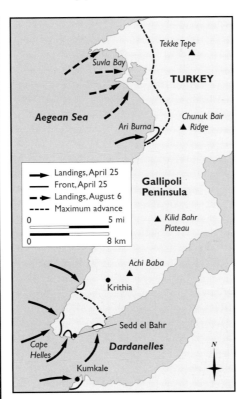

(3 km) at the cost of 3000 casualties. The Turks, who are rushing reinforce-ments to the peninsula, launch a succession of counterattacks.

MAY 1

EASTERN FRONT, *GALICIA*

The German attack toward Gorlice and Tarnow begins, heralded by a four-hour barrage from more than 600 artillery pieces, which fire both con-ventional and gas shells. German and Austro-Hungarian forces advance along a 28-mile (45-km) front, smashing the Russian Third Army. Gorlice falls on the following day and Tarnow on the 6th. The German forces capitalize on their early gains and continue their advance deep into Galicia over the following weeks.

SEA WAR, *ATLANTIC*

The *U-30* sinks the first US merchant ship, the *Gulflight*, without warning.

MAY 6

WESTERN FRONT, *BELGIUM*

The commander of the British Second Army at Ypres, General Sir Horace Smith-Dorrien, is removed from his post after suggesting that a tactical withdraw would reduce pressure on the salient. His superior, Field Marshal Sir John French, disagrees strongly and continues to order counterattacks,

The Cunard Liner LUSITANIA

▲ *The British liner* Lusitania, *bound for England from New York, was sunk by a German submarine without warning off the coast of Ireland. Its loss hardened US public feeling against Germany.*

none of which recaptures any significant territory. Smith-Dorrien's replacement is General Herbert Plumer.

MIDDLE EAST, *TURKEY*
The British at Gallipoli again attempt to capture the town of Krithia from the Turks. The advance stalls quickly, gaining only 600 yards (550 m) at a cost of 6500 casualties. The British commander, General Sir Ian Hamilton, receives more reinforcements.

MAY 7

SEA WAR, *ATLANTIC*
The *Lusitania* is sunk without warning by the German submarine *U-20*. Among the dead are 124 US citizens.

MAY 8

WESTERN FRONT, *BELGIUM*
In the Second Battle of Ypres the Germans capture Frenzenberg Ridge and hold it despite facing counterattacks.

MAY 9

WESTERN FRONT, *FRANCE*
General Sir Douglas Haig, commander of the British First Army, attacks on either side of Neuve-Chapelle. His aim is to secure Aubers Ridge, which lies some 3000 yards (2740 m) from the town. The British are supporting a major French offensive in Artois. The opening barrage is poorly coordinated and does little to undermine the German defenses. There are also concerns over the quality and quantity of the shells provided for the artillery. The attack, which makes little progress, grinds to a halt the next day. British casualties amount to 11,600 men.

While the British batter away at Aubers Ridge, the French open the Second Battle of Artois. Led by the corps of General Henri-Philippe Pétain, the French advance some four miles (6 km) in 90 minutes to reach the key Vimy Ridge, a vital piece of high ground. Mounting losses convince Pétain that further frontal attacks on the ridge would be too costly, however. The fighting continues and centers on the town of Souchez.

MAY 11

MIDDLE EAST, *MESOPOTAMIA*
The commander of the much-enlarged British forces in Mesopotamia, General Sir John Nixon, outlines a major offensive devised to advance on and capture Baghdad. He is unaware that the Turks are also building up their strength in the region.

MAY 12

AFRICA, *SOUTHWEST AFRICA*
South African troops led by General Louis Botha occupy Windhoek, the capital of German Southwest Africa. In a meeting with the German governor on the 20th, Botha demands unconditional surrender.

▼ *A lone soldier looks out across no-man's land during the Festubert battle.*

MAY 13

POLITICS, *BRITAIN*
The government agrees to intern all enemy aliens who are of military age.

MAY 15

WESTERN FRONT, *FRANCE*
The commander of the British Expeditionary Force, Field Marshal Sir John French, remains under severe pressure to support the major French

▲ *German wounded and prisoners take shelter in a shell crater with their British captors at Aubers Ridge.*

offensive in Artois and orders his First Army under General Sir Douglas Haig to attack Festubert. The British attack under cover of darkness for the first time and the onslaught is preceded by a 60-hour bombardment of the German trench line. There are early

MAY 19

gains by the British, but a mixture of rain, mist, and a stiffening of German resistance prevent any exploitation. The British shortage of artillery shells becomes increasingly acute.

MAY 19

MIDDLE EAST, *TURKEY*

The Australians and New Zealanders at Gallipoli, some 17,000 men, defeat a major counterattack by 40,000 Turks, inflicting over 3000 casualties.

MAY 23

POLITICS, *ITALY*

The government announces that Italy is at war with Austria-Hungary – but not Germany. The subsequent fighting is concentrated in two mountainous areas in northern Italy – the Trentino and along the Isonzo River. The major effort is directed across the Isonzo toward the Austro-Hungarian port of Trieste, but the Italians are also hoping to initiate an advance to help hard-pressed Serbia.

MAY 24

WESTERN FRONT, *BELGIUM*

A German attack at Ypres directed against the British-held Bellewaarde Ridge enjoys early success, but many of the initial gains are lost to British counterattacks. The fighting ends on the 25th and marks the last act of the

Second Battle of Ypres. The British have had 58,000 casualties since the opening of the offensive, the Germans 35,000, and the French around 10,000. The Ypres salient has been reduced to a depth of just three miles (5 km).

▲ Australian infantrymen await the order to attack the Turks at Gallipoli.

▼ Winston Churchill, (center, with cane) pictured after his dismissal from Britain's government over the Gallipoli fiasco.

▲ *French troops, captured during the fighting around the Ypres salient in Belgium during the spring of 1915.*

MAY 25

POLITICS, *BRITAIN*
A coalition government is formed, drawing together 12 Liberals and eight Tories in the cabinet. Liberal firebrand David Lloyd George is made minister for munitions.

MAY 26

POLITICS, *BRITAIN*
First Lord of the Admiralty Sir Winston Churchill is dismissed from his post by Prime Minister Herbert Asquith after the failure of the naval attack on the Dardanelles. In November Churchill is dropped from the government altogether because of the failure of the land operation on the Gallipoli Peninsula. He goes to fight on the Western Front.

SEA WAR, *ADRIATIC*
Italy introduces a naval blockade of Austria-Hungary.

MAY 27

WESTERN FRONT, *FRANCE*
The British attack at Festubert ends. The British commander-in-chief, Field Marshal Sir John French, contacts the government stating that there can be no further attacks until his stock of artillery shells is replenished. The British have won territory a mile in depth across a 3000-yard (2700-m)

front but at a high price – some 16,000 casualties. German losses total 5000 men.

AIR WAR, *GERMANY*
French Voisin bombers carry out their first major long-range raid, dropping bombs on poison-gas producing facilities at Ludwigshafen.

MAY 31

MIDDLE EAST, *MESOPOTAMIA*
Under orders from General Sir John Nixon, General Sir Charles Townshend defeats a Turkish force at Qurna. Townshend is in command of a division-size force supported by a flotilla of gunboats and is under orders to test the feasibility of an advance on Baghdad. A second amphibious assault captures Amara on June 3. Townshend, however, is stricken with illness.

JUNE 1

POLITICS, *GERMANY*
The government makes an official apology to the United States for the sinking of the tanker *Gulflight* by one of its submarines off the Scilly Isles on May 1.

JUNE 2

POLITICS, *GERMANY*
Kaiser Wilhelm II backs plans to launch a limited encirclement of the Russian forces in the salient around Warsaw, despite opposition from Hindenburg and Ludendorff. The plan calls for General Max von Gallwitz's new German Twelfth Army to strike south toward Warsaw, while the German and Austro-Hungarian forces in the south engaged in exploiting

▶ *British General Sir Charles Townshend, who was ordered to advance on Baghdad despite a lack of resources.*

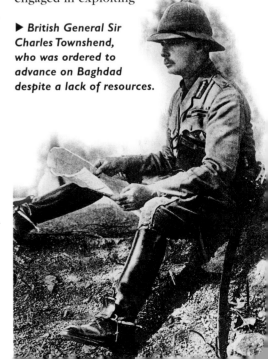

JUNE 3

lack of progress lead to the sending of further reinforcements. However, doubts about the operation grow.

JUNE 6–7

AIR WAR, *BRITAIN*
German Zeppelin airships launch a major raid against east coast ports and London. Zeppelin *L9* strikes the port of Hull, where 64 casualties result from a 20-minute attack. The key mission is against London. Three Zeppelins complete their attack but their fortunes are mixed. *LZ38* returns

◀ *British women at work in an armaments factory, a growing part of the country's war effort.*

▼ *German troops enter Przemysl.*

the recent Gorlice–Tarnow break-through should advance north.
HOME FRONT, *BRITAIN*
The British government passes the Munitions of War Act, which leads to the mass employment of women workers – 46,000 rush to enhance the country's war production in the first week after the act becomes law.

JUNE 3

EASTERN FRONT, *GALICIA*
Capitalizing on their breakthrough at Gorlice–Tarnow the previous month, the Germans and Austro-Hungarians recapture the fortress of Przemysl.

JUNE 4

MIDDLE EAST, *TURKEY*
The British at Gallipoli attempt to capture the Turkish-held town of Krithia for the third time. Some 30,000 men attack but gain only a few hundred yards at a cost of 6500 casualties. Mounting losses and the

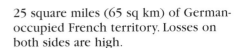

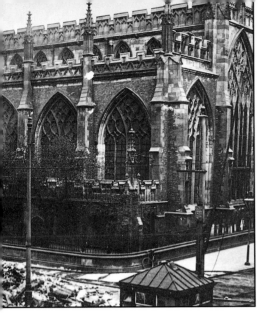

◄ *British firefighters and rescue workers comb through the ruins of a house in Hull after a German airship raid.*

to its base near Brussels, but is destroyed by bombs dropped from British naval aircraft; elsewhere Flight Sub-Lieutenant R. Warneford chases Zeppelin *LZ34* from Ostend to Ghent in Belgium and, despite heavy protective fire, destroys it by dropping bombs on it from above; and the *LZ39* returns home safely.

JUNE 16

WESTERN FRONT, *FRANCE*
The Second Battle of Artois carries on with the French launching a major 20-division attack against the Germans, who have received large reinforcements. The offensive is aimed at Vimy Ridge, but only one French division gains a brief foothold on the commanding heights.

JUNE 18

WESTERN FRONT, *FRANCE*
Although fighting will continue until the end of the month, the Second Battle of Artois grinds to a halt. The French claim to have recaptured some

◄ *French gunners stand ready to open fire during the Second Battle of Artois.*

▼ *Austro-Hungarian troops man trenches high above the Isonzo River.*

25 square miles (65 sq km) of German-occupied French territory. Losses on both sides are high.

JUNE 22

EASTERN FRONT, *GALICIA*
The Austro-Hungarian Second Army recaptures the fortress of Lemberg, which has been occupied by the Russians since September 1914. This victory is a result of the recent Gorlice–Tarnow breakthrough engineered by General August von Mackensen, who is promoted to the rank of field marshal the same day.

JUNE 23–JULY 7

WESTERN FRONT, *ITALY*
The Italians open the First Battle of the Isonzo, marking the beginning of a series of 11 engagements in northeast Italy along the border with Austria-Hungary that will continue until 1918. The offensive plans to capture the Austro-Hungarian port of Trieste, two-thirds of whose inhabitants are Italians. However, the Italians have to overcome considerable physical obstacles, chiefly the Isonzo River itself, which meanders along the border and is backed by precipitous mountains.

The 200,000 Italians, who initially outnumber the Austro-Hungarians by approximately two-to-one in men and artillery pieces, make some progress in the opening phase of the battle but their main offensive, which begins on

JUNE 24

the 30th, ends in failure. Italian forces attack on a 20-mile (32-km) front, but gain only a single foothold on the east bank of the Isonzo.

A renewal of the attack on July 5 achieves little. The Italian armies, the Second under General Pietro Frugoni and the Duke of Aosta's Third, spearhead the onslaught. Despite a superiority of six-to-one, they advance little more than a mile. Casualties are heavy – the Italians lose 5000 men, some 4000 alone in the battle for Gorizia; Austro-Hungarian losses total 10,000.

JUNE 24

POLITICS, *FRANCE*
Meeting at Chantilly, the French commander-in-chief, General Joseph Joffre, and the British Expeditionary Force's Field Marshal Sir John French agree that the Western Front is the decisive theater of war and plan to launch a major offensive in late summer. Both need time to gather reinforcements.

HOME FRONT, *UNITED STATES*
Some 70,000 attend the National German–American meeting at New York's Madison Square Garden.

▼ The bodies of Italian dead are examined by a party of Austro-Hungarians at the end of the First Battle of the Isonzo.

▲ A column of Italian infantry, known as Bersagliari, moves through a village on the way to the First Battle of the Isonzo.

JULY 2

HOME FRONT, *UNITED STATES*
A bomb planted by a German student from Cornell University destroys a reception room in the Senate. The perpetrator, who later commits suicide in prison on the 6th, also shoots and wounds the pro-British banker William Pierpoint Morgan.

JULY 9

AFRICA, *SOUTHWEST AFRICA*
The remaining German forces in German Southwest Africa surrender to the South Africans.

HOME FRONT, *BRITAIN*
Secretary of War Lord Kitchener makes a speech at London's Guildhall calling for greater recruitment to the country's armed forces. By the end of the month, two million men have answered his call to arms. Many are enthusiastic volunteers, who form units based on their home towns.

JULY 11

POLITICS, *UNITED STATES*
Secretary of State Robert Lansing privately writes: "Germany must not be allowed to win this war, or to break even."

SEA WAR, *AFRICA*
The German raider *Königsberg*, holed up in the Rufiji River, is badly damaged after 90 minutes of shelling by two British monitors, whose fire is directed by a spotter plane. The *Königsberg* is scuttled by its crew, but its valuable main guns are salvaged by the Germans and used in land operations in East Africa.

JULY 13

EAST FRONT, *POLAND*
General Max von Gallwitz's German

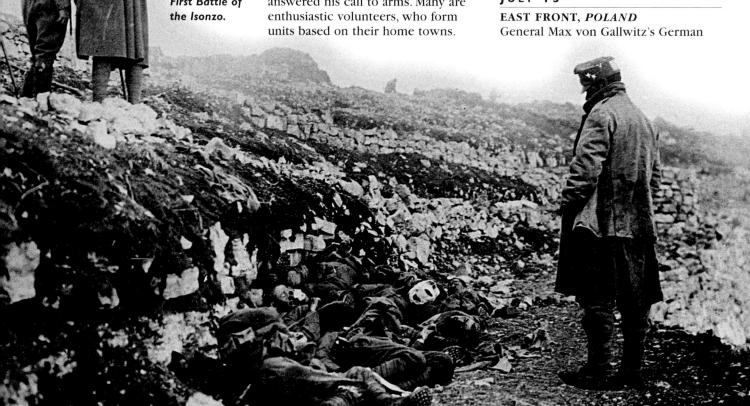

Twelfth Army, a force of some 120,000 men, launches its offensive directed toward Warsaw by attacking on a 25-mile (40-km) front. The army has advanced some five miles (8 km) by the 17th. Russian morale is reported to be falling and German troops enter Warsaw on August 5. The salient around the Russian held-city is collapsing rapidly under the attacks from the north and south.

JULY 17

POLITICS, *BRITAIN*
Women march demanding to make a fuller contribution to the war effort.

POLITICS, *BULGARIA*
Although declaring its continued neutrality, Bulgaria signs a secret treaty with Germany and Austria-Hungary. As part of the deal Bulgaria receives some 600 square miles (1550 sq km) of frontier territory from Turkey.

▲ *The shattered German surface raider* Königsberg *lies scuttled on the bed of the Rufiji River in East Africa. After sustaining damage from British warships, its captain ordered his vessel to be disabled. However, its armaments were saved for use on land.*

▼ *A lone German soldier keeps watch over a party of Russian prisoners captured around Warsaw.*

WESTERN FRONT, *ITALY*

The Italians and Austro-Hungarians clash in the Second Battle of the Isonzo. The commander-in-chief of the Italian Army, General Luigi Cadorna, has sent more artillery to the front in the hope of achieving the decisive breakthrough to Trieste. For their part the outnumbered Austro-Hungarians have reinforced their positions with just two divisions – but it is enough.

The battle begins with a shorter, more accurate barrage by the Italians, and their Second and Third Armies make some initial progress, taking 4000 Austro-Hungarian prisoners by the 22nd. However, a lack of shells and heavy artillery combine to slow the advance, which breaks down in front of the still intact Austro-Hungarian trench systems protected by barbed wire. The few gains that the Italians make are recaptured by the Austro-Hungarians. The battle ends on the 3rd.

JULY 24

MIDDLE EAST, *MESOPOTAMIA*

British Major General George Gorringe, who has been ordered to advance up the Euphrates River in support of General Sir Charles Townshend's push along the adjacent Tigris River in the direction of Baghdad, defeats the Turkish at Nasiriya, 100 miles (160 km) from Basra.

▼ *Austro-Hungarian artillery fires at Italian positions during the fighting along the Isonzo River.*

▲ *General Luigi Cadorna, chief of the Italian General Staff, 1914–17.*

AUGUST 1

POLITICS, *GERMANY*

Germany's war planners agree on the need to defeat Serbia as soon as possible, preferably with the aid of Bulgaria. Defeat of Serbia will free their forces to redouble their efforts on the Eastern Front.

AIR WAR, *FRANCE*

German pilot Max Immelmann scores his first air victory, in part due to his

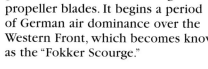

aircraft, a Fokker EI fitted with an interrupter device that allows machine-gun rounds to be fired through its propeller blades. It begins a period of German air dominance over the Western Front, which becomes known as the "Fokker Scourge."

AUGUST 4

ESPIONAGE, *BELGIUM*

The Germans arrest British-born nurse Edith Cavell, who is implicated in

◄ A Fokker E1 monoplane fighter. It easily outperformed its rivals and helped establish German air superiority in 1915.

aiding more than 200 prisoners-of-war to escape. Cavell is convicted by a German court martial, which convenes on October 7, and is executed five days later. Her last words are: "Patriotism is not enough. I must have no hatred or bitterness toward anyone."

AUGUST 6

MIDDLE EAST, *TURKEY*
In an attempt to break the deadlock at Gallipoli, the British launch an amphibious assault on Suvla Bay on the north of the peninsula adjacent to the original landing beach at Ari Burna. The plan is to outflank the Turkish defenders to the south, who have confined the British to the tip of the peninsula. The landings are to be made in conjunction with an

▼ British naval ratings escort the coffin carrying the remains of executed nurse Edith Cavell on its arrival in England.

AUGUST 12

Australian and New Zealand attack against the high ground known as Chunuk Bair.

Although the ANZACs attack with great determination, their few gains are won at a high cost. They briefly capture the summit of Chunuk Bair on the 8th, but a Turkish counterattack led by Mustafa Kemal evicts them two days later. The landings at Suvla are unopposed, but the local commander, Sir Frederick Stopford, fails to take advantage of the situation, allowing Turkish reinforcements to gain the high ground overlooking Suvla Bay.

AUGUST 12

TECHNOLOGY, *BRITAIN*
British inventors begin work on what will become the world's first tracked

▲ British forces led by General Sir Charles Townshend begin their advance toward Turkish-held Kut-el-Amara.

▼ A party of Turkish prisoners captured during a British attack on the town of Krithia on the Gallipoli Peninsula.

armored vehicle. Nicknamed "Little Willie," it makes its debut on September 8. Suggestions by Winston Churchill on December 24 that the secret weapon should be described as a water tank is accepted and the term "tank" enters the common language.

AUGUST 17

MIDDLE EAST, *TURKEY*
The commander of the Gallipoli operation, General Sir Ian Hamilton, asks the British secretary of war, Lord Kitchener, for a further 95,000 reinforcements. There is growing political dismay at the lack of progress and the growing list of casualties at Gallipoli.

AUGUST 19

SEA WAR, *IRISH SEA*
Submarine *U-24* sinks the liner *Arabic*; among the 44 killed are three US citizens. US war protests mount.

AUGUST 20

POLITICS, *ITALY*
Declares war on Turkey.

AUGUST 21

POLITICS, *RUSSIA*
Czar Nicholas II takes personal command of the Russian armed forces, sacking his commander-in-chief, Grand Duke Nicholas, despite the latter's steadying influence during the recent and ongoing German and Austro-Hungarian encircling offensive against the salient around Warsaw. The grand duke is sent to command the forces fighting in the Caucasus, while the czar makes General Mikhail Alekseyev his chief-of-staff.

AUGUST 25

EASTERN FRONT, *RUSSIA*
Driving into the rear of the Warsaw salient from the south, General Alexander von Linsingen's forces take Brest-Litovsk from the Russians.

AUGUST 26

POLITICS, *GERMANY*
The authorities announce that merchant ships will not be attacked without warning and also order their U-boats not to sink liners without warning four days later.

AUGUST 27

MIDDLE EAST, *MESOPOTAMIA*
British General Sir Charles Townshend, recently returned from sick leave in India, is ordered to advance on Kut-el-Amara, a major Turkish base on the Tigris River, some 300 miles (480 km) to the north of the main British base of Basra. Townshend believes his force of some 11,000 troops is inadequate.

▲ *An early British attempt to test the ability of tracked vehicles to cross small obstacles. The vehicle is a Killen Strait Tractor fitted with a wire-cutter.*

▼ *Australian troops advance at the run with fixed bayonets against the Turkish trenches at Gallipoli.*

DECISIVE WEAPONS

THE STOKES MORTAR

In October 1914 British troops on the Western Front complained bitterly of a German trench device that could lob a shell to a range of 600 yards (550 m) to which they could not reply. In response the British simply made copies of a captured German *Minenwerfer* ("mine-thrower"), but also asked their arms manufacturers to come up with similar devices.

By mid-1915 the government had been inundated with potential designs, but most were far from practical. Like the *Minenwerfer* many of these were no more than mini-howitzers – large, costly, and often of little use in the confines of a trench system. However, one individual, engineer Wilfred Stokes, had a practical, if revolutionary, design. His weapon consisted of a short barrel, which fitted to a bedplate, and a bipod, which could be slid up or down the barrel to give the correct firing elevation. In trials the mortar was remarkably accurate. Stokes then designed a shell that exploded on impact, rather than by a preset fuse.

Stokes's device was simple, cheap, easily manhandled, and could be brought into use rapidly. It also proved its worth in 1918, when the stalemate of trench warfare ended. The Germans had to abandon their heavy trench mortars, while each Stokes mortar and its ammunition could be brought forward by a few men.

Two examples of the successful mortar created by Wilfred Stokes. Their portability and high rate of fire became the basis for all subsequent designs.

▲ *German six-inch (15-cm) howitzers are moved to a new firing position somewhere on the Western Front.*

His offensive, which begins on September 12, is severely hampered by intense heat, a lack of river transport, and the need to detach one of his two infantry divisions to protect his tenuous lines of communication. However, he arrives outside Kut-el-Amara on September 16. The Turkish defender of Kut, Nur-ud-Din Pasha, commands 10,000 entrenched troops backed by nearly 40 artillery pieces.

AUGUST 28

POLITICS, *RUSSIA*
Rebuffing offers of peace from Germany, the government announces that peace cannot be agreed until all German soldiers have left Russia.

SEPTEMBER 6

POLITICS, *BULGARIA*
Bulgarian representative Colonel Gancev meets with General Erich von Falkenhayn, chief of the German General Staff, and Austria-Hungary's chief-of-staff, General Franz Conrad von Hötzendorf. They sign a military pact that binds them to crush Serbia. The Bulgarians issue a mobilization order on the 22nd.

SEPTEMBER 18

POLITICS, *GERMANY*
The government, bowing to mounting US protests about its unrestricted submarine campaign, decides to withdraw its U-boats from the southwest approaches to Britain and the English Channel. Many are transferred to the Mediterranean, where they begin a major campaign in early October.

EASTERN FRONT, *RUSSIA*
The Germans captures Vilna, marking the high point of the offensive against the salient around Warsaw that began in June. In the space of just a few months the Russians have been pushed out of Galicia and Poland, retreating some 300 miles (480 km). Although there is further fighting on the Eastern Front, little territory is lost or gained by both sides in the final months of the year. Heavy rains turn the roads into a morass and movement becomes all but impossible.

The Russians have taken a severe pounding but have escaped total encirclement, chiefly due to the efforts of the recently sacked Grand Duke Nicholas. However, their losses have been great and will total some two million men by the year's end. German and Austro-Hungarian casualties are suspected to be a little over one million men.

SEPTEMBER 24

MIDDLE EAST, *CAUCASUS*
Russia's Grand Duke Nicholas arrives in the region as overall commander but retains General Nikolai Yudenich as his main senior officer. They begin planning for a major offensive against the Turks in 1916.

SEPTEMBER 25

WESTERN FRONT, *FRANCE*

Following a three-day bombardment by 2500 artillery pieces, two French armies attack the Germans on a 15-mile (24-km) front, opening the Second Battle of Champagne, one of three major Anglo-French offensives to begin simultaneously on the Western Front. The aim is to give aid to Russia, which is under ferocious attack, and wear down the German forces.

Early gains are made – in the center the French advance some 3000 yards (2700 m) – and on the second day they break through to the German second line. The fighting continues into November, but becomes increasingly bogged down.

The second French attack, known as the Third Battle of Artois, also begins and they capture the town of

▲ French guards move German prisoners to the rear at the height of the Second Battle of Champagne.

Souchez. After five days of heavy fighting they briefly capture the commanding heights of Vimy Ridge – for the third time. However, subsequent gains are limited and bought at a high price as German resistance stiffens. The fighting continues into November, but the French are unable to capitalize on their early successes. French casualties are estimated at some 48,000 men; the Germans have losses totaling 30,000.

Also as part of the grand offensive, General Sir Douglas Haig's First Army launches an attack between Lens and the La Bassée Canal, opening the Battle of Loos. The British, short of artillery ammunition, use gas for the first time in the war. However, adverse winds

blow some of the gas back over the British lines and the terrain – strongly fortified villages and slag-heaps – makes progress difficult. The first-day advance totals 4000 yards (3660 m) and the assault troops capture part of the Hohenzollern Redoubt, Loos village, and Hill 70.

The German second line holds, however. French troops earmarked to support the British are slow to advance and their attack on the morning of the 26th is defeated. German counterattacks recapture the Hohenzollern Redoubt. The fighting continues into October.

SEPTEMBER 27

POLITICS, *GREECE*

The Greek government agrees to allow 150,000 Anglo-French troops to occupy Salonika, which will act as a base for operations in support of Serbia. The force will be commanded by two generals, France's Maurice Sarrail and Britain's Bryan Mahon.

SEPTEMBER 27–28

MIDDLE EAST, *MESOPOTAMIA*

British General Sir Charles Townshend launches his forces against the Turks defending Kut-el-Amara. The attack is successful, with the Turks suffering 5300 casualties, including 1300 men taken prisoner. However, the Turkish commander, Nur-ud-Din Pasha, makes a measured retreat to the next blocking position south of Baghdad, Ctesiphon. British losses reach 1230 men.

▼ The build-up of forces in the Greek province of Salonika continues. Here, French troops wait to move out.

◀ British wounded trudge through the streets of a shell-blasted town during the the Battle of Loos, October 13.

Gallipoli, storms damage several piers used for the unloading of supplies and the evacuation of casualties.

OCTOBER 9

BALKANS, *SERBIA*
Austro-Hungarian troops occupy the capital Belgrade, while others attack Montenegro, Serbia's ally.

OCTOBER 11

POLITICS, *BRITAIN*
Secretary of War Lord Kitchener evaluates the risks of evacuating Gallipoli and states that "abandonment would be the most disastrous event in the history of the British Empire." The commander at Gallipoli, General Sir

SEPTEMBER 30

MIDDLE EAST, *TURKEY*
The British 10th Division is withdrawn from the stagnating battle for Gallipoli and sent to Salonika, Greece.

OCTOBER 2

POLITICS, *BULGARIA*
Bulgaria agrees to fight alongside Austria-Hungary and Germany in the forthcoming invasion of Serbia.

OCTOBER 6

WESTERN FRONT, *FRANCE*
The Second Battle of Champagne continues with a renewed French offensive against the German front line. French gains are limited. The fighting drags on into November but is stalemated. French losses to October 6 total 144,000 men; the Germans suffer 85,000 casualties.

BALKANS, *SERBIA*
Two German and Austro-Hungarian armies open the invasion of Serbia by attack across the northern border. The initial advance is followed by two Bulgarian armies striking from the east on the 14th – one moves on Nis; the other makes for Skopje. The joint operation is commanded by Field Marshal August von Mackensen. Outnumbered by nearly two-to-one, the Serbian Army escapes being surrounded but is forced to retreat to the southwest.

OCTOBER 8

MIDDLE EAST, *TURKEY*
To add to the problems faced by the troops occupying the trenches at

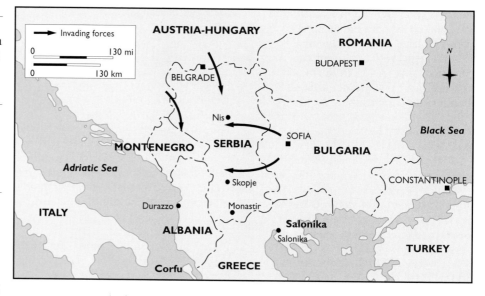

Ian Hamilton, estimates he will lose some 50 percent of his troops in such an enterprise.

OCTOBER 13

AIR WAR, *BRITAIN*
In the heaviest Zeppelin raid of the year five, German airships strike against various targets. In London, bombs dropped by *L13, L14,* and *L15* cause about 150 casualties. Elsewhere, there are 49 other civilians either killed or wounded.

OCTOBER 13–14

WESTERN FRONT, *FRANCE*
The British 46th Division captures part of the German-held Hohenzollern Redoubt at the end of the Battle of Loos and successfully beats off German counterattacks. British casualties total 62,000 men, while the Germans have about 26,000 men killed, wounded, or captured. The commander of the British Expeditionary Force, Field Marshal Sir John French, is widely blamed for the poor handling of his reserves during the battle and calls to replace him grow ever more strident.

OCTOBER 14

POLITICS, *BALKANS*
Bulgaria and Serbia declare war against each other.

◀ *The twin-pronged attack on Serbia in 1915 involved troops from Bulgaria, Germany, and Austria-Hungary.*

▼ *A German cavalry detachment advances through Serbia.*

▲ *A German Zeppelin airship is framed by two searchlights while on a bombing raid on London.*

OCTOBER 15

POLITICS, *BRITAIN*
The government declares war on Bulgaria, which has invaded Serbia. Montenegro, a close ally of threatened Serbia, follows suit.

OCTOBER 16

POLITICS, *FRANCE*
The government declares war on Bulgaria.
MIDDLE EAST, *TURKEY*
The commander of the Gallipoli forces, General Sir Ian Hamilton, receives notice that he is to be replaced by General Sir Charles Monro, who takes charge on the 28th. His first request is for winter clothing.

OCTOBER 18–NOVEMBER 4

WESTERN FRONT, *ITALY*
The Italians again hammer away at the Austro-Hungarians defending the line of the Isonzo River as they continue their attacks toward Trieste. Despite having stockpiled over one million shells for the three-day barrage by 1200 artillery pieces that opens their attack on the outnumbered Austro-Hungarians, the Italians make little progress. What little ground they gain is swiftly retaken. Heavy rain and mud also slow the Italian offensive.

The attacks are called off on November 4. Losses are large. The Italians have 67,000 men killed, wounded, or taken prisoner; the Austro-Hungarians suffer 42,000 casualties.

OCTOBER 19

POLITICS, *ITALY/RUSSIA*
Both declare war on Bulgaria.

OCTOBER 24

BALKANS, *SERBIA*
Invading Bulgarian forces effectively prevent any link up between the Anglo-French forces advancing northward from Salonika and the embattled Serbian Army.

NOVEMBER 5

NOVEMBER 5

BALKANS, *SERBIA*
The Bulgarian First Army captures the city of Nis, a vital railroad junction. Its fall means that a rail line now stretches unhindered from Germany and Austria-Hungary to Turkey.

NOVEMBER 7

SEA WAR, *MEDITERRANEAN*
The Austrian submarine *U-38* shells and then torpedoes the liner *Ancona* bound for New York from Italy. Among the 208 dead are 25 US citizens. The Austrian response to the protests of the US government is considered inadequate.

NOVEMBER 10–DECEMBER 2

WESTERN FRONT, *ITALY*
The Italians and Austro-Hungarians fight the Fourth Battle of the Isonzo. The Italian offensive is heralded by an intense four-hour bombardment. Although attacking in force, the

▼ *Ctesiphon, the scene of the battle between Turkish and British forces.*

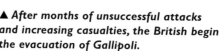
▲ *After months of unsuccessful attacks and increasing casualties, the British begin the evacuation of Gallipoli.*

Italians make only limited gains and resort to leveling one of their key objectives – the town of Gorizia – with artillery fire on the 18th.
   The fighting dies down on December 2, with the Italians having made little further progress. Again, the list of casualties on both sides is high: an estimated 49,000 Italians and 30,000 Austro-Hungarians.

NOVEMBER 11

MIDDLE EAST, *MESOPOTAMIA*
The British continue their advance toward the Turkish-held positions around Ctesiphon. The Turkish commander, Nur-ud-Din Pasha, has received large reinforcements, which bring his strength up to 18,000 men supported by 45 artillery pieces. In contrast the British commander, General Sir Charles Townshend, has 10,000 infantry, 1000 cavalry, and 30 artillery pieces with which to attack.

NOVEMBER 20

POLITICS, *CANADA*
The government declares war on both Turkey and Bulgaria.

NOVEMBER 22

POLITICS, *UNITED STATES*
The administration rejects a German offer of $1000 for each US passenger killed following the torpedoing of the *Lusitania* on May 7.

MIDDLE EAST, *TURKEY*
Lord Kitchener, the British secretary of war, who has been on a fact-finding mission to Gallipoli since the 10th, advises evacuation. He sails home on the 24th. No firm decision is made until December 7, when the British government agrees to evacuate the positions at Suvla Bay and Ari Burna.

NOVEMBER 22–26

MIDDLE EAST, *MESOPOTAMIA*
The British attack the Turkish positions at Ctesiphon, which lies some 20 miles (32 km) south of their main objective, Baghdad. The initial advance successfully pierces the Turkish front, but the British commander, General Sir Charles Townshend, lacks the reserves to exploit this success and Turkish counterattacks stabilize the situation. As the Turks receive more reinforcements, Townshend orders a withdrawal back to Kut-el-Amara on the 25th. Turkish losses total 6200 men, while Townshend's smaller force takes 4600 casualties. The Turkish pursuit is limited and the exhausted British reach Kut-el-Amara on December 3.

NOVEMBER 23

BALKANS, *SERBIA*
The badly-mauled Serbian Army, some 200,000 men, begins a 100-mile

◄ *Specialist Italian mountain troops, known as Alpini, trek to their mountain-top positions.*

(160-km) retreat to the west and southwest, aiming to reach Albania. Four columns embark on a crossing of the mountains that separate the two countries. Short of food and warm clothing, thousands of Serbians die.

DECEMBER 3

POLITICS, *FRANCE*
General Joseph Joffre becomes commander-in-chief of all the French forces on the Western Front.

DECEMBER 6

POLITICS, *FRANCE*
British and French strategists reconvene at Chantilly and agree to plan a general offensive on the Western Front in 1916. They also agree to maintain their large – and growing – presence in Salonika.

▼ *A Serbian heavy artillery battery prepares to open fire on advancing Austro-Hungarian forces.*

DECEMBER 7

MIDDLE EAST, *MESOPOTAMIA*
The Turks lay siege to the much-weakened British forces at Kut-el-Amara. The British reject a call to surrender on December 9 and are later informed that a relief force is being prepared to come to their rescue. Several attacks later in the month are defeated by the town's garrison and the Turks begin to entrench.

DECEMBER 8

MIDDLE EAST, *TURKEY*
The evacuation of the Suvla Bay and Ari Burna bridgeheads at Gallipoli begins. Despite much foreboding, they are carried out with great success due to meticulous work of the plan's creator, General William Birdwood. The Turks do not interfere with the evacuation and some 83,000 men, 186 artillery pieces, 1700 vehicles, and some 4500 transport animals are whisked away. The process is completed by the 20th. Troops remain in position at Cape Helles on the tip of the peninsula, however.

DECEMBER 12

SEA WAR, *ADRIATIC*
Allied warships begin the evacuation of Serbian forces from Albania. The operation will continue into 1916.

DECEMBER 17

POLITICS, *BRITAIN*
Field Marshal Sir John French is dismissed as the commander of the British Expeditionary Force. His replacement is General Sir Douglas Haig.

DECEMBER 21

POLITICS, *GERMANY*
Twenty-two out of 44 Social Democrats in the Reichstag (German parliament) vote against further loans to finance the war.

DECEMBER 26

SEA WAR, *NORTH SEA*
The German commerce-raider *Möwe* leaves Bremen. It sinks 14 vessels before returning on March 4, 1916.

DECEMBER 27

MIDDLE EAST, *TURKEY*
The British government agrees to evacuate Cape Helles on the Gallipoli Peninsula. It begins the next day.

DECEMBER 28

POLITICS, *BRITAIN*
The government agrees to introduce adult male conscription.

DECEMBER 29

POLITICS, *WESTERN FRONT*
France's General Joseph Joffre and Britain's General Sir Douglas Haig meet. They discuss a 1916 attack along the Somme River sector on the Western Front.

1916

In a year of large and costly offensives, the Germans attempted to smash the French Army at Verdun. They failed, but it required the British and Russians to relieve some of the pressure. On the Somme the Germans survived, despite suffering as many losses as the British and French. The Russians almost forced the surrender of Austria-Hungary but had to divert forces to aid new ally Romania. The year also saw vain attempts to reach an acceptable peace.

JANUARY 1

MIDDLE EAST, *ARABIA*
In Turkish-controlled Arabia Hussein, Grand Sherif of Mecca, agrees to an alliance with Britain and later requests money to purchase rifles and food. The British government accepts his request and the rebellion begins in May.

AFRICA, *CAMEROONS*
British troops occupy Yaunde, the capital of this German West African colony. The campaign, supported by other colonial nations, had begun in August 1914. However, the German defenders are far from subdued by the fall of the capital and slowly retreat into the Spanish colony of Muni, some 125 miles (200 km) from Yaunde.

SEA WAR, *TECHNOLOGY*
The British introduce the depth-charge as part of their ongoing battle against enemy submarines. However, they will be in short supply until 1917.

JANUARY 2

SEA WAR, *BLACK SEA*
The British end their highly successful submarine campaign against Turkish shipping. Some 50 percent of Turkey's merchant ships have been sunk and the remainder are short of fuel.

JANUARY 4

POLITICS, *AUSTRIA-HUNGARY*
Chief of the General Staff Conrad von Hötzendorf confides to Prime Minister

▼ British and local troops operating a 4.5-inch (115-mm) howitzer in the German colony of Cameroons in West Africa.

▶ *Local porters carry equipment belonging to the small German army operating in East Africa commanded by General Paul von Lettow-Vorbeck. The Germans avoided pitched battles and carried out hit-and-run raids against isolated enemy garrisons and railroads.*

▼ *Turkish troops prepare to entrain for Baghdad, Mesopotamia, to increase the pressure on the British garrison besieged in Kut-el-Amara and the force sent to relieve it.*

by German General Paul von Lettow-Vorbeck, who wages a successful and protracted guerrilla war.

JANUARY 8

BALKANS, *MONTENEGRO*
Some 50,000 mainly Austro-Hungarian troops launch a major offensive, which is heralded by a 500-gun barrage and supported by air and naval attacks.

▼ *General Paul von Lettow-Vorbeck led the German and local troops operating against British, Belgian, and Portuguese colonies in East Africa.*

Count István Tisza that "There can be no question of destroying the Russian war machine; England cannot be defeated; peace must be made in not too long a space, or we shall be fatally weakened, if not destroyed."

MIDDLE EAST, *MESOPOTAMIA*
The British launch their first attempt to reach Kut-el-Amara, which has been besieged by the Turks since December 1915. The relief column, General Fenton Aylmer's 19,000-strong Tigris Corps, is opposed by more than 30,000 Turks. Aylmer's force clashes with the Turks at the Battle of Sheikh Saad on the 9th.

JANUARY 6

AFRICA, *EAST AFRICA*
South African General Jan Christiaan Smuts takes over operations in the region from British General Sir Horace Smith-Dorrien, who is ill with pneumonia. Smuts embarks on a campaign to capture the German colonies in East Africa. He is close to success by the end of the year but fails to destroy the small army commanded

▼ *Austro-Hungarian troops advance through Serbia in overwhelming strength. The country was quickly overrun.*

JANUARY 10

▶ The British prototype tank, known as "Mother," is put through its paces. There was a growing belief in Britain that tanks could end the deadlock on the Western Front.

Austro-Hungarian progress is rapid and Montenegro is forced to capitulate to the invaders on the 17th.

MIDDLE EAST, *TURKEY*
The British evacuation of the Gallipoli Peninsula is completed when the last troops (17,000 men and around 40 artillery pieces) are taken off the beaches at Cape Helles. There are no casualties during the complex operation. However, the campaign has cost the British, Commonwealth, and French some 252,000 casualties and the Turks some 250,000 men.

JANUARY 10

MIDDLE EAST, *ARMENIA*
The Turkish Third Army is forced back to the city of Erzerum following the Battle of Köprüköy on the border between Russia and Turkey, which heralds a major offensive by Russian commander General Nikolai Yudenich.

JANUARY 12

BALKANS, *ALBANIA*
The evacuation of the Serbian Army from the port of Durazzo begins. The troops are heading for Corfu, which has been occupied by French marines, despite neutral Greece's protests.

JANUARY 15

POLITICS, *UNITED STATES*
Outrage is widespread when details of payments made to pro-German agents by Germany's military attaché

in Washington, Franz von Papen, are made public. Papen has already been recalled to Germany at the request of the US government.

JANUARY 16

MIDDLE EAST, *MESOPOTAMIA*
General Fenton Aylmer, leader of the British relief column making for Kut-el-Amara, is informed by the besieged garrison's commander, General Sir Charles Townshend, that he has rations for just two or three weeks.

JANUARY 21

MIDDLE EAST, *MESOPOTAMIA*
The British relief force heading for the besieged garrison of Kut-el-Amara is halted by the Turks at the Battle of Hanna. On the same day the garrison is put on half rations, although the discovery of an unknown store of barley alleviates matters somewhat. Over the following weeks the British rush

◄ Admiral Reinhard Sheer, commander-in-chief of the German High Seas Fleet from late January.

DECISIVE WEAPONS

ZEPPELIN AIRSHIPS

The first Zeppelin airship raid against Britain took place on the night of January 19–20, 1915, and by 1918, 55 similar raids, most in 1915–16, had been made. In total, some 200 tons (203,000 kg) of bombs were dropped by airships and killed some 250 people. At first the British could do little to counter the high-altitude raids.

However, the advent of coordinated anti-aircraft defenses, chiefly bands of anti-aircraft guns with searchlights and high-altitude fighters, made the Zeppelins more vulnerable. They were increasingly replaced by long-range bombers, particularly the twin-engined Gotha, which made its first attack in April 1917. Zeppelins continued to be used elsewhere as bombers and also acted in the maritime reconnaissance role.

Zeppelins, named after Count Ferdinand von Zeppelin who produced aluminum-framed airships in the first decade of the twentieth century, were covered by an outer skin, which contained gas-filled bags that gave lift. By 1914 Germany had a fleet of 18 Zeppelins, operated by both the army and navy. Most could reach an altitude of 20,000 feet (6100 m) and had a speed of 80 mph (130 k/h).

Two Zeppelins lie at anchor in one of the vast hangars built to protect them from the weather.

more troops to the theater and make plans to renew the relief operation, which recommences on March 7.

JANUARY 24

POLITICS, *GERMANY*
Admiral Reinhard Sheer is promoted to commander-in-chief of the German High Seas Fleet. Sheer, an advocate of offensive action against Britain's Home Fleet, later proposes luring the British navy into a decisive engagement in the North Sea, a strategy approved by Kaiser Wilhelm II the following month.

JANUARY 27

POLITICS, *GERMANY*
General Erich von Falkenhayn, the chief of the German General Staff, finalizes plans for an offensive against the French forces holding the fortress-city of Verdun in eastern France. Falkenhayn first proposed the attack in December 1915 and received the wholehearted backing of Kaiser Wilhelm II. Falkenhayn is planning to inflict massive casualties on the French at Verdun to sap their morale and will to fight on. The operation is scheduled to begin on February 12

and the Germans have positioned an extra 1220 artillery pieces around the city and delivered over 2.5 million shells to the front by the 1st.

JANUARY 29

AIR WAR, *FRANCE*
Paris suffers its second and last raid by Zeppelin airships, which produces 54 casualties. The French capital will not be attacked from the air again until January 1918.

TECHNOLOGY, *BRITAIN*
The first prototype tank, known as "Mother," starts a series of trials in great secret. These are successful and the commander of the British Expeditionary Force in France, General Haig, orders 40 on February 11. This figure is later increased to 100.

JANUARY 31

AIR WAR, *BRITAIN*
German airships launch their first attack on central and northwest England, key industrial areas. Seven Zeppelins are involved but the damage caused is small. One of the returning raiders, *L11*, goes down in the North Sea on February 2.

FEBRUARY 1

SEA WAR, *ENGLISH CHANNEL*
The British *Franz Fischer* becomes the first merchant ship to be sunk by air power, succumbing to an attack by Zeppelin bombs. It is one of only three ships to be sunk by the airships in the entire conflict.

FEBRUARY 7

AIR WAR, *WESTERN FRONT*
The British deploy their first single-seater fighter squadron.

FEBRUARY 9

BALKANS, *ALBANIA*
The evacuation of the remnants of the Serbian Army from various ports in Albania is completed.

FEBRUARY 11

POLITICS, *GERMANY*
Kaiser Wilhelm II permits German submarines to attack armed steamers, but forbids attacks on passenger liners. The order comes into force on the 29th. On the same day it is agreed to postpone the imminent offensive against the French at Verdun on the Western Front due to rain and snow. It is rescheduled for the 21st.

FEBRUARY 14

POLITICS, *BRITAIN/FRANCE*
Britain and France confirm that there can be no peace with Germany without the restoration and guarantee of Belgian neutrality. Their military planners agree to launch their Somme offensive on July 1.

FEBRUARY 16

MIDDLE EAST, *ARMENIA*
In a continuation of his winter offensive, Russian General Nikolai Yudenich captures the Turkish-held city of Erzerum and continues his advance.

FEBRUARY 21

WESTERN FRONT, *VERDUN*
The German offensive is heralded by a nine-hour barrage from 1240 artillery pieces, which fire both high-explosive and gas shells against an eight-mile (13-km) section of the French front line to the north of Verdun. This is followed by an advance by 6000

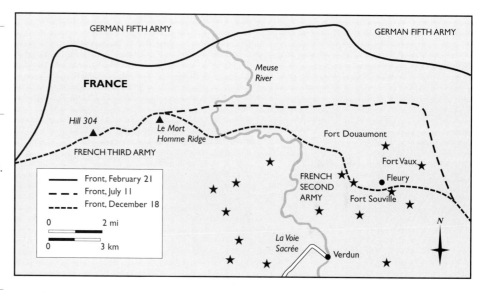

specialist German assault troops, some equipped with flame-throwers. These lead the way forward for the main force of some 140,000 men from Crown Prince William's Fifth Army. The French lose some ground in the face of these attacks.

▲ *Verdun, which lasted from February until November, was an attritional struggle and both the French and German forces suffered heavy casualties.*

▼ *German infantrymen advance in open order at the beginning of Verdun.*

FEBRUARY 22

POLITICS, *RUSSIA*
In an ill-judged move, the Russian high command appoints General Aleksey Kuropatkin as commander-in-chief of the North Front. The cautious Kuropatkin, aged 68, is a veteran of the Russo-Japanese War (1904–05). He will keep his post until July.

WESTERN FRONT, *VERDUN*
The French command agrees to create what becomes known as *La Voie Sacrée* ("The Sacred Way"). This is a narrow road stretching from Bar-Le-Duc to Verdun, and becomes the main

◄ *German artillerymen operating one of the 128 eight-inch (21-cm) howitzers deployed against Verdun.*

▲ *French reinforcements are rushed to Verdun along the vital supply route known as* La Voie Sacrée *("The Sacred Way").*

route for supplies and reinforcements entering Verdun. The road comes under frequent German artillery fire but damage is quickly repaired by teams of laborers earmarked for the vital task. Around Verdun itself German attacks, which gain some ground, are met by fierce French counterattacks.

FEBRUARY 23

POLITICS, *BRITAIN*
The government forms the Blockade Ministry under Lord Robert Cecil. Its role will be to coordinate efforts to cut off the flow of supplies by sea to Germany.

POLITICS, *PORTUGAL*
Acting on a British request, the government interns more than 70 German vessels and refuses German demands that they be released.

FEBRUARY 24

POLITICS, *RUSSIA*
The Russian high command decides to launch an offensive on the Eastern Front to relieve some of the pressure on the French, who are fighting for their lives at Verdun. The French

commander-in-chief, General Joseph Joffre, confirms the necessity of an immediate offensive on March 2.

WESTERN FRONT, *VERDUN*
The Germans cut through the second line of French defenses around Verdun and advance on the third, where one of the city's key positions, Fort Douaumont, lies.

FEBRUARY 25

WESTERN FRONT, *VERDUN*
One of the key French positions at Verdun, Fort Douaumont, just four miles (6 km) from the city, falls to German troops. Late in the day General Henri-Philippe Pétain takes charge of the French forces at Verdun.

Pétain re-invigorates the French troops and relies on defensive tactics rather than costly counterattacks, issuing the slogan *"Ils ne passeront pas"* ("They Shall Not Pass"). He also improves the flow of supplies to the front, brings better coordination to French artillery fire, and institutes a system whereby units suffering heavy casualties are withdrawn from the fighting to rest and recuperate. French morale does not break.

TECHNOLOGY, *FRANCE*
The French Army requests 400 tanks from manufacturer Schneider.

MARSHAL HENRI-PHILIPPE PÉTAIN

Pétain (1856–1951), who was commissioned in the late 1870s, saw no active service until World War I. However, in 1914 he was rapidly promoted, reaching the rank of general. His greatest moment came in 1916, when he was placed in charge of the French forces facing the Germans at Verdun.

Pétain, who excelled at defensive fighting, saw that the situation was critical but not irretrievable. He immediately set about improving the conditions for his troops: the flow of supplies and reinforcements to Verdun was increased; units were rotated into and out of the trenches on a more regular basis; and the strength of his artillery was increased. These reforms improved French morale and enabled them to hold the Germans and go over to the offensive.

In 1917 the French Army mutinied and Pétain, who had an excellent rapport with soldiers, was made commander-in-chief. He used harsh discipline against ringleaders but also introduced reforms, effectively ensuring that the army would fight on. In 1918 Pétain's defensive skills bore fruit during the defeat of the German spring offensive.

After World War I he was promoted to the rank of marshal. In 1940, after France had been invaded, Pétain was made prime minister and signed an armistice with Germany. Between 1940 and 1944 Pétain was head of the collaborationist Vichy regime in southern France, although it seems unlikely that he wielded much power due to the onset of senility. In 1945 he was convicted of treason and sentenced to death by the provisional government of Charles de Gaulle, who had also served at Verdun. This was later commuted to life imprisonment.

FEBRUARY 28

WESTERN FRONT, *VERDUN*
To add to the miseries of the French and German troops at Verdun, a sudden thaw turns the shell-blasted battlefield into a morass.

FEBRUARY 29

POLITICS, *GERMANY*
The German chancellor, Theobald von Bethmann Hollweg, suggests to Kaiser Wilhelm II that an unrestricted submarine campaign will precipitate US involvement in the war.

WESTERN FRONT, *ITALY*
Italian soldier Benito Mussolini is promoted to the rank of corporal for his good service record.

MARCH 2

POLITICS, *BRITAIN*
The government announces that all singled men aged 18–41 are liable for compulsory military service.

POLITICS, *GERMANY*
Germany's military planners inform several of their army commanders in occupied France and Belgium that they are to create a body of 50,000 forced laborers.

WESTERN FRONT, *VERDUN*
One of the French defenders of Fort Vaux, Captain Charles de Gaulle, is wounded and captured by the Germans. Along with Fort Douaumont, Vaux is one of the city's key defenses.

MARCH 4

POLITICS, *GERMANY*
Admiral Alfred von Tirpitz, secretary of state for the navy, fails to convince Kaiser Wilhelm II and his advisers that the need for unrestricted submarine warfare is overwhelming. Tirpitz feels that his position is undermined.

▼ Le Mort Homme *Ridge ("Dead Man" Ridge) at Verdun shows the results of prolonged artillery fire.*

MARCH 6

POLITICS, *BRITAIN*
The government forms the Women's National Land Service Corps to boost agricultural production and free male farm workers for military service.

WESTERN FRONT, *VERDUN*
The Germans open a new offensive to the northwest of the city. While the fighting around Fort Vaux continues, the Germans attempt to capture *Le Mort Homme* Ridge ("Dead Man" Ridge) and Hill 304.

MARCH 9

POLITICS, *GERMANY*
Declares war on Portugal, which is refusing to release interned German vessels. Austria-Hungary follows on the 15th.

▲ *French troops shelter in one of trenches dug on Verdun's Le Mort Homme Ridge ("Dead Man" Ridge).*

MARCH 11

WESTERN FRONT, *ITALY*
The Italians launch the Fifth Battle of the Isonzo. The attack against the Austro-Hungarians is in part designed to help relieve some of the pressure on the French at Verdun.

However, the Italian offensive is dogged by poor weather and their lack of artillery. Little ground is won

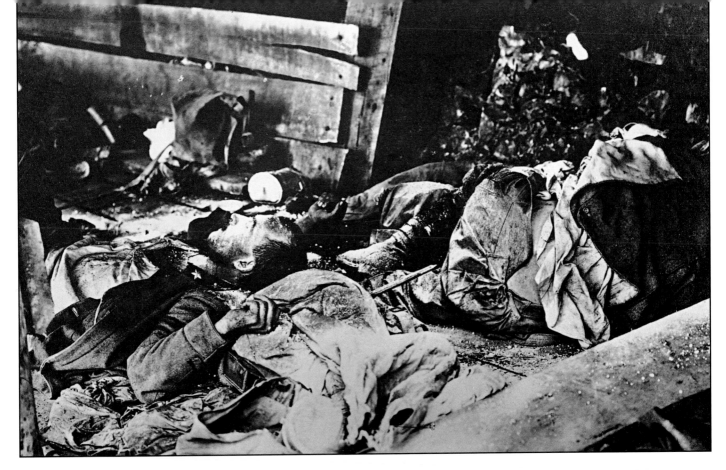

▲ Italian troops killed in the fighting along the Isonzo River on the border between Austria-Hungary and Italy.

or lost by either side in the battle and the fighting in the sector dies down at the end of the month.

MIDDLE EAST, *MESOPOTAMIA*
Following his botched handling of his forces during the Battle of Dujaila Redoubt on the 8th, General Fenton Aylmer is replaced as commander of the Tigris Corps, which is tasked with breaking the Turkish siege of Kut-el-Amara, by General George Gorringe. The British advance is delayed and does not recommence until April 5.

MARCH 12

POLITICS, *GERMANY*
Admiral Alfred von Tirpitz, head of the navy, resigns. He believes he has not been fully consulted over the role and deployment of the navy's increasingly important submarine fleet.

MARCH 15

POLITICS, *UNITED STATES*
President Woodrow Wilson orders General John Pershing to invade northern Mexico to track down rebel leader Pancho Villa. Villa's rebels have

▶ Russian prisoners indicate the German victory at Lake Naroch. Some 120,000 were killed, wounded, or captured.

executed 16 mining engineers, all US nationals, at Santa Isabel and attacked Columbus, New Mexico. Despite fighting a number of skirmishes, Pershing fails to capture Villa.

MARCH 18

EASTERN FRONT, *RUSSIA*
The Russians launch a major offensive designed to aid the French, who are

struggling to halt the major German offensive on Verdun. The Russian attack, which becomes known as the First Battle of Lake Naroch, involves a two-pronged advance into the Lake Naroch and Vilna areas. These are heralded by more than 1200 artillery pieces bombarding German positions for eight hours. The Russian Second Army then moves against the German

MARCH 19

Tenth Army. Some 350,000 Russian soldiers face just 75,000 German troops supported by 300 guns.

Despite their numerical superiority, the Russians make little progress – gaining just one mile (1.6 km) across a front of two miles (3.2 km) for the loss of 15,000 men. So heavy are their losses, the Russians resort to attacking under cover of darkness. However, subsequent Russian advances become bogged down in waterlogged terrain. The battle rages until mid-April.

AIR WAR, *WESTERN FRONT*
German fighter pilot Ernst Udet gains the first of his 62 confirmed victories in air combat.

MARCH 19

MIDDLE EAST, *EGYPT*
General Sir Archibald Murray replaces General Sir John Maxwell as commander of the British forces in Egypt.

MARCH 22

SEA WAR, *ATLANTIC*
U-68 becomes the first submarine to be sunk by depth-charge attack following an engagement with the British *Farnborough* off the coast of southwest Ireland. The *Farnborough* is a Q-ship, an armed vessel that is disguised to look like an ordinary merchant ship.

APRIL 4

EASTERN FRONT, *RUSSIA*
General Aleksey Brusilov, one of Russia most capable commanders, is placed in charge of the Southwest Front, which comprises four armies.

APRIL 5

SEA WAR, *ADRIATIC*
In the largest sea evacuation to date, warships complete the removal of Serbia forces from Albania – some 260,000 troops. Remarkably, there are no Serbian losses. However, 19 French, British, and Italian warships have been sunk in air and submarine attacks.

APRIL 6

MIDDLE EAST, *MESOPOTAMIA*
The British relief force making for Kut-el-Amara makes slow progress. At the First Battle of Sannaiyat, some 16 miles (24 km) east of Kut, the Turks are forced to retreat just 500 yards (450 m), but the British suffer heavy casualties and are little nearer to

▲ *A lone German infantryman at Verdun keeps watch over Fort Vaux, one of the city's key defenses, from the remains of a captured French trench.*

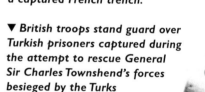

▼ *British troops stand guard over Turkish prisoners captured during the attempt to rescue General Sir Charles Townshend's forces besieged by the Turks at Kut-el-Amara.*

▼ *A German sentry moves a party of Russian machine-gunners captured at the Battle of Lake Naroch.*

▲ *Units of the Serbian Army arrive in Salonika, Greece, following their recent evacuation from Albania.*

their objective. A renewal of the fighting at Sannaiyat on the 9th sees the British lose their hard-won gains.

APRIL 9

WESTERN FRONT, *VERDUN*

The Germans launch a major offensive to the northwest of Verdun, against the high ground. Most of the attacks are repulsed by the French but the Germans capture front-line trenches on *Le Mort Homme* Ridge ("Dead Man" Ridge). General Henri-Philippe Pétain tells his troops: *"Courage, on les aura"* – "Courage, we'll get them."

APRIL 11

BALKANS, *CORFU*

The Serbian Army sets sail to join the ever-growing forces stationed in Salonika, Greece.

APRIL 14

EASTERN FRONT, *RUSSIA*

The Russian offensive around Lake Naroch ends. The battle, which began in mid-March, has resulted in an enormous Russian casualty list, some 122,000 men, but has produced few tangible results. The outnumbered Germans list 20,000 losses. Czar Nicholas II, who now formulates Russia's war strategy, meets with General Aleksey Brusilov, who agrees to launch a major summer offensive.

▲ *A British aircraft is readied to drop supplies to the garrison at Kut-el-Amara.*

Brusilov informs his four army commanders to prepare for a major attack by May 11. He tells them that they can expect no reinforcements.

APRIL 15

MIDDLE EAST, *MESOPOTAMIA*
British aircraft begin dropping food supplies to the besieged garrison of Kut-el-Amara. The garrison's commander, General Sir Charles Townshend, has stated that his stocks of food will be exhausted by the 29th.

The British column heading for Kut-el-Amara has been repulsed by the Turks the previous day.

APRIL 18

MIDDLE EAST, *ARMENIA*
Russia forces capture the Turkish Black Sea port of Trebizond, marking a key moment in their ongoing offensive.

APRIL 20

ESPIONAGE, *IRELAND*
Roger Casement, a supporter of Irish independence from Britain, lands from a German submarine with weapons

for the nationalists. He is captured on the 21st and later charged with high treason. He is convicted on June 29 and executed on July 3.

APRIL 21

POLITICS, *IRELAND*
Irish nationalists rebel against British rule. The rebellion, which becomes known as the Easter Rising, centers on Dublin, where the insurgents take

▼ *The aftermath of the fighting in Dublin, where British troops put down an uprising by Irish nationalists.*

▶ Members of the British garrison of Kut-el-Amara photographed after they have been released from Turkish captivity following an exchange of prisoners.

▼ Karl Liebknecht addresses a crowd of German workers in Berlin. Liebknecht formed the Spartacus League, which opposed the continuation of the war.

over and fortify several of the city's public buildings. The British declare martial law and their troops quickly recapture nationalist-held buildings.

The uprising ends on May 1. More than a dozen captured nationalists will be tried and later executed by the British. Seventy-nine receive prison terms. However, British fears that Irish troops fighting on the Western Front might be adversely affected by the rebellion prove unfounded.

APRIL 23

MIDDLE EAST, *MESOPOTAMIA*
With his food virtually exhausted and the advance of the relief force stalled, the commander of the British garrison at Kut-el-Amara, General Sir Charles Townshend, asks permission to begin surrender discussions with the Turks.

APRIL 25

SEA WAR, *NORTH SEA*
Four German battlecruisers shell the ports of Great Yarmouth and Lowestoft on the east coast of England for 20 minutes, causing around 20 mainly civilian casualties. At Great Yarmouth the German warships are forced to withdraw following the sudden arrival of British naval forces.

APRIL 29

MIDDLE EAST, *MESOPOTAMIA*
The British at Kut-el-Amara surrender. Some 13,000 are taken prisoner. Around 2500 sick and wounded are released by the Turks but the rest march into captivity. Some 4800 will die due to disease, illness, and neglect.

MAY 1

POLITICS, *GERMANY*
Radical politician Karl Liebknecht, along with Rosa Luxemburg a founder of the communist Spartacus League, is arrested during an antiwar protest by 10,000 Berlin workers.

ESPIONAGE, *HOLLAND*
Dutch-national Margaretha Zelle, who performs as an exotic dancer with the stage name of Mata Hari ("Eye of the Day"), is allegedly recruited as a spy by the Germans.

WESTERN FRONT, *VERDUN*
General Henri-Philippe Pétain is promoted to the command of France's Center Army Group. His replacement at Verdun is General Robert Nivelle, who is considered to be a more aggressive figure. Nivelle plans to launch major counterattacks against the Germans around Verdun.

◀ Mata Hari, the Dutch-born exotic dancer, was allegedly a spy for the Germans, although doubts have been expressed over the truth of the accusation.

May 2

May 2

BALKANS, *GREECE*
French forces, part of the large multi-national force building up in Salonika, advance to and occupy Florina close to the Serbian border and some 25 miles (40 km) from the enemy-occupied city of Monastir. Other troops are advancing with the French.

AIR WAR, *BRITAIN*
A raid by eight German Zeppelins against targets along the east coast causes 39 casualties. However, one of the raiders, *L20*, is wrecked by a fierce storm near Stavanger, Norway, as it is returning to its home base on the 3rd.

May 5

MIDDLE EAST, *ARABIA*
Backed by the British, Hussein, the Grand Sherif of Mecca, begins an uprising in the Turkish province. Hussein commands a force of 50,000 men, but has just 10,000 rifles. The Turkish presence in Arabia numbers 10,000. An early attack by his son Feisal on Medina is repulsed. However, the rebellion forces the Turks to withdraw some of their troops facing the British in Egypt to protect their communications.

May 9

POLITICS, *BRITAIN/FRANCE*
The British and French, with the agreement of Russia, sign the secret Sykes–Picot Agreement. It is named after its two chief negotiators, Britain's Sir Mark Sykes and France's Georges Picot. The convention agrees plans for the dismemberment of the Turkish Empire after an allied victory. Turkish-held territories across the Middle East are to be divided between and administered by the various allies. The agreement is made known to Italy in August, and it is agreed in 1917 that Italy will also receive Middle East lands.

May 13

MIDDLE EAST, *ARABIA*
In the first success of their rebellion against the Turks, Arabs fighting for

▲ *French colonial troops from what is now Vietnam prepare to advance deeper into Greece from their camp in Salonika.*

▼ *British vessels at anchor in the southern Italian port of Taranto. They are part of the Otranto barrage across the Adriatic.*

◄ *Italian troops occupy a mountain-top post in the Trentino, where the Austro-Hungarians launched a major attack in mid-May.*

▶ *An Austro-Hungarian trench mortar opens fire on the Italians in the Trentino.*

Hussein, Grand Sherif of Mecca, capture the holy city of Mecca. A further Turkish defeat follows on the 16th, when the city of Jeddah falls following naval and air attacks.

SEA WAR, *ADRIATIC*
The Austro-Hungarian submarine *U-6* becomes the only confirmed victim of the warships manning the Otranto barrage. The barrage comprises a semi-continuous line of small vessels stretching across the southern Adriatic. Its role is to deny German and Austro-Hungarian warships access into and egress out of the sea.

MAY 14

POLITICS, *CHINA*
The government agrees to supply France with 200,000 laborers to support its war effort.

MAY 15

WESTERN FRONT, *ITALY*
The Austro-Hungarians launch a major offensive in the Trentino region on the

north Italian border, which catches the Italians unprepared. The long-planned attack is opened on a 20-mile (32-km) front and, despite the mountainous terrain, the Austro-Hungarians make some progress, chiefly thanks to their specialist mountain troops. The Austro-Hungarian Eleventh and Third Armies, commanded by Archduke Eugene,

smash through the lines of General Roberto Brusati's Italian First Army in the next few days. On the 20th the Italian commander-in-chief, General Luigi Cadorna, orders the men of the First Army to fight to the death.

MAY 17

POLITICS, *UNITED STATES*
President Woodrow Wilson announces that the US may have to intervene in the war and should certainly have a role in any peace-making process.

MAY 20

POLITICS, *ITALY*
The Italian government, which is

▼ *Italian troops killed by Austro-Hungarian artillery fire in the Trentino.*

facing a crisis in the Trentino region due to an ongoing Austro-Hungarian offensive, asks the Russians to launch an immediate diversionary attack on the Eastern Front.

MAY 25

POLITICS, *BRITAIN*
The Military Service Act comes into force. All men between the ages of 18–41 are liable for military service and those previously rejected on whatever grounds are to be re-examined.

MAY 26

WESTERN FRONT, *ITALY*
The Austro-Hungarians maintain the momentum of their offensive in the Trentino by shifting the focus of their attacks toward the Asiago Plateau. Its

▲ *The British battlecruiser* Queen Mary *disappears in a cloud of smoke after being hit by shells from the German Derfflinger at Jutland.*

◄ *Admiral Sir John Jellicoe, commander of the British Home Fleet at Jutland.*

battlecruisers led by Admiral Sir David Beatty sets sail from Rosyth. The British plan to rendezvous at the Jutland Bank off the coast of Denmark. The German High Seas Fleet does not set sail until the 31st.

MAY 31

SEA WAR, *NORTH SEA*
The Battle of Jutland, fought between the British Home Fleet and the German High Seas Fleet, begins in the early afternoon, when rival light cruisers on picket duty spot each

capture will open the way into the lowlands of northern Italy. The Italians abandon the plateau on the 29th. However, the Austro-Hungarian offensive is slowing due to the problems of moving supporting artillery through the mountainous terrain.

MAY 27

POLITICS, *UNITED STATES*
President Woodrow Wilson suggests the creation of an international body with the authority to maintain peace and the freedom of the seas.

MAY 30

SEA WAR, *NORTH SEA*
Forewarned by the intelligence-gatherers of Room 40, the British Home Fleet puts to sea to intercept a major sortie by the German High Seas Fleet. The larger part of the Home Fleet, commanded by Admiral Sir John Jellicoe, sails from its bases at Scapa Flow and Invergordon. A strong force of

other and open fire. The main action opens shortly before 1600 hours when Admiral Sir David Beatty's battlecruisers open fire on German Admiral Franz von Hipper's battlecruisers. Beatty attempts to sail south to cut Hipper off from his base in Germany. Hipper undertakes a withdrawal to the southeast, hoping to lure Beatty into an unequal struggle against the main part of the High Seas Fleet.

During this running fight Beatty is at a disadvantage as the low sun in the west highlights his own ships, while the German battlecruisers are partly hidden by haze and mist. In the ensuing action Beatty comes off worst: the *Indefatigable* is struck by salvoes from the *Von der Tann*, falls out of the line, and then disappears in a massive explosion. Twenty-five

minutes later, the *Derfflinger* lands a salvo on the *Queen Mary*, which is ripped apart by an internal explosion – only nine men survive of a crew of more than 1200.

Beatty's own flagship, the *Lion*, also suffers severe damage, and his battlecruisers are perilously close to the battleships of the High Sea Fleet. He orders his depleted force to turn away from the German fleet and head north, where the British Home Fleet is in position. His withdrawal is covered by ships commanded by Rear Admiral Sir Horace Hood.

Meanwhile, Admiral Sir John Jellicoe has sent three battlecruisers to aid Beatty in his withdrawal. At 1735 these open fire on Hipper's ships, badly damaging the *Lützow* and hitting two light cruisers, the *Wiesbaden* and *Pillau*. Jellicoe, whose battle plans are made on poor and intermittent intelligence from his advance warships, now attempts a maneuver that will place his battleships in a position that will give them an enormous advantage over the main German fleet – in effect cutting the Germans off from their bases and allowing the British fleet to pound their warships to destruction.

The High Seas Fleet faces a line of British warships some nine miles (14 km) long, but continues the fight. One of the first ships to succumb is Hood's flagship, the *Invincible*, which is blown apart by the *Derfflinger* and *Lützow* at a

range of 10,500 yards (9500 m). The German fleet's commander, Admiral Reinhard Sheer, sensing the danger, opts to execute a turn away from the British, which will allow him to escape. However, Jellicoe is equal to this move and again attempts to block the German line of withdrawal.

To gain time for his main fleet, Sheer orders his light units, chiefly torpedo-boats and destroyers, and Hipper's battlecruisers – despite the odds – to attack. Sheer's attempt to escape under the cover of darkness is successful, but his fleet has several losses: the old battleship *Pommern* is sunk by a torpedo; two light cruisers – the *Frauenlob* and *Rostock* – also sink; and the *Elbing* is sliced in half by the battleship *Posen* as it attempts to cross the bow of the larger ship. The battlecruiser *Lützow* has to be abandoned and is later sunk by a torpedo to prevent it from falling into British hands.

Nightfall effectively ends the Battle of Jutland and the German fleet is able to return through the minefields that

▼ The British battlecruiser Indefatigable *sinks after being hit by the German battlecruiser* Von der Tann *at Jutland. The British warship was blown apart.*

intelligence between ships and the poor design of some of the vessels, which led to several suffering devastating internal explosions after being hit by German shells.

◄ *Warships of the German High Seas Fleet head out into the North Sea to confront the British at Jutland.*

▼ *Russian troops advance through barbed wire under fire during the opening moves of General Aleksey Brusilov's offensive.*

protect the waters around its bases. However, one battleship, the *Ostfriesland*, is damaged by striking a mine on the morning of June 1.

In Germany, Jutland, or the Battle of the Skaggerak, is seen as a victory as three British battleships, three cruisers, and eight destroyers have

▼ *Damage inflicted on the German battlecruiser* Seydlitz *by the British during the Battle of Jutland.*

been sunk for the loss of a single battleship, as well as four cruisers and five destroyers.

However, the British fleet, although mauled, is still able to fight on and make sure that the High Seas Fleet remains bottled up in its home ports. The British handling of the battle is seen as poor, although they came close to inflicting a severe defeat on Sheer. Most concern is expressed over the badly-handled transfer of orders and

JUNE 1

MIDDLE EAST, *ARMENIA*
The Turks begin planning an attack against General Nikolai Yudenich's Russian forces. The operation is devised by Enver Pasha, the Turkish commander, and calls for a broad-front offensive. The Third Army under Vehip Pasha is ordered to advance along the coast of the Black Sea, while Ahmet Izzim Pasha's new Second Army makes for the Russian-held city of Bitlis. However, the Russian commander,

▲ *Serbian artillery in action during the fighting in Salonika, Greece. A spent shell case is being ejected from the gun.*

General Nikolay Yudenich, moves to counter the threat when the operation starts at the beginning of July.

JUNE 2

WESTERN FRONT, *BELGIUM*
A German attack against the Ypres salient, which becomes known as the Battle of Mount Sorrel, makes initial progress, but many of their gains are lost due to Canadian counterattacks.
SEA WAR, *NORTH SEA*
It is announced that the British Home Fleet is again ready for action despite its recent action at Jutland.

JUNE 3

BALKANS, *SALONIKA*
The British and French declare a state of siege in Salonika and remove all the region's Greek officials from their posts. They demand that the possibly pro-German Greek government is changed and its army mobilizes.

JUNE 4

EASTERN FRONT, *RUSSIA*
Russian forces led by General Aleksey Brusilov, the commander-in-chief of the Southwest Front, launch a major offensive against the Austro-Hungarian and German armies in former Russian Poland and Austria-Hungary itself. The starting date for the offensive had been planned for June 15 following

◀ *The territory regained by the Russians during the Brusilov Offensive, their most successful attack of the war.*

recent Austro-Hungarian successes against the Italians, whose high command has requested a Russian effort to draw Austro-Hungarian troops away from the fighting in Italy.

The Russian attack, which becomes known as the Brusilov Offensive, had been scheduled to coincide with the British onslaught along the Western Front's Somme River sector. Both the British and Russian attacks had been designed to relieve some of the pressure on the French at Verdun.

Brusilov plans to advance on a broad front of some 200 miles (320 km). His Third and Eighth Armies are ordered to strike against the Austro-Hungarian Fourth Army to the south of the Pripet Marshes. Farther south the Russian Seventh Army is directed against the Austro-Hungarian Seventh Army.

The operation is heralded by a bombardment from close to 2000 Russian artillery pieces and early progress is excellent, particularly in the north and south, where the Austro-Hungarians virtually collapse. Only in the center, where the Russians face German units, is the advance stalled. The battle continues into September.

JUNE 5

SEA WAR, *NORTH SEA*
The British cruiser *Hampshire* is sunk by a mine laid by the German

Map labels:
■ WARSAW
Poland
Brest-Litovsk
Pripet Marshes
N
RUSSIA
Ukraine
Przemysl ●
Tarnopol
Galicia
Czernowitz
AUSTRIA-HUNGARY
Bessarabia
Transylvania
—— Front, June
- - - Front, August
0   95 mi
0   150 km
Moldavia
ROMANIA
BULGARIA

▲ *The remains of the aircraft of German ace Max Immelmann, who was shot down and killed over France on June 18.*

submarine *U-75* as it is making its way to Russia. Among the many dead is Secretary of War Lord Kitchener, who was to meet with Czar Nicholas II to discuss the flow of supplies between Russia and Britain. The incident is blamed on rough seas, poor mine-sweeping operations, and the ill-coordinated rescue operation.

JUNE 7

WESTERN FRONT, *VERDUN*
After weeks of bitter fighting and at high cost the Germans capture Fort Vaux from the French.

JUNE 8

WESTERN FRONT, *ITALY*
The Austro-Hungarians withdraw two divisions from their forces committed to the on-going Trentino offensive. They are rushed to the Eastern Front, where the Russian offensive led by General Aleksey Brusilov is making considerable territorial gains.

JUNE 10

POLITICS, *NEW ZEALAND*
The government passes a bill permitting compulsory military service.
POLITICS, *GERMANY*
The chief of the General Staff, General Erich von Falkenhayn, orders four German divisions in northern Russia and five from Verdun on the Western Front to move by rail to reinforce the defense against Brusilov's Offensive, which is close to totally defeating the

Austro-Hungarians. More will follow – 15 divisions will have been sent to the Eastern Front by mid-September.

JUNE 17

WESTERN FRONT, *ITALY*
The Austro-Hungarians call a stop to their Trentino offensive in the face of a mounting Italian counterattack, which began on the 16th. Backed by 800 artillery pieces, the Italians make steady but unspectacular gains. The campaign has cost the Italians 147,000 men, including 40,000 taken prisoner. The Austro-Hungarians, who pull back to more defensible positions over the next few days, admit to losses totaling 81,000, including 26,000 prisoners.
AIR WAR, *WESTERN FRONT*
Henri Navarre, France's first fighter ace, is shot down and badly wounded. He never takes to the air again. The following day German ace Max Immelmann is killed in air combat. He has 15 combat victories to his credit.

JUNE 23

WESTERN FRONT, *VERDUN*
There is intense German pressure against the French defenses around Verdun. The attacks concentrate on the French positions to the northeast of the city, where the Germans, advancing between Forts Douaumont and Vaux, move ever closer to Fleury and Fort Souville. Their capture would effectively seal the fate of Verdun.

▶ *Italian artillerymen attempt to place a three-inch (75-mm) gun on the summit of a mountain in the Trentino to help block the Austro-Hungarian offensive.*

JUNE 24

WESTERN FRONT, *SOMME*
The British begin their bombardment of the German trenches. Some 2000 British artillery pieces fire an estimated 1.7 million shells on the first day. However, as many as a third fail to explode, and many others are too light to inflict much damage on the German barbed wire or their strongly-constructed defenses. The barrage continues over the following week, further alerting the Germans to the impending offensive.

JUNE 27

POLITICS, *GREECE*
Under pressure from both Britain and France, the Greek government agrees to mobilize its armed forces.

JULY 1

WESTERN FRONT, *SOMME*
The British offensive begins at 0730 hours on an intensely hot day following the firing of 224,000 shells in an hour. Shortly before the advance begins, 10 huge underground mines are exploded beneath the German trenches, burying many of their occupants. Both the British commanders and the ordinary soldiers, most of whom are enthusiastic volunteers, believe that the first stage of the offensive, which becomes known as the Battle of Albert, will be an overwhelming success.

▼ *A British mine explodes underneath the German trenches near Beaumont Hamel at the beginning of the Somme attack.*

▲ *A German aerial photograph records the devastated remains of the French-held Fort Souville outside Verdun.*

The advance takes place along a front of some 25 miles (40 km). There are early gains to the east and southeast of the town of Albert: Montauban and Mametz, where the British Fourth Army led by General Henry Rawlinson attacks, and west of Péronne, where French colonial troops make some progress.

However, progress to the north of Albert is nothing short of disastrous. The attacking British infantry are confronted by uncut German barbed wire and intact defenses, particularly around Beaumont Hamel and Thiepval. Advancing at a walk and burdened

▲ German prisoners captured on the third day of the British Somme offensive carry one of their wounded comrades.

down with equipment, they meet a wall of machine-gun fire. By the end of the day British casualties total more than 57,000, of which 19,000 are killed. It is the greatest loss ever suffered by the British Army in a single day's combat. German losses are thought to be around 8000 men.

The British also find it difficult to rush reinforcements up to the exhausted troops holding what ground has been gained. There is poor communication between troops in advance positions and their head-quarters. German counterattacks are frequently successful. The British attempt to continue their offensive.

JULY 2

WESTERN FRONT, *VERDUN*

General Erich von Falkenhayn, chief of the German General Staff, orders the reduction of the German offensive at Verdun and the transfer of troops and artillery pieces to the Somme River, where the British have recently launched a major offensive. The fighting at Verdun, although less intense for the moment, continues.

SEA WAR, *ADRIATIC*

Austro-Hungarian agents in Taranto, southern Italy, use explosives to capsize the Italian battleship *Leonardo da Vinci*, killing 248.

JULY 4

POLITICS, *GERMANY*

Admiral Reinhard Sheer concludes his report to Kaiser Wilhelm II on the recent Battle of Jutland with the

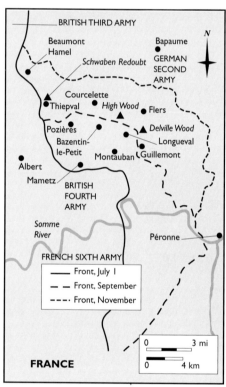

BRITISH THIRD ARMY

Beaumont Hamel

Bapaume

Schwaben Redoubt

GERMAN SECOND ARMY

Courcelette

Thiepval *High Wood* Flers

Pozières

Delville Wood

Bazentin-le-Petit

Longueval

Montauban Guillemont

Albert

Mametz

BRITISH FOURTH ARMY

Somme River

Péronne

FRENCH SIXTH ARMY

—— Front, July 1
– – – Front, September
- - - Front, November

0   3 mi
0   4 km

FRANCE

N

▲ The Battle of the Somme, designed by the British to aid the French at Verdun and possibly knock Germany out of the war, produced huge casualties.

◀ *The execution of Serbian guerrillas by Austro-Hungarians.*

will be later promoted to command all of the British forces in the region (August 28). Before contemplating any renewal of the advance on Turkish-held Baghdad, he begins to build up his fleet of river steamers, which are vital for keeping his forces supplied in the field. He is anxious to avoid the logistical problems that dogged the first advance on the city.

statement that "A victorious end can only be achieved by using the submarines against British trade."

JULY 5

BALKANS, *SERBIA*
Serbian guerrilla units begin operating against the Austro-Hungarian occupation forces. Similar developments also take place in Montenegro.

JULY 7

POLITICS, *BRITAIN*
Liberal politician David Lloyd George becomes secretary of war following the recent death of Lord Kitchener.

JULY 10

EASTERN FRONT, *RUSSIA*
The Russian authorities announce that they have captured some 300,000 German and Austro-Hungarian prisoners since the opening of the Brusilov Offensive on May 4.

JULY 11

MIDDLE EAST, *MESOPOTAMIA*
General Sir Frederick Maude takes over the 95,000-strong Tigris Corps from General George Gorringe. Maude

JULY 14–20

WESTERN FRONT, *SOMME*
Four British divisions, preceded by a short barrage, achieve surprise,

▶ *David Lloyd George was made the British secretary of war in July after the death of Lord Kitchener.*

▲ *A British supply depot replenishes the ammunition stocks of an infantry unit on the Somme.*

▼ *The beginning of the Somme offensive – British infantrymen move forward slowly and methodically into a maelstrom of German machine-gun fire.*

Yudenich now turns his attention to Ahmet Izzim Pasha's Second Army, which is advancing on Bitlis.

JULY 29

POLITICS, *GERMANY*
Germany, Austria-Hungary, and Bulgaria agree to take direct military action against Romania.

AUGUST 1

WESTERN FRONT, *SOMME*
The British offensive is a month old and their casualties total 158,000 plus another 40,000 elsewhere on the Western Front. German losses on the Somme amount to 160,000 men.

BALKANS, *SALONIKA*
Some 5000 Russian troops arrive in Salonika, thereby contributing to the ever-growing presence in the province. Some 11,000 Italian troops arrive on the 11th.

AUGUST 2

AIR WAR, *BRITAIN*
Sixteen German airships attack London and southeast England. The results are poor due to bad weather

taking 4000 German prisoners along with the villages of Longueval and Bazentin-le-Petit. On the following day the South African Brigade, just 3000 men, attacks and secures most of Delville Wood. The brigade is surrounded and is faced by three German divisions but manages to hold out until it is relieved on the 20th. The brigade has just 778 survivors. Delville Wood is abandoned but is later recaptured and held.

JULY 19

MIDDLE EAST, *EGYPT*
Turkish troops, some 15,000 men commanded by German General Kress von Kressenstein, launch their second attack against the British-held Suez Canal. They advance to within 10 miles (16 km) of Romani, a rail junction, and then establish defensive positions.

JULY 23

WESTERN FRONT, *SOMME*
The British attempt to restart their offensive in an attack that becomes known as the Battle of Pozières Ridge. Australian and New Zealand troops lead the advance toward Pozières to the northeast of Albert. The village is secured by the 25th, but the fighting then degenerates into stalemate.

JULY 25

MIDDLE EAST, *ARMENIA*
Russian General Nikolai Yudenich inflicts a major defeat on Vehip Pasha's Turkish Third Army at Erzincan, thereby blunting one of the two main attacks launched by Enver Pasha.

▲ *The first contingent of Russian troops to arrive in Salonika parades through the streets of a Greek town.*

▼ *British intelligence officers sift through the wreckage of a German Zeppelin airship shot down near London.*

and technical problems. One of the raiders, *SL11*, is shot down by British pilot Lieutenant Leefe Robinson.

AUGUST 4

WESTERN FRONT, *ITALY*
The Italians launch the Sixth Battle of the Isonzo, but the key attack by the Duke of Aosta's Third Army does not begin until the 6th. The main assault opens at 1400 hours, after the Austro-Hungarian front line has been pounded by artillery for nine hours. The Italians gain some ground, chiefly Gorizia, which falls on the 8th.

MIDDLE EAST, *EGYPT*
The Turks commanded by German General Kress von Kressenstein attack the British-held rail junction at Romani, a little to the east of the Suez Canal. The surprise advance makes initial progress but is halted by New Zealand and other mounted forces. Turkish casualties are high in the battle – some 5000 men. The British losses total 1100.

AUGUST 5

MIDDLE EAST, *ARMENIA*
In the only noteworthy success of the Turkish offensive against General Nikolai Yudenich's Russian forces, Mustafa Kemal's corps captures Bitlis and then Mus on the following day. However, these gains will soon be lost.

AUGUST 8

POLITICS, *PORTUGAL*
The Portuguese government agrees to increase its military backing for the war against the Central Powers.

AUGUST 12

EASTERN FRONT, *RUSSIA*
General Aleksey Brusilov announces details of his continuing offensive. He claims to have captured 375,000 German and Austro-Hungarian prisoners as well as more than 400 artillery pieces, 1300 machine guns, and taken 15,000 square miles (38,850 sq km) of territory. Russian casualties total

▲ *Italian mountain troops move forward against the Austro-Hungarians during the fighting along the Isonzo River. The crew of a howitzer waits to advance once the infantry column has passed.*

▼ *Three wounded Turkish prisoners are escorted to the rear by British troops following fighting in the vicinity of the Suez Canal.*

550,000 men. Many of these troops were intensely loyal to Czar Nicholas II, but their replacements are less steadfast in their support for the Russian monarchy.

AUGUST 17

POLITICS, *ROMANIA*
The government agrees to join the war against the Central Powers with the aim of gaining territory.

WESTERN FRONT, *ITALY*
The Italians end the Sixth Battle of the Isonzo, their most successful attack

▼ *German artillerymen on the Eastern Front lounge by their three-inch (77-mm) field gun awaiting orders. The gun's camouflaged ammunition caisson is nearly empty, suggesting that there has been recent action.*

against the Austro-Hungarians to date. They have won territory and inflicted losses totaling 49,000. Italian casualties number 51,000.

BALKANS, *GREECE*
The Bulgarians launch a pre-emptive attack into the northern Greek region of Macedonia. There are early gains – the town of Florina falls on the 18th – and various enemy forces are pushed back to a line along the Sturma River.

AUGUST 18

SEA WAR, *NORTH SEA*
For one of the last times before its surrender in 1918 the German

▲ *Russian prisoners captured by the Germans during the Brusilov Offensive trudge into captivity.*

High Seas Fleet launches a major attack against Britain. The plan is to shell the port of Sunderland on the east coast of England and lure the British Home Fleet, which will sail from its bases to deal with the threat posed by the High Seas Fleet, into several groups of waiting submarines.

However, one German warship, the *Westfalen*, is torpedoed by a British submarine at the start of the sortie. The British commanders, thanks to their intelligence-gatherers in

Room 40, are aware of the attack, and Admiral Sir John Jellicoe has, in fact, already sailed to counter the threat.

AUGUST 19

SEA WAR, *NORTH SEA*
Two British cruisers, the *Nottingham* and *Falmouth*, part of the counter to the recently-launched sortie by the German High Seas Fleet, are sunk by German submarines. Their loss forces the British to break off their confrontation with the High Seas Fleet, which in turn heads for its home ports.

HOME FRONT, *GERMANY*
Coalminers in the Ruhr region go on strike to protest against inflation and shortages of food.

▲ *Serbian machine-gunners hold defensive positions outside the southern Serbian city of Monastir during their advance from Greece.*

◄ *A German submarine watches the Italian merchant ship that it has just intercepted burn. In 1916 such submarines sank 964 vessels of all types. Just 22 submarines were lost.*

▼ *Romanian troops advance into the southern Austro-Hungarian province of Transylvania, where there was a significant ethnic Romanian population. However, the territory captured by the Romanian forces was soon lost to swift counterattacks.*

AUGUST 20

SEA WAR, *MEDITERRANEAN*
The German submarine *U-35* commanded by Lothar von Arnauld de la Perière returns to its base at Cattaro in the Adriatic after a record-breaking 25-day cruise. It has sunk 54 ships, most Italian, in the Mediterranean. Many have been sent to the bottom by gunfire. Its captain will become the most successful submarine commander of all time.

AUGUST 27

POLITICS, *ROMANIA*
The government declares war on Austria-Hungary and mobilizes its armed forces, which immediately invade the Austro-Hungarian province of Transylvania, which has a large ethnic Romanian population. Germany and Turkey come to the aid of their ally and both declare war on Romania over the next few days.

STRATEGY & TACTICS

DEFENSE-IN-DEPTH

By late 1916 Germany's military planners were becoming seriously short of manpower on the Western Front due to recent losses, particularly at Verdun and on the Somme, and their commitments in several other war theaters. One of their solutions to this problem was to give up some territory on the Western Front and fall back to a more easily defensible – and shorter – front line. A shorter front would require few troops to defend it and free those not needed for service elsewhere.

Central to this revised strategy was a new defensive doctrine known as defense-in-depth, which called for a comparatively thinly-held front line, backed by lines of more extensive defenses stretching in depth to several miles. The aim was that the well-fortified but lightly-held front line would delay and break up any enemy attack, allowing time for fresh reserves to be rushed to the threatened sector. With fewer troops in the front line it was believed that the massive preliminary bombardments by the enemy would cause fewer casualties than in the past.

The plan was the brainchild of Marshal Paul von Hindenburg and the defenses were nicknamed after him, although their actual name was the Siegfried Line. Preliminary work on the Hindenburg Line began in late 1916. Its builders took advantage of any favorable high ground. The line, when completed in spring 1917, stretched from Arras, through St. Quentin to Soissons, and shortened the Western Front by some 25 miles (40 km). This contraction allowed around 14 divisions to be withdrawn from the front line.

The line itself consisted of a 600-yard (550-m) forward "outpost zone," which consisted of a series of positions held by a dozen or so men each. These were intended to break up or delay any enemy attack. The second line, the "battle zone," was 2500 yards (2300 m) in depth and contained two trench lines, each dotted with prefabricated concrete machine-gun posts with interlocking zones of fire. This was the main line of defense and was held in greater strength. Troops were protected by deep underground bunkers. Both zones were masked by thick belts of barbed wire.

Behind the "battle zone" were one or two "rear zones" 6000 yards (5500 m) in depth in total, where reserves could be mustered for counterattacks if an enemy advance appeared successful.

AUGUST 28

POLITICS, *ITALY*

Declares war on Germany.

AUGUST 29

POLITICS, *GERMANY*

Marshal Paul von Hindenburg replaces General Erich von Falkenhayn as chief of the General Staff. Falkenhayn has been criticized for his offensive against the French at Verdun. It was to have inflicted massive casualties on the French and destroyed their will to fight on. Neither has happened and German casualties are as high as the French. Falkenhayn goes to the Eastern Front, where he takes charge of the Ninth Army. General Eric Ludendorff, Hindenburg's confident, is made his deputy. Both men believe a new strategy is needed on the Western Front – defense-in-depth.

AUGUST 31

POLITICS, *GERMANY*

The government's war minister receives a letter from Marshal Paul von Hindenburg demanding a doubling of

◄ *General Erich von Falkenhayn (center, with cane), the ex-chief of the German General Staff, with Ninth Army officers.*

▲ *German dead lie outside the shell-blasted remains of their machine-gun post near the Somme village of Guillemont.*

ammunition output by May 1917. Hindenburg also requests a three-fold increase in machine-gun and artillery production. He later meets leading industrialists to discuss his armaments needs and shortages of manpower. Hindenburg also presses for the immediate commencement of an unrestricted submarine campaign.

SEPTEMBER 1

POLITICS, *BULGARIA*
The government declares war on Romania.

SEPTEMBER 3

WESTERN FRONT, *SOMME*
Under mounting French pressure and needing to offer aid to Romania, which has recently joined the war, General Sir Douglas Haig agrees to yet another major renewal of the offensive, which has degenerated into a series of localized battles since its beginning.

◄ *While one man keeps watch out of a forward trench, other Bulgarian soldiers eat their rations.*

Supported by a French attack south of Albert, the main British effort is directed against the village of Guillemont, which is captured by the 20th Division. However, attacks on German positions at High Wood and against the Schwaben Redoubt fail.

BALKANS, *ROMANIA*
German Field Marshal August von Mackensen, commanding a German–Bulgarian–Turkish force known as the Danube Army, invades southern Romania from Bulgaria.

BALKANS, *GREECE*
The troops in Salonika launch a counter-offensive against the Bulgarian forces operating in Macedonia, which they invaded in mid-August. They make early gains and push both Bulgarian and German forces back.

SEPTEMBER 5

WESTERN FRONT, *SOMME*
After two months of fighting, the British, with French support, secure all of the German second-line defenses. However, these were expected to fall in the opening phase of the battle.

SEPTEMBER 8

SEPTEMBER 8

WESTERN FRONT, *FRANCE*

Marshal Paul von Hindenburg and his deputy General Erich Ludendorff visit the Western Front, where the German forces are facing heavy fighting at Verdun and the Somme. Both realize that a new Western Front strategy needs to be implemented soon, particularly as German forces are been siphoned off to prosecute campaigns on the Eastern Front and in the Balkans. They finalize a new tactical doctrine, which becomes known as defense-in-depth.

SEPTEMBER 13

WESTERN FRONT, *VERDUN*

France's president, Raymond Poincaré, visits the city and bestows on it the Legion of Honor. The French are planning to launch a major counter-attack against the Germans.

SEPTEMBER 14

WESTERN FRONT, *ITALY*

The Seventh Battle of the Isonzo opens at 0900 hours with the Italian Third Army attacking on a six-mile (10-km) front. The fighting will continue until the 17th. The Italians make some early gains, but bad weather and strong Austro-Hungarian resistance combine to thwart any major progress.

◄ *Germany's Baron Manfred von Richthofen, the top-scoring fighter pilot of World War I with 80 victories to his credit.*

SEPTEMBER 15

WESTERN FRONT, *SOMME*

The British again attempt to break the deadlock by launching what becomes known as the Battle of Flers-Courcelette, two villages to the northeast of Albert. Fourteen divisions are involved in the battle and tanks appear on the Western Front for the first time. The advance goes well, gaining some 2500 yards along a six-mile (10-km) front. Both villages are captured, but the slow-moving tanks, although causing some initial panic among the German defenders, are far from successful. Many are knocked out, become stuck in mud and ditches, or suffer mechanical failure during the advance. Nevertheless, General Sir Douglas Haig, the British commander on the Western Front, requests that another 1000 tanks be built on the 19th.

AIR WAR, *ADRIATIC*

Two Austro-Hungarian flying-boats make military history by becoming the first aircraft to sink a submarine. Their victim is the French boat *Foucault*.

▲ *British troops and a Mark I tank pictured during a lull in the fighting around Flers-Courcelette on the Somme.*

SEPTEMBER 16

WESTERN FRONT, *FRANCE*

Marshal Paul von Hindenburg announces the construction of a massive fortified position, which becomes known as the Hindenburg Line. The construction is to take place between five (8 km) and 30 miles (48 km) behind the existing front line. Work begins on the 23rd.

SEPTEMBER 17

BALKANS, *GREECE*

French and Russian troops recapture the Macedonian town of Florina from the Bulgarians. The various contingents are planning to capture Monastir, some 20 miles (32 km) inside Serbia.

MIDDLE EAST, *EGYPT*

Capitalizing on their victory against the Turks at the Battle of Romani in early August, New Zealand and Australian mounted units successfully attack Mazar some 45 miles (72 km) east of Romani. The Turks are forced to retreat some 20 miles (32 km) to positions near El-Arish.

AIR WAR, *WESTERN FRONT*

German pilot Baron Manfred von Richthofen scores his first victory.

SEPTEMBER 16

BALKANS, *ROMANIA*

General Erich von Falkenhayn takes charge of the German Ninth Army. His immediate objective is to force the Romanians out of the Austro-Hungarian province of Transylvania and then secure several passes through the Transylvanian Alps. Their capture will allow his army to push into Romania itself.

SEPTEMBER 26

WESTERN FRONT, *SOMME*

A British attack spearheaded by 13 tanks succeeds in capturing the village of Thiepval. Fighting continues along much of the Somme front, with the British and French making some small gains at high cost over the following weeks. However, thick mud and strong German resistance make progress slow.

MIDDLE EAST, *ARMENIA*

The Turks abandon the recently occupied town of Mus, marking the end of their offensive against General Nikolai Yudenich's Russian forces. It has been a failure as the Russians still control most of Armenia. As the campaigning season ends, the Russians and Turks forces go into winter quarters.

OCTOBER 6

POLITICS, *FRANCE*

The government requisitions uncultivated land and livestock to improve agricultural output.

POLITICS, *GERMANY*

The authorities agree to resume attacks on merchant vessels, irrespective of their nationality, although it is specifically forbidden for submarine commanders to torpedo ships without warning them first.

OCTOBER 7

POLITICS, *UNITED STATES*

Democrat and serving president Woodrow Wilson is re-elected. He has campaigned on a ticket of maintaining US neutrality, despite increasing friction with Germany.

OCTOBER 8

POLITICS, *GERMANY*

The authorities agree to form an air force by uniting "all means of air

▲ *Female supporters campaign for US President Woodrow Wilson, who was re-elected in November.*

▼ *British stretcher-bearers carry a wounded man away from the fighting around Thiepval on the Somme.*

OCTOBER 9

▶ *French bystanders cover their ears as a 12-inch (30-cm) rail gun fires on German positions.*

combat and air defense with the army, in the field and in the home areas, into one unit."

SEA WAR, *ATLANTIC*
The German submarine *U-53* marks an escalation of the naval war by becoming the first boat to sink enemy vessels off the East Coast of the United States. Three British, one Dutch, and one Norwegian ships are its victims.

OCTOBER 9

WESTERN FRONT, *ITALY*
The Italians open the Eighth Battle of the Isonzo, with their Second and Third Armies striking the Austro-Hungarian Fifth Army. Again, the fighting is indecisive. The Italians gain just two miles (3 km) at a cost of 24,000 casualties. The battle ends on the 12th.

OCTOBER 10

POLITICS, *RUSSIA*
Czar Nicholas II orders that the highly successful offensive led by General Aleksey Brusilov is brought to a conclusion. However, the fighting drags on into mid-October.

BALKANS, *MACEDONIA*
German General Otto von Below is made the local army group commander and establishes his headquarters at Skopje. He is granted reinforcements from the Western and Eastern Fronts.

OCTOBER 16

MIDDLE EAST, *ARABIA*
Captain T.E. Lawrence, a member of the British Arab Bureau, arrives at Jeddah. His mission is to liaise between the leaders of the Arab revolt and the British establishment. He becomes the adviser to Prince Feisal, who is attempting to unite

▶ *Colonel T. E. Lawrence, the British liaison officer with the Arabs in Turkish Arabia.*

the various Arab tribes against the Turks. Lawrence, an advocate of the creation of an independent Arab state, will become known as "Lawrence of Arabia" because of his exploits.

OCTOBER 19

BALKANS, *ROMANIA*
The Danube Army commanded by German Field Marshal August von Mackensen, which has been

advancing steadily along the coast of southern Romania from Bulgaria since early September, gains a decisive breakthrough and advances on the key port of Constanza at the mouth of the Danube River on the Black Sea, which falls on the 22nd.

OCTOBER 24

WESTERN FRONT, *VERDUN*
The French launch their counterattack. Its aim is to capture territory to the northeast of Verdun. Advancing under cover of mist, the French recapture Fort Douaumont, taking 6000 prisoners. German attacks are defeated.

OCTOBER 21

POLITICS, *GERMANY*
The government agrees to establish the War Munitions Office to boost the country's output of much-needed ammunition, particularly for artillery. The body begins work on November 1.

▲ *The invasion of Romania was a chiefly German affair. The Romanian Army was no match for the invaders.*

▼ *French troops man a captured German machine gun amid the ruins of Verdun's Fort Douaumont.*

OCTOBER 28

AIR WAR, *WESTERN FRONT*
One of Germany's leading air aces, with 40 victories, and an outstanding tactician, Oswald Boelcke, is killed in a midair collision with a colleague.

NOVEMBER 1

WESTERN FRONT, *FRANCE*
The French commander-in-chief, General Joseph Joffre, outlines his plans for a combined Anglo-French offensive in 1917 to his British counterpart, General Sir Douglas Haig.

NOVEMBER 1–4

WESTERN FRONT, *ITALY*
The Ninth Battle of the Isonzo begins with attacks by the Italian Second and Third Armies against Austro-Hungarian positions east of the town of Gorizia. Bad weather and heavy casualties (28,000 men) force the Italian commander-in-chief, General Luigi Cadorna, to halt the attacks.

NOVEMBER 2

WESTERN FRONT, *VERDUN*
The Germans abandon what little remains of Fort Vaux, which is fully under French control by the 5th.

NOVEMBER 4

POLITICS, *ARABIA*
Despite several British and French protests, Hussein, Grand Sherif of Mecca, is crowned as king of the Arabs at Mecca.

▶ *German air ace Oswald Boelcke was killed in a midair collision on the Western Front in November.*

to the northeast of Albert. The British attack, heralded by the destruction of the German Hawthorn Redoubt by the detonation of an underground mine, is directed toward the village of Beaumont Hamel, which is captured. The fighting in the sector continues until the 18th.

NOVEMBER 15

POLITICS, *FRANCE*
The various allies confer at Chantilly, where General Joseph Joffre, the French commander-in-chief, chairs a meeting that discusses a joint offensive on the Western, Eastern, and Italian Fronts to begin in early

◄ *British troops negotiate the shell-cratered landscape along the Somme River at the close of their offensive during late 1916.*

▼ *Russian troops await the order to occupy Monastir in southern Serbia after its evacuation by Bulgarian forces.*

NOVEMBER 5

POLITICS, *FRANCE*
The government attempts to show its solidarity with occupied Serbia by sponsoring a national Serbian Soldiers' Flag Day.

POLITICS, *POLAND*
Germany and Austria-Hungary, conquerors of this former Russian territory, announce the creation of the "Kingdom of Poland," hoping to recruit Poles into their armed forces. Some Poles do join up, but many do not believe the German and Austro-Hungarian offer of independence goes far enough.

NOVEMBER 10

SEA WAR, *BALTIC*
Seven German destroyers are sunk in a Russian minefield.

NOVEMBER 12

POLITICS, *MEXICO*
A high-ranking German diplomat remarks to a Mexican official that "The imperial government would see with the greatest of pleasure the Mexican government's consent to a [submarine] base in its territory."

NOVEMBER 13

WESTERN FRONT, *SOMME*
The newly-created British Fifth Army commanded by General Sir Hubert Gough initiates the Battle of the Ancre

February 1917. It is believed that the Germans and Austro-Hungarians will be unable to counter such a widespread simultaneous offensive.

HOME FRONT, *GERMANY*
Germany's growing manpower shortage is highlighted when the 1918 conscription class, all under 19 years, is called up to fight. Medical reports note that many are undernourished, partly reflecting the growing success of the British naval blockade, which is preventing many supplies from overseas reaching Germany.

NOVEMBER 18

WESTERN FRONT, *SOMME*
The Battle of the Ancre ends, effectively concluding the British offensive on the Somme. British casualties are enormous; some 420,000 men. The French have lost 205,000 troops and the Germans some 500,000. At the end of their attacks the British have still not captured some of their first-day objectives. For example, they are still three miles (5 km) from Bapaume. Despite having gained little territory, the British have inflicted equally massive casualties on the Germans during the fighting and

contributed to their decision to withdraw to the Hindenburg Line.

WESTERN FRONT, *VERDUN*
General Robert Nivelle is given permission by General Joseph Joffre, the French commander-in-chief, to launch a final offensive. Nivelle has regained much of the territory to the northeast of Verdun lost to the Germans in the first months of the year and his stock with both the public and senior commanders is high. Part of his success is due to using a creeping barrage in which French troops advance behind a wall of artillery fire, which itself moves forward at a predetermined rate.

NOVEMBER 19

BALKANS, *SERBIA*
Serbian and French forces recapture the city of Monastir, which has been abandoned by its Bulgarian and German defenders who have fallen back a little way to the north.

NOVEMBER 21

POLITICS, *AUSTRIA-HUNGARY*
Emperor Franz Joseph dies at the age of 86. He is succeeded by his great nephew, 26-year-old Archduke Charles.

▲ *A German supply column negotiates a ford in Romania during the advance of the Ninth Army toward Bucharest.*

SEA WAR, *MEDITERRANEAN*
The British hospital ship *Britannic*, a companion-ship of the ill-fated *Titanic*, succumbs to a mine laid by a German submarine. The *Britannic* is not carrying wounded at the time and there are just 78 casualties among the crew of the former luxury passenger liner.

NOVEMBER 23

POLITICS, *GREECE*
The Greek provisional government in Salonika declares war on Germany and Bulgaria after much prompting by the French and British, who have substantial troops in the region.

BALKANS, *ROMANIA*
German Field Marshal August von Mackensen's Danube Army launches a second invasion of Romania to support his forces already attacking along the Black Sea coast. Units strike across the Danube River along a 30-mile (48-km) front. The plan is to link up with the German Ninth Army commanded by General Erich

von Falkenhayn, who is advancing through northwest Romania after negotiating the fortified passes of the Transylvanian Alps. Their objective is the Romanian capital, Bucharest. The two forces make contact on the 26th, by which stage they are less than 50 miles (80 km) from Bucharest. The struggle for the Romanian capital begins at the end of the month. The defeat of Romania will give the Central Powers access to its oil fields.

NOVEMBER 25

SEA WAR, *ATLANTIC*
The German submarine *U-52* sinks the French battleship *Suffren* as its sails off the coast of southern Portugal. There are no survivors.

NOVEMBER 28

AIR WAR, *BRITAIN*
Long-range German bombers launch the first daylight attack on London. A lone aircraft drops six small bombs on the center of the capital, wounding 10 civilians.

NOVEMBER 29

POLITICS, *BRITAIN*
Admiral Sir David Beatty is appointed to command the Home Fleet in place of Admiral Sir John Jellicoe, who is made First Sea Lord on December 4.

DECEMBER 1

POLITICS, *ROMANIA*
The government abandons the capital, Bucharest, and moves to Jassy.

DECEMBER 5

POLITICS, *BRITAIN*
Prime Minister Herbert Asquith resigns as head of the country's coalition government and is replaced by Liberal

▲ *German Field Marshal August von Mackensen celebrates the capture of Bucharest.*

David Lloyd George on the 7th. Lloyd George acts swiftly to reform and regularize Britain's war effort by establishing various powerful boards and committees.

POLITICS, GERMANY
The Auxiliary Service Law comes into effect. All males ages between 17 and 60 are compelled by the authorities to work in war-related industries.

DECEMBER 6

BALKANS, ROMANIA
German Field Marshal August von Mackensen, celebrating his 67th birthday, makes a triumphant entry into Bucharest mounted on his favorite white charger. There has been a three-day truce to allow the Romanians the opportunity to evacuate their capital. Romanian forces retreat into the northeast of their country in the direction of the border with Russia. They are pursued, although worsening weather slows the German advance.

▼ *A British gunboat on the Tigris River bombards Turkish positions at the opening of General Sir Frederick Maude's push to reach Baghdad, which began in mid-December.*

DECEMBER 11

BALKANS, SALONIKA/SERBIA
French General Maurice Sarrail, nominally the commander of all the forces operating in the theater is ordered to cease all offensive operations and place his forces in their winter quarters. Monastir remains under frequent artillery fire.

▲ *French troops march through the recently-captured city of Monastir in southern Serbia.*

DECEMBER 12

POLITICS, FRANCE
General Joseph Joffre is replaced as French commander-in-chief of the Armies of the North and Northeast by General Robert Nivelle, the hero of Verdun. On the same day General Ferdinand Foch is replaced as commander of the North Army Group by General Louis Franchet d'Esperey. Foch goes into semiretirement, but will soon return to active service.

POLITICS, GERMANY
The government sends a "peace note" to the various powers allied against it. It is rejected as being "empty and insincere" on the 30th.

DECEMBER 13

MIDDLE EAST, MESOPOTAMIA
The British commander, General Sir Frederick Maude, begins an offensive along the Tigris River. His force of 48,000 men is supported by more than 170 artillery pieces, 24 aircraft, and numerous armed river steamers. The Turks are able to muster 20,000 troops and 70 artillery pieces. However, heavy rains slow the British advance.

DECEMBER 15

DECEMBER 15

WESTERN FRONT, *VERDUN*
The French attack to the northeast of Verdun. Within a few days, the Germans have been forced away from key positions, including Forts Douaumont and Vaux. Although the fighting around Verdun will continue into 1917, this attack ends the main battle. Losses are enormous: 360,000 French troops and 336,000 Germans. The German plan to destroy the French Army at little cost has failed.

DECEMBER 19

POLITICS, *BRITAIN*
Prime Minister David Lloyd George makes his first speech. He rejects recent peace proposals, stating that "We shall put our trust rather in an unbroken army than in broken faith."

DECEMBER 21

MIDDLE EAST, *EGYPT*
Australian and New Zealand mounted units force the Turks to abandon their positions around El-Arish.

DECEMBER 26

POLITICS, *FRANCE*
General Joseph Joffre resigns as the French commander-in-chief but is

▲ German prisoners, some of the more than 17,000 captured at Verdun, are escorted to the rear by French troops.

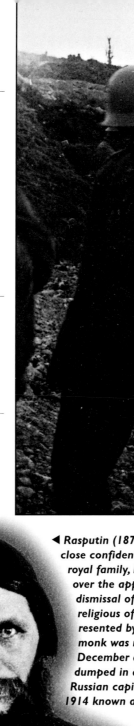

◀ Rasputin (1871–1916) became a close confident of the Russian royal family, but his influence over the appointment and dismissal of political and religious officials was greatly resented by many nobles. The monk was murdered in late December and his body dumped in a river in the Russian capital Petrograd, until 1914 known as St. Petersburg.

▼ A victim of a German submarine sinks by the stern, one of 1157 vessels of all nations sunk during 1916.

KEY PERSONALITIES

FIELD MARSHAL SIR DOUGLAS HAIG

Douglas Haig (1861–1928) was the commander of the British forces on the Western Front between 1915 and 1918. In 1914 Haig was given command of I Corps, which he led during the Battles of Mons, the Marne, and First Ypres. Promoted to lead the First Army in December 1914, he played a prominent role in the Battle of Neuve-Chapelle. Haig is believed to have been involved in the dismissal of the increasingly unpopular Field Marshal Sir John French, the commander of the British Expeditionary Force, in December 1915.

Haig's period as commander-in-chief remains controversial. He was always looking for a decisive breakthrough on the Western Front. At the Battle of the Somme in 1916 and at Third Ypres in 1917 he persisted in attacking – at very great cost – even though chances of making a breakthrough were small. However, Haig proved adept in organizing, training, and supplying his forces, and was receptive to new ideas and technologies, such as the tank.

Haig's calmness during the German spring offensive of 1918 enabled the French and British to block the attack, and between August and November it was the British under Haig who won a string of victories against the Germans that effectively destroyed their army on the Western Front. Also, Haig was a prime-mover behind the creation of a joint Anglo-French command structure in 1918 – one led by the French.

promoted to the rank of marshal. On the following day General Ferdinand Foch is made chief military adviser to the French government.

DECEMBER 29

WESTERN FRONT, *SOMME*
General Sir Douglas Haig completes his report on the prolonged battle. He claims that the British have fought half of the German Army, and have taken 38,000 prisoners and captured 125 artillery pieces of various calibers.

DECEMBER 31

POLITICS, *BRITAIN*
General Douglas Haig, the commander-in-chief of the British forces on the Western Front, is promoted to the rank of field marshal.

POLITICS, *RUSSIA*
Monk and mystic Rasputin, who many Russians believe has an untoward influence on the royal family, particularly the czarina, is murdered by a group of nobles.

SEA WAR, *ATLANTIC*
At the end of a successful month German submarines are credited with sinking 167 vessels. Of this total 70 belong to neutral countries. However, there are still calls for a greater effort.

1917

The year was dominated by the outbreak of the Russian Revolution, which would release Germans troops for service elsewhere, and the declaration of war on Germany by the United States. Italy came close to being knocked out of the war and the French Army mutinied, leaving Britain to bear the brunt of the campaign on the Western Front. German allies Austria-Hungary and Turkey were also in growing military and political decline.

JANUARY 8–9

MIDDLE EAST, *EGYPT*
The British forces massing in Egypt under the command of General Sir Archibald Murray begin to clear the Turks out of the Sinai Peninsula, prior to launching an invasion of Palestine. They win an important victory at the Battle of Magruntein, capturing some 1600 Turkish prisoners and a handful of artillery pieces. Murray's forces suffer a total of 487

▶ *A British-crewed howitzer in action during the fighting against the Turks in the Sinai Peninsula.*

▲ *A column of Turkish cavalry moves out from a town in Palestine to confront the advancing British.*

casualties. He now begins to plan an invasion of Palestine; his first targets will be the series of Turkish-held ridges stretching from Gaza on the Mediterranean coast to Beersheba in the interior, a distance of some 20 miles (32 km). Murray's ultimate objective is Jerusalem.

JANUARY 19

POLITICS, *MEXICO*
The German diplomatic representative receives a secret telegram penned by German Foreign Secretary Arthur Zimmermann. Its suggests forming a defensive alliance with Mexico if the United States declares war on Germany. The note concludes: "Mexico is to reconquer the lost territory in New Mexico, Texas, and Arizona." (All of these US states were

administered by Mexico, then
a Spanish colony, in the past.) The
message also suggests that Mexico
should encourage Japan, which has
plans to carve out an empire in the
Pacific, to join the Central Powers.
Unbeknown to the Germans, the
British intercept and decode the
sensitive message.

JANUARY 22

POLITICS, *UNITED STATES*
President Woodrow Wilson calls on
all the combatant nations fighting in

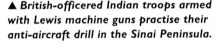
▲ British-officered Indian troops armed
with Lewis machine guns practise their
anti-aircraft drill in the Sinai Peninsula.

◄ German submarines and destroyers are
readied to attack enemy shipping.

World War I to agree to "peace without
victory." The British and French reject
the offer, finding some of the demands
made by Germany unacceptable.

JANUARY 27

POLITICS, *UNITED STATES*
General John Pershing, who has
been in charge of 4800 US troops
attempting to capture rebel leader
Pancho Villa in Mexico for some 10
months, is ordered to return to the
United States.

JANUARY 31

POLITICS, *GERMANY*
After many months of often acrimo-
nious debate the government agrees
to launch an unrestricted submarine
warfare campaign. This allows the 111

FEBRUARY 22–23

MIDDLE EAST, *MESOPOTAMIA*
General Sir Frederick Maude, the commander of the British forces pushing northward toward Baghdad, launches a major attack on the Turks at Kut-el-Amara. He conducts a feint drive against the Turkish right to cover his forces crossing the Tigris River, and then unleashes powerful attacks on both Turkish flanks. The Turkish commander, Kara Bekr Bey, orders his forces to retreat toward Baghdad following his defeat at what becomes known as the Second Battle of Kut. Kut-el-Amara is abandoned to the British on the 25th.

FEBRUARY 23

WESTERN FRONT, *FRANCE*
German forces begin their withdrawal to the newly-built defenses-in-depth of the Hindenburg Line, some 20 miles (32 km) behind the existing front and stretching from Arras to Soissons.

Between the old front line and their new positions the Germans destroy towns, villages, and lines of communications, cut down forests, and poison water supplies. The movement is secret and completed by April 5.

German U-boats currently available to sink any vessels at will. It is believed that such a campaign will starve Britain into surrender within as little as five months.

The German high command recognizes that the decision will have profound consequences on Germany's diplomatic relations with the United States, which is likely to declare war if its neutral vessels are sunk. However, it is thought that the United States will be unable to make any significant impact on the war in Europe for at least two years by which time the German planners believe that the Central Powers will have won the war.

A note concerning the submarine campaign is passed to the US Secretary of State Robert Lansing; it announces that all ships will be "stopped with every available weapon and without further notice."

FEBRUARY 3

POLITICS, *UNITED STATES*
The administration cuts its diplomatic ties with Germany following the latter's announcement that its navy will conduct unrestricted submarine warfare. President Woodrow Wilson announces: "This government has no alternative consistent with the dignity and honor of the United States." Other nations follow suit, including many in Latin American, and China. On the same day as Wilson's speech an American merchant ship, *Housatonic*, is sunk without warning.

▼ A section of the German Hindenburg Line with huge barbed-wire defenses.

◄ Students and army deserters fire on police during the "February Revolution" in Petrograd, the Russian capital.

MIDDLE EAST, *MESOPOTAMIA*
British forces under General Sir Frederick Maude, having brushed aside the Turkish Sixth Army under Halil Pasha and after three days of skirmishing along the Diyala River, enter Baghdad. Keen to prevent the Turks from regrouping, Maude sends some of his troops to scout along various rivers. However, the onset of intense summer heat will eventually bring a halt to operations until September.

MARCH 12

POLITICS, *RUSSIA*
Workers, left-wing politicians, agitators, and strike leaders meeting in the Russian capital form the Petrograd Soviet (Council of Workers' Deputies). One of its first acts is to issue "Order No. 1," which deprives Russian officers of their authority. Two days later the Duma (parliament) itself establishes a provisional government headed by Prince Lvov, although real power is wielded by Minister of War Alexander Kerensky. Neither body accepts the authority of the other, initially weakening the forces opposed to Czar

▼ British troops march into Baghdad, Mesopotamia, on March 11 following its capture from the Turks.

FEBRUARY 24

POLITICS, *BRITAIN*
The US ambassador to Britain, Walter Hines Page, is given a copy of the message written by German Foreign Secretary Arthur Zimmermann suggesting that Mexico should enter an alliance with Germany if the United States declares war on Germany. The ambassador passes the transcript of the so-called "Zimmermann Telegram" to the US State Department. Its contents cause an uproar when they are printed in newspapers on March 1.

MARCH 1

POLITICS, *AUSTRIA-HUNGARY*
Emperor Karl replaces General Franz Conrad von Hötzendorf as chief of the General Staff with General Arthur Arz von Straussenburg.

MARCH 8

POLITICS, *RUSSIA*
Riots, strikes, and mass demonstrations break out in Moscow. People are demonstrating against shortages of food and fuel, and the autocratic style of the government. The police use lethal force against the demonstrations, but the unrest continues over the following days. By the 10th an estimated 25,000 workers are on strike. Army units called in to deal with the growing unrest refuse to fire on the demonstrators. (The events become known as the "February Revolution" as the Russian calendar of the time was 11 days behind the Western one.)

MARCH 11

POLITICS, *RUSSIA*
Czar Nicholas II refuses to accede to calls for urgent political reforms from the president of the Duma (Russian parliament) and reacts by ordering the Duma to disband. However, it continues to sit in the increasingly lawless capital, Petrograd, whose garrison has rebeled the previous day. (The capital had been known as St. Petersburg until 1914, when it was give the less German-sounding name of Petrograd.)

KEY PERSONALITIES

VLADIMIR ILICH LENIN

Born in Simbirsk in 1870 with the name Vladimir Ilich Ulyanov, Lenin was the leader of the revolutionary Bolshevik Party, which played a dominant part in Russian politics in 1917 and won the subsequent Russian Civil War (1918-21).

Lenin studied law at university and developed his belief in revolutionary Marxism while in St. Petersburg during the 1890s. He was arrested in 1895 and sent into a three-year internal exile in Siberia. After his release he traveled to Western Europe, where he emerged as leader of the Bolshevik majority grouping within the Russian Social Democratic Workers' Party in 1903. Returning to Russia, he took part in the unsuccessful revolution of 1905 and then returned to Western Europe, basing himself in Switzerland from 1907.

In March 1917 he returned to Russia, which was in turmoil after the "February Revolution." The Bolsheviks emerged as the leading political force in Russia following the "November Revolution" the same year. Lenin led the Bolsheviks during the Russian Civil War, although Minister of War Leon Trotsky effectively commanded the ultimately victorious Red Army.

After the Civil War Lenin was primarily concerned with extending the Bolsheviks' control of Russia and developing the country's economy. However, he suffered from poor health and had a debilitating stroke in 1922. He died in 1924. Following a period of instability and infighting within the Russian leadership, Lenin's successor – Joseph Stalin – assumed power in 1927.

▲ *Russia's Czar Nicholas II abdicated as his war-weakened country descended into chaos in March.*

Nicholas II and his advisers. The chaos, which the army is both unwilling and unable to curtail, spreads throughout Russia. Pressure mounts on the czar to abdicate. One revolutionary in exile, Vladimir Lenin, the head of the radical Bolsheviks, misses the coup but is swiftly speeded back to Russia in a sealed train provided by the Germans.

POLITICS, *UNITED STATES*
The US authorities announce President Woodrow Wilson's decision to arm all US merchant ships sailing in areas where German submarines are known to be active. His order is a counter to Germany launching an unrestricted submarine warfare campaign at the end of January.

MARCH 15

POLITICS, *RUSSIA*
Czar Nicholas II abdicates. Proposals to replace him with his son Aleksey are rejected by the czar, who favors his own brother, Grand Duke Mikhail.

MARCH 17

SEA WAR, *ENGLISH CHANNEL*
German destroyers launch one of their periodic sorties against enemy shipping plying the narrow seas between Britain and France. They are able to sink a pair of British destroyers and a single merchant ship in quick succession with no loss to themselves.

MARCH 18

SEA WAR, *ATLANTIC*
Three American vessels, the *City of Memphis*, *Vigilancia*, and *Illinois*, are sunk by German submarines; the incidents further anger the United States.

▼ *The US merchant ship Illinois, sunk on March 18, was a victim of Germany's unrestricted submarine campaign.*

MARCH 26

MIDDLE EAST, *PALESTINE*
British General Sir Archibald Murray begins his invasion of the Turkish province by attempting to break through the Gaza–Beersheba line with some 16,000 troops. The attack, led by units under the command of General Sir Charles Dobell, fails due to poor British planning, a lack of

▲ *A Turkish artillery battery fires on the British in Palestine, while a wounded man is carried away on a stretcher.*

communication between the infantry and cavalry units involved, acute water shortages, and Turkish resistance.

The Turks, who have a similar number of troops committed to what becomes known as the First Battle of Gaza, suffer some 2500 casualties in the fighting, while the British record losses of nearly 4000 men. Murray is, however, authorized to launch a second effort against the Turks.

APRIL 2

POLITICS, *UNITED STATES*
President Woodrow Wilson addresses Congress concerning the country's deteriorating relationship with Germany. Wilson states: "I advise that the Congress declares the recent course of the Imperial German government [the unrestricted submarine campaign and the Zimmermann correspondence] to be in fact nothing less than war against the government and

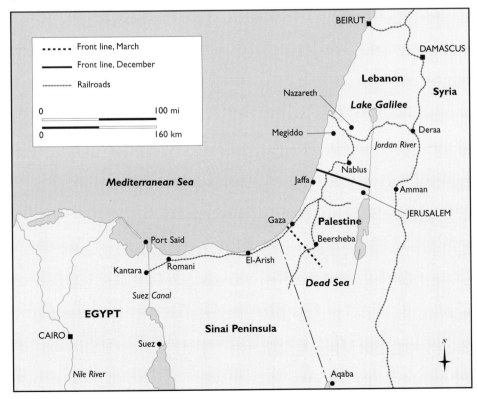

◄ *The 1917 campaign in Palestine. After a poor start the British were able to take Jerusalem from the Turks by December.*

Front line, March

Front line, December

Railroads

0   100 mi

0   160 km

BEIRUT

DAMASCUS

Lebanon

Nazareth

Lake Galilee

Syria

Megiddo

Deraa

Jordan River

Nablus

Jaffa

Amman

Mediterranean Sea

JERUSALEM

Gaza

Palestine

Beersheba

Port Said

Dead Sea

Kantara   Romani   El-Arish

Suez Canal

EGYPT

Sinai Peninsula

CAIRO

Suez

Aqaba

Nile River

▲ *President Woodrow Wilson addresses Congress on April 2, asking those present to support war against Germany.*

people of the United States ...[and] to exert all its power and employ all its resources to bring the government of the German Empire to terms and to end the war." Congress is asked to back what is a declaration of war.

APRIL 3

POLITICS, *RUSSIA*
Russian revolutionary Vladimir Ilich Lenin returns to Petrograd from exile. He intends to overthrow the Provisional Government and create a state headed by the Bolsheviks, but must first take control of various soviets (workers' councils). This is achieved by October.

▲ *German prisoners are marched to the rear as British troops move forward during the fighting at Arras.*

◄ *The crew of a British 12-in (30-cm) howitzer prepares to open fire at the beginning of the Battle of Arras.*

APRIL 6

POLITICS, *UNITED STATES*
President Woodrow Wilson's administration declares war on Germany. However, the US Army will have to be expanded before it can contribute to the war. The navy is more prepared. The United States does not become a full ally of the British, French, and Russians, preferring to be an "Associate Power." Wilson sees the war as a moral crusade and does not want to be associated with the motives of the other states arrayed against Germany.

APRIL 9

WESTERN FRONT, *FRANCE*
The British open the Battle of Arras, intending to force the Germans to withdraw troops from the Aisne River sector of the Western Front, which is about to be attacked by the French under General Robert Nivelle.

Three British armies are committed to the enterprise. In the center, around Arras, lies General Sir Edmund

Allenby's Third Army. It will lead the offensive. To the north, poised to strike at Vimy Ridge, is the First Army under General Sir Henry Horne containing the Canadian Corps led by General Sir Julian Byng. South of Allenby, General Sir Hugh Gough's Fifth Army is to strike at the Hindenburg Line around Bullecourt. Facing the onslaught are the troops of General Ludwig von Falkenhausen's German Sixth Army.

The British herald their attack with a five-day bombardment. They achieve considerable gains on the first day, particularly the Third Army's Canadian Corps, whose spirited assault captures Vimy Ridge, and its XVII Corps, which advances some four miles (6 km). However, Gough makes little progress.

The pilots of the British Royal Flying Corps suffer heavy losses due to the inferiority of their aircraft in comparison with the German Albatross D.III and the German tactic of diving on them from altitude. Some 33 percent of British pilots become casualties during April.

APRIL 11

WESTERN FRONT, FRANCE
The British continue the Battle of Arras in the face of growing resistance from the reinforced German Sixth Army under General Ludwig von Falkenhausen. The British 37th Division captures the village of Monchy le Preux and elements of General Sir Hugh Gough's Fifth Army break into the Hindenburg Line at Bullecourt the next day. However, the battle is becoming a stalemate.

The British commander-in-chief, Field Marshal Sir Douglas Haig, opts to continue the Arras offensive into the middle of May, and the fighting centers on Bullecourt. Haig's decision is made in part to draw the German Army's

▼ *Canadian troops commanded by General Sir Julian Byng consolidate their recently-won gains on Vimy Ridge.*

▼ *British troops investigate a German observation post disguised as a shell-blasted tree stump.*

▲ *The opening of the Nivelle Offensive – French troops advance against the German-held Chemin des Dames ridges.*

▲ *Paul René Fonck, France's top fighter pilot, practises his marksmanship skills at his home airfield.*

attention away from the sectors of the Western Front held by the French, whose armies are in disarray following widespread mutinies. At the close of the offensive British casualties total some 150,000 men killed, wounded, or captured. German losses are 100,000.

APRIL 15

AIR WAR, *WESTERN FRONT*
Paul René Fonck joins one of France's top fighter units, Groupe de Chasse No. 12, better known as *Les Cigognes* ("The Storks"). He is destined to become the country's top ace, scoring

75 victories by the end of the war, although his unofficial score is 127. On two occasions in 1918 – May 9 and September 26 – Fonck, an extra-ordinarily lethal marksman, shoots down six enemy planes in a day.

APRIL 16–20

WESTERN FRONT, *FRANCE*
General Robert Nivelle opens a major offensive, which he has promised will smash the German defenders on the Western Front at little cost. However, Nivelle's superiors are not convinced of his plan and only agree to it after

▼ *A German six-inch (15-cm) howitzer is prepared to fire on the French at the beginning of their Nivelle Offensive.*

he has threatened to resign. The attack involves offensives in Champagne and along the Aisne River.

Committed to the enterprise are the French Fifth Army under General Olivier Mazel and General Charles Mangin's Sixth Army. They are supported by General Marie-Emile Fayolle's First Army and the Tenth Army commanded by General Denis Duchêne. Nivelle has 102,000 men and 7000 artillery pieces. Opposing them are two German armies: the First under General Fritz von Below and General Max von Boehn's Seventh.

The French advance takes place along a front of some 40 miles (64 km) between Soissons and Reims, with the bulk of the troops committed to capturing the Chemin des Dames, a series of thickly-wooded ridges running parallel to the front line. Nivelle intends to use a creeping

artillery barrage to cover the main attacks. However, the Germans are fully aware of the onslaught, which becomes known as the Nivelle Offensive, as there has been little secrecy and the Germans have captured plans for the attack. Shortly before it begins, German aircraft destroy many French balloons used for artillery observation and strafe columns of French troops and tanks.

The German Seventh Army blocks the French advance into the Chemin des Dames, as does von Below's First Army to the east. French troops are met by heavy artillery fire and well-defended machine-gun positions. Their losses are heavy, some 118,000 men by the 20th.

By the 20th it is also clear that Nivelle is not going to achieve a decisive breakthrough. Despite capturing some 20,000 Germans, French territorial gains are limited, although a section of the Hindenburg Line on the Chemin des Dames falls by the end of the month. The fighting, which becomes increasingly bogged down, continues into May.

APRIL 17

WESTERN FRONT, *FRANCE*
A day after the opening of General Robert Nivelle's offensive, which has made little progress and produced severe casualties, the troops of the French 108th Regiment mutiny and abandon their trenches in the face of the enemy.

The mutiny spreads until some 68 of the French Army's 112 divisions are involved. Officers report a total of 250 cases of troops refusing to obey orders; some 35,000 men are

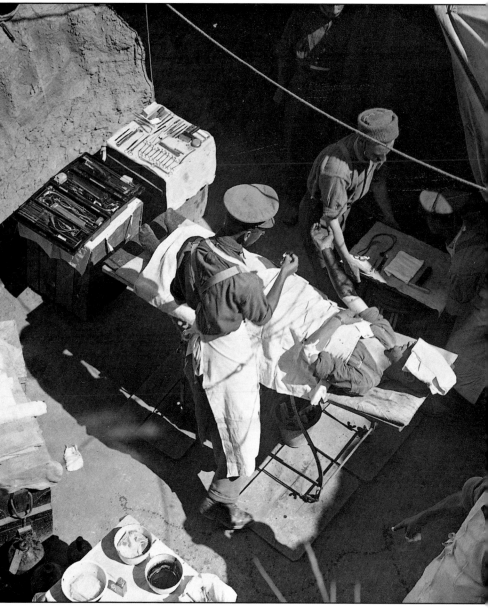

▲ *A wounded British soldiers receives medical treatment in Palestine. A bullet has been removed from his arm.*

implicated in the mutiny. Many mutineers are willing to defend their positions, but refuse outright to advance against the enemy.

APRIL 17-19

MIDDLE EAST, *PALESTINE*
British General Sir Archibald Murray again attempts to invade the Turkish province by breaking through the enemy positions stretching between Gaza and Beersheba. As in the First Battle of Gaza fought in the previous March, the main effort is made by troops commanded by General Sir Charles Dobell. Dobell's frontal attack against well-entrenched Turkish forces

ends in high losses and no gains. British casualties reach a total of 6500 men, more than three times the recorded Turkish figure.

This action, the Second Battle of Gaza, has profound consequences on the British command structure in the region. First to pay the price of failure is Dobell, who is sacked by Murray. However, Murray's future is also in doubt as his recent failures at Gaza have angered the British government whose prime minister, David Lloyd George, has personally backed the attacks in Palestine.

APRIL 20-21

SEA WAR, *ENGLISH CHANNEL*
An attack by German destroyers on coastal shipping is foiled by two British destroyers, *Broke* and

Swiftsure, which sink two enemy destroyers. Their success halts German naval raids in the Channel until 1918.

APRIL 23

MIDDLE EAST, *MESOPOTAMIA*
Troops under British General Sir Frederick Maude, who captured Baghdad on March 11, continue their advance against the Turks by taking Samarra on the Tigris River. A Turkish counterattack is beaten off, but Maude is forced to end operations until September due to the intense heat.

AIR WAR, *ENGLISH CHANNEL*
Three British long-range Handley Page 0/100 bombers attack a flotilla of German torpedo-boats off Ostend, Belgium. Several boats are hit and damaged. However, subsequent losses in daylight operations force the bombers to abandon their daylight maritime patrol activities and concentrate on the strategic bombing of German targets under cover of darkness. One of their key roles will be to attack the airfields from which Germany's Gotha bombers operate.

MAY 5

TECHNOLOGY, *FRANCE*
The bulky and unmaneuverable Saint Chamond tank makes its first appearance in battle. It has a crew of nine, who operate four machine guns and a three-inch (75-mm) main gun.

MAY 7

AIR WAR, *WESTERN FRONT*
Captain Albert Ball, one of Britain's leading aces with more than 40 air victories to his credit, is shot down and killed.

▲ *A French Saint Chamond tank in action. It was plagued by several design weaknesses, but 400 were built.*

▼ *An aerial view of the French Nivelle Offensive. It was France's only major attack on the Western Front in 1917.*

MAY 7–8

SEA WAR, *ENGLISH CHANNEL*
British warships bombard Zeebrugge, Belgium, which is a major base for German destroyers and submarines. The attack does little damage, but other such operations follow.

MAY 9

WESTERN FRONT, *FRANCE*
General Robert Nivelle's attack along the Chemin des Dames is brought to a close. It has failed spectacularly. The French have been unable to break through the German defenses and have suffered enormous losses, some 187,000 men as opposed to around 163,000 German casualties. Ordinary French soldiers, who see little point in suffering such rates of attrition for no concrete advantage, are suffering from low morale, and some front-line units have mutinied.

MAY 9–23

BALKANS, *GREECE*
Serbian and French troops, some of

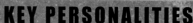

the 600,000 in the theater, launch an attack in Macedonia. Their aim is to break through the enemy and swing west across the Vardar River, while British troops attack around Lake Doiran. The offensive makes little progress and casualties total 14,000 men by the 23rd. There is growing disquiet over the competence of the commander, France's Maurice Sarrail.

▲ *A convoy of merchant ships and warships crosses the Atlantic. Losses to German submarines declined steadily once this system was introduced in May. Equally, German submarine losses began to soar as the escorts became effective.*

MAY 10

POLITICS, *BRITAIN*
Prime Minister David Lloyd George forces the British navy to institute the convoy system to protect merchant ships from enemy submarines. Recent losses to enemy submarines, which are rising alarmingly, are threatening to isolate Britain.

Henceforth, vessels will sail across the North Atlantic in large groups rather than singly and be protected by numerous warships. The system has an immediate impact – German submarine losses rise, while the rate of merchant ship sinkings declines equally dramatically.

MAY 12

POLITICS, *UNITED STATES*
General John Pershing is appointed the commander of the American Expeditionary Force, which is being formed to fight on the Western Front. It will take time to increase the strength of the US Army, but Pershing expects the number of American troops in France to reach one million by May 1918 and is planning for a force of three million if the war continues. Pershing also intends to make sure that his units will fight as a separate force and not be split into small units and placed under French or British command.

WESTERN FRONT, *ITALY*
The chief of the Italian General Staff, General Luigi Cadorna, finally initiates the delayed Tenth Battle of the Isonzo

KEY PERSONALITIES

GENERAL OF THE ARMIES JOHN PERSHING

Pershing (1860–1948) was commissioned as a junior officer in 1886 after graduating from West Point, and his early military experience was gained in several campaigns against Native Americans. After various peacetime appointments he saw overseas service in the Spanish–American War (1898–99), as a military observer in the Russo-Japanese War (1904–05), and in the Philippines. Between March 1916 and January 1917 Pershing led an unsuccessful punitive expedition into Mexico in pursuit of revolutionary Pancho Villa, whose forces had crossed the border and killed US citizens in Columbus, New Mexico.

When the United States entered World War I, Pershing was made commander of the American Expeditionary Force (AEF), which was earmarked for France, on May 12. He arrived in Europe on June 23 (below, center) and oversaw the massive build-up of US force in France, which began in earnest that summer and continued well into 1918. By May the AEF numbered more than 425,000 men. By the end of the war two million US troops had served overseas.

Pershing was successful in maintaining the AEF as an independent force with its own commanding officers and one able to carry out independent large-scale offensive operations. Pershing also oversaw the AEF's three main attacks on the Western Front in 1918: the Aisne–Marne (July–August), St. Mihiel (September), and Meuse–Argonne (September–November). He was made a six-star general and given the unique rank of general of the armies in 1919.

DECISIVE WEAPONS

THE GOTHA BOMBER

The German-built Gotha bomber, which began operating in early 1917, marked a new era in air warfare – for the first time heavier-than-air vessels could strike against an enemy at long range. This two-engined aircraft with a three-man crew was capable of speed of 80 mph (128 k/h), had a ceiling of 15,000 feet (4600 m), and could carry around 660 lb (300 kg) of bombs. Its defensive armament comprised two or three machine guns. Development work on the aircraft began in 1914 and the prototype took to the air in January 1915.

In April 1917 Gothas began attacking England from their bases in occupied Belgium. The Gothas' chief target became London in an operation known as *Türkenkreuz* ("Turkish Cross"). Their first attacks, which culminated in 14 Gothas bombing central London and killing 104 people with one direct hit on June 13, took place in daylight. Despite numerous British fighters being scrambled to meet the intruders, none was shot down. The lack of response caused public uproar.

However, the British strengthened their anti-aircraft defenses around the capital and the Gothas had to attack under cover of darkness. Between September 1917 and May 1918 the bombers flew 19 night missions against London. They killed some 830 people and wounded more than 1900. Sixty Gothas were lost during these attacks, although few fell to the British defenses. Most suffered from mechanical failures or crashes. The British conquered the Gotha threat by launching their own bomber offensive directed against the Gotha bases in Belgium.

Bombs in position under the fuselage and wing of a Gotha GV bomber prior to a mission against London.

in northeast Italy. The offensive had originally been timed to coincide with two attacks on the Western Front by the French and British in mid-April, but muddled planning and lack of organization have combined to delay the Italian effort.

The Tenth Battle of the Isonzo lasts for 17 days and the Italians fail to make any significant gains in the face of mountainous terrain and stubborn Austro-Hungarian resistance. The Italians record around 160,000 men killed, wounded, or taken prisoner by the close of their offensive, while the Austro-Hungarians report 75,000 casualties. Despite the lack of success on the Isonzo Front, Cadorna resolves to continue his efforts to break through to the Austro-Hungarian port of Trieste.

MAY 15

POLITICS, *FRANCE*

General Robert Nivelle, whose recent offensive on the Western Front has failed with massive casualties and provoked a widespread mutiny in the French Army, is sacked as commander-in-chief. He is replaced by General Henri-Philippe Pétain, the hero of Verdun. Pétain moves quickly to quell the mutiny.

Over the following months he tours the front listening to the grievances of the ordinary soldiers, agrees to improve their conditions, and arrests some of the ringleaders. The record of

disobedience peaks in July but is virtually over by the following month, although isolated incidents continue into early 1918. Some 50 men are tried and executed. Thanks to an efficient system of press censorship the Germans do not hear of the mutiny until it is virtually over and are unable to take advantage of the situation.

SEA WAR, *ADRIATIC*

Austro-Hungarian warships commanded by Captain Miklós Horthy, later the dictator of Hungary, attack several Italian vessels sailing off the Albanian coast. Fourteen are sunk before British, French, and Italian warships intervene, forcing Horthy to withdraw.

MAY 18

POLITICS, *UNITED STATES*

Congress passes the Selective Service Act, which allows for the registration and selective draft of men aged between 21 and 30.

MAY 23

AIR WAR, *BRITAIN*

Marking a new chapter in strategic bombing, 16 long-range German Gotha bombers attack London from their bases in Belgium. Darkness foils the attack on the capital, but the

▼ *A blindfolded volunteer draws out the assigned numbers of some of those Americans to fight on the Western Front.*

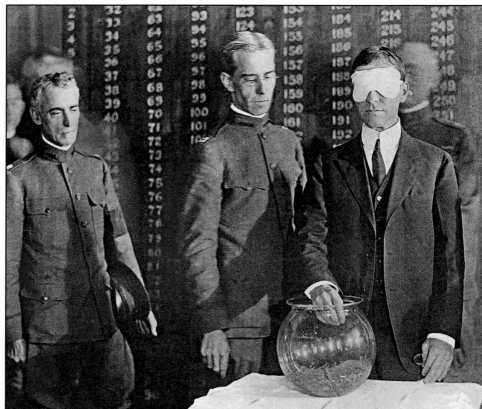

twin-engined aircraft drop their bombs to the east, killing some 100 Canadian troops at a military base.

JUNE 2

AIR WAR, *WESTERN FRONT*
Canadian fighter ace Billy Bishop carries out a singlehanded attack on a German airfield for which he will be awarded the Victoria Cross, Britain's highest award for valor. By the end of the conflict Bishop will be credited with 72 air victories.

▼ *A panorama of the German-held trenches captured by the British during the attack on Messines Ridge, Belgium.*

JUNE 4

POLITICS, *RUSSIA*
General Aleksey Brusilov is appointed commander-in-chief by the Provisional Government to replace General Mikhail Alekseev. However, it is clear that the Russian Army is disintegrating.

JUNE 7

WESTERN FRONT, *BELGIUM*
Field Marshal Sir Douglas Haig's British Expeditionary Force launches an attack against the German troops holding the high ground of Messines Ridge in southwest Belgium. Haig is planning to stage a major offensive

▲ *Canadian ace Billy Bishop pictured in front of his French-built Nieuport 17 fighter.*

between the North Sea and the Lys River in the hope of breaking through the German lines around Ypres to the north, but before he can contemplate such an attack the dominating ridge at Messines has to be captured.

The German defenses have been under constant artillery barrage from 2000 artillery pieces for 17 days, and shortly before the British infantry advance, a series of huge underground mines are exploded under the battered enemy positions.

JUNE 12

The troops committed to the painstakingly-planned British attack are drawn from General Sir Herbert Plumer's Second Army and in a day's fighting they capture the ridge at a cost of 17,000 casualties. The German defenders suffer 25,000 casualties, of whom some 7500 are taken prisoner. The capture of the ridge paves the way for Haig's grand offensive, which is known as the Third Battle of Ypres, or Passchendaele. It begins in late July.

JUNE 12

POLITICS, *GREECE*

King Constantine I, whose has pro-German sympathies (he is the brother-in-law of Germany's Kaiser Wilhelm II), is forced to abdicate. The new king is Constantine's second son, Alexander, who is more sympathetic to Britain and France. He appoints Eleuthérios Venizélos as his prime minister. They allow allied forces to move into Thessaly in northern Greece.

JUNE 13

AIR WAR, *BRITAIN*

Fourteen German long-range Gotha bombers return to attack London in daylight, striking the center of the capital, killing 104 people, and wounding more than 400 without loss. Public outrage forces the government to improve its anti-aircraft defenses around the capital. This strengthening forces the Gothas to mount their attacks under cover of darkness.

JUNE 24

WESTERN FRONT, *FRANCE*

US General John Pershing lands with the first contingents of the American Expeditionary Force. Other units will follow; some 180,000 men by the end of the year.

JUNE 27

POLITICS, *GREECE*

The government enters the war against the Central Powers.

JUNE 29

POLITICS, *BRITAIN*

The government replaces the commander of its forces in Egypt, General Sir Archibald Murray, with General Sir Edmund Allenby. Murray's failure to cut through the Turkish forces holding the Gaza–Beersheba

◄ *Civilians and military rescue workers survey the aftermath of a German bomber raid on central London.*

line on two previous occasions has brought about his downfall. His replacement, a cavalry officer with a reputation for clear-headed leadership and military flair, is ordered by the government to break through the enemy defenses and take "Jerusalem by Christmas."

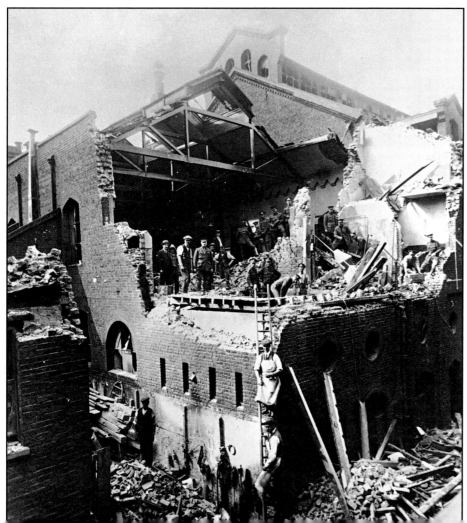

▲ US troops parade through central London, tangible evidence of the United States' commitment to the war.

JULY 1

EASTERN FRONT, RUSSIA
Despite growing political turmoil, the Russian commander-in-chief, General Aleksey Brusilov, launches a major offensive toward Lemberg at the behest of Minister of War Alexander Kerensky, who gives his name to the

▲ British General Sir Edmund Allenby was ordered to seize Jerusalem from the Turks by Christmas 1917.

attack. This, the Kerensky Offensive, begins well for the Russians. Their Eleventh and Seventh Armies make progress against German General Felix von Bothmer's Southern Army, and the Austro-Hungarian Second Army is also under intense pressure. In the south the Russian Eighth Army under General Lavr Kornilov attacks on the 7th and presses forward toward the oil fields at Drohobycz against the Austro-Hungarian Third Army.

However, there are growing signs that ordinary Russian soldiers are no longer willing to obey their officers. Many units have established their own

JULY 1 1917

▲ The course of the war on the Eastern Front in 1917–18.

▼ A German howitzer bombards the retreating Russians during their disastrous Kerensky Offensive.

135

soviets (workers' councils) and these are usurping the authority of the officers. The Kerensky Offensive begins to collapse as the Germans lay plans for a counteroffensive.

JULY 11

WESTERN FRONT, *BELGIUM*
The British begin a major air campaign over Ypres. Their intention is to sweep the Germans from the skies prior to the opening of a major offensive at the end of the month.

JULY 18

WESTERN FRONT, *BELGIUM*
The British begin the preliminary bombardment for their forthcoming attack in the Ypres salient. Some 1400 artillery pieces unleash high-explosive

▲ *Mata Hari, the convicted Dutch-born German spy, awaits execution at the hands of a French firing squad.*

and gas shells on the German trenches outside the city. The barrage will continue until the last day of the month, when the Third Battle of Ypres, also known as Passchendaele, begins with nine divisions leading the ground offensive.

However, the British barrage badly craters the low-lying ground, which has a high water table, and destroys the natural and manmade drainage systems.

▼ *German pilots prepare for a sortie over British-held Ypres in Belgium. The aircraft are Fokker DR.1 triplanes.*

JULY 19

POLITICS, *GERMANY*
Members of the Reichstag (parliament) pass a peace resolution, which effectively backs the plans for an end to the war proposed by US President Woodrow Wilson.

EASTERN FRONT, *RUSSIA*
German forces under the overall command of General Max Hoffmann launch their counteroffensive against the Russian forces involved in the recent Kerensky Offensive, which began on July 1. The Russian armies are riven by political unrest and begin to disintegrate. Many units simply refuse to advance or attack, and rates of desertion soar. The Germans quickly regain much of the territory lost during the initial Russian attacks, and rebuff a limited counterattack by the Russian Fourth Army and contingents of Romanians on the 22nd.

JULY 20

POLITICS, *BALKANS*
In a move that paves the way for the formation of what will become the state of Yugoslavia, the Serbian government-in-exile agrees the Pact of Corfu. It calls for Croats, Montenegrins, Serbs, and Slovenes to be united in a single state, which is to be headed by the Serbian royal family.

POLITICS, *RUSSIA*
Former Minister of War Alexander Kerensky is made head of the Provisional Government, although its status is not recognized by various left-wing revolutionary groups.

JULY 24

ESPIONAGE, *FRANCE*
Dutch-national Margaretha Zelle, who is better known by her stage name Mata Hari, stands trial on charges of spying for the Germans. She was arrested by French security personnel in Paris on February 13. Although the evidence is ambiguous, she is convicted and later executed.

JULY 26

AIR WAR, *WESTERN FRONT*
Faced with increasing numbers of more advanced enemy fighters, the Germans reorganize their own fighter forces by amalgamating various squadrons to form

▶ *British troops attempt to free a light field piece from the mud at Ypres.*

◄ *British troops examine a captured German heavy machine gun at Ypres. They are wearing body armor.*

to the northeast of Ypres toward Pilckem Ridge. Support is offered by the French First Army under General François Anthoine to the north and General Sir Herbert Plumer's Second Army to the south. The initial attacks are moderately successful, but strong German counterattacks limit British gains to around two miles (3 km).

AUGUST 2

POLITICS, *RUSSIA*
General Lavr Kornilov replaces General Aleksey Brusilov as the Russian commander-in-chief. Kornilov's chief problem is to restore discipline in the rapidly disintegrating Russian Army. However, he has little faith in the Provisional Government headed by Alexander Kerensky.

WESTERN FRONT, *BELGIUM*
The British offensive around Ypres, which began on July 31, is temporarily suspended due to unseasonal heavy rain. The heavily-cratered battlefield is turning into a sea of thick mud. It is hoped that the postponement will give time for the ground to dry out.

AUGUST 16–18

WESTERN FRONT, *BELGIUM*
The British offensive at Ypres, halted temporarily on the 2nd to allow the waterlogged ground to dry,

units consisting of 50 or so aircraft. One of the most famous, its aircraft painted in vivid colors, is nicknamed "Richthofen's Circus" after its commander, the charismatic ace Baron Manfred von Richthofen.

JULY 31

WESTERN FRONT, *BELGIUM*
Field Marshal Sir Douglas Haig launches what becomes known as the Third Battle of Ypres, or Passchendaele. His aims are ambitious: to smash through

General Sixt von Arnim's German Fourth Army, push several miles along the coast, and then swing northward to capture the ports of Ostend and Zeebrugge, from where German submarines and destroyers are operating. Once the ports have fallen, Haig intends to recommence his drive to evict the Germans from Belgium.

The main force committed to the operation consists of General Sir Hubert Gough's British Fifth Army, which is to attack

AUGUST 17

▲ *The battlefield of Third Ypres pictured with abandoned British tanks.*

recommences. The focus of the fighting is around the village of Langemarck, which is attacked by General Sir Hubert Gough's Fifth Army. Progress is slow due to the difficult conditions and the stubborn German defense. British progress is limited to a few hundred yards.

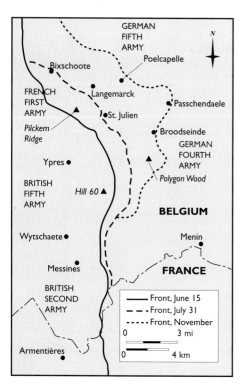

GERMAN
FIFTH
ARMY

Bixschoote
Poelcapelle

FRENCH
FIRST
ARMY
Langemarck
Passchendaele

St. Julien

Pilckem
Ridge
Broodseinde

GERMAN
FOURTH
ARMY

Ypres
Polygon Wood

BRITISH
FIFTH
ARMY
Hill 60

BELGIUM

Wytschaete
Menin

Messines
FRANCE

BRITISH
SECOND
ARMY

Front, June 15
Front, July 31
Front, November

0   3 mi

Armentières
0   4 km

AUGUST 17
POLITICS, *BRITAIN*
General Jan Christiaan Smuts makes a report to the government concerning means of improving the country's defenses against German air attack. Chief among his proposals is the creation of a single air force that is independent of either the British Army or navy. This will involve amalgamating the Royal Flying Corps and the Royal Naval Air Service. His report is accepted immediately. Air Marshal Sir Hugh Trenchard, a keen advocate of an independent air force and commander of the Royal Flying Corps, will be appointed its first commander.

AUGUST 18–SEPTEMBER 15
WESTERN FRONT, *ITALY*
The Italian commander-in-chief, General Luigi Cadorna, orders his forces to launch what becomes the Eleventh Battle of the Isonzo against the Austro-Hungarians. Two Italian armies are committed to the enterprise. The Second Army under General Luigi Capello, attacks to the north of the town of Gorizia, while the Duke of Aosta's Third Army attacks to the south

▶ *French fighter ace Georges Guynemer (second from right) pictured in front of his Morane-Saulnier Type L fighter.*

◀ *The Third Battle of Ypres was the major British offensive of 1917.*

between Gorizia and Trieste. The Italian forces total some 52 divisions backed by 5000 artillery pieces.

General Svetozan Borojevic von Bojna's Austro-Hungarian Fifth Army swiftly halts the Duke of Aosta's advance, but the Italians make greater progress to the north. Here, the Italian Second Army takes the Bainsizza Plateau. Italian casualties are again very severe – around 166,000 men killed, wounded, or taken prisoner; the Austro-Hungarians admit to losses of 85,000. However, the Austro-Hungarian commanders believe that their troops are on the point of collapse and that they do not have the military resources to save the situation. They call on the German high command to send forces to stabilize the front.

SEPTEMBER 1
EASTERN FRONT, *RUSSIA*
Capitalizing on the growing unrest in Russia, the Germans launch an offensive directed against the port of Riga. Committed to this enterprise is the Eighth Army commanded by General Oskar von Hutier, who is opposed by the Russian Twelfth Army. Hutier uses new tactics – a brief preliminary bombardment followed by attacks by specialist stormtrooper assault infantry units, which push forward rapidly supported by mobile artillery and bypass enemy strongpoints.

Hutier's assault across the Dvina River is highly successful; the Russian Twelfth Army melts away. The Germans, whose casualties are

▲ *German troops rest in front of a church in the city of Riga, which they captured from the Russians in early September.*

minimal, take 9000 Russian prisoners. Many other Russian soldiers have simply deserted their posts.

SEPTEMBER 9–14

POLITICS, *RUSSIA*

General Lavr Kornilov launches a rebellion against the Bolsheviks, who dominate the Provisional Government in Petrograd, and are led by Vladimir Lenin and Leon Trotsky. However, Kornilov's attempted coup fails as his wavering forces are defeated by armed workers organized by the Bolsheviks.

SEPTEMBER 11

AIR WAR, *WESTERN FRONT*

Georges Guynemer is killed while operating over the Belgian city of Ypres. Guynemer, the top-scoring French ace of the war, gained his first victory in June 1915 and flew with the Third Squadron of the elite *Les Cigognes* ("The Storks") group.

SEPTEMBER 20

WESTERN FRONT, *BELGIUM*

The focus of the British offensive around Ypres switches to the south of

▼ *General Oskar von Hutier, one of the pioneers of Germany's successful stormtrooper tactics.*

STRATEGY & TACTICS

GERMAN STORMTROOPERS

By 1917 it was clear to some senior commanders on all sides that the established offensive doctrine of long preliminary bombardments followed by measured infantry attacks to capture all of an enemy's positions on a set step-by-step timetable was not working. Long artillery barrages warned the enemy, rarely destroyed his defenses or ability to fight back, and never produced massive casualties. Some tacticians began to consider new ways of fighting a battle based on surprise and rapid movement. Chief among these were two German officers on the Eastern Front, General Oskar von Hutier and Colonel George Bruchmüller.

They concluded that a sudden, unexpected artillery bombardment against key enemy positions using both gas and high-explosive shells would be more effective than a long barrage, particularly if the artillery pieces involved were brought into position shortly before the attack to avoid them being spotted.

They also argued that enemy positions surviving this initial rain of shells should be avoided to prevent the offensive from breaking down; far better that specially-trained assault units, their ranks filled with men known as stormtroopers, should infiltrate as quickly as possible into the enemy's rear areas, sowing confusion and disrupting communications as they went, rather than fighting against surviving strongpoints. Ideally, artillery, which in the past had failed to keep up with sudden breakthroughs, had to maintain pace with the infantry assault. Aircraft would support the advancing stormtroopers, shooting up enemy targets and pockets of resistance.

These ideas were not entirely unique. The British won a local victory at Messines Ridge on the Western Front in June 1917 using a brief bombardment. Equally, the French had used a similar tactic during the Nivelle Offensive in April. However, both Hutier and Bruchmüller saw that the surprise bombardment was clearly not enough: the specialist troops and mobile artillery were also essential.

The new German tactics were first tested on the Eastern Front in September 1917 and at Caporetto against the Italians in October. They were stunningly successful on both occasions. In the spring of 1918 the same tactics came very close to achieving a great German victory on the Western Front.

▲ *Turkish prisoners captured by the British at the Battle of Ramadi in Mesopotamia are led to the rear.*

the salient, where General Sir Herbert Plumer's Second Army is ordered to attack. The methodical Plumer decides to set limited objectives for a series of attacks that if successful will see his forces occupy the ridges to the south of Ypres. He opts to attack on a narrow front led by a creeping barrage.

Three battles follow: Menin Road (September 20–25), Polygon Wood (September 26), and Broodseinde (October 4). The British are aided by the drying out of the ground, a factor which has dogged progress since the opening of the Third Battle of Ypres in late July. Despite much heavy fighting, in which the Germans use mustard gas for the first time, Gough's limited, step-by-step attacks are successful. However, heavy rain again falls over the battlefield. The British commander-in-chief, Field Marshal Sir Douglas Haig, opts to continue.

SEPTEMBER 23

AIR WAR, *WESTERN FRONT*
German ace Werner Voss, who is credited with 48 victories in less than a year, is killed by British fighters led by James McCudden, who will win 57 victories before his death in 1918.

SEPTEMBER 27–28

MIDDLE EAST, *MESOPOTAMIA*
British and Commonwealth forces under the command of General Sir

Frederick Maude advance northward along the Euphrates River and confront the Turks at the Battle of Ramadi. The Turks are defeated and pursued by the British deep into central Mesopotamia. Maude's intention, once he has secured central Mesopotamia, is to drive northward along the Tigris River in the direction of Mosul, a vital oil-producing center.

OCTOBER 9–12

WESTERN FRONT, *BELGIUM*
The focus of the British offensive at Ypres switches back to the northeast of the town, but an attack led by Australian troops fails to make any significant progress. However, the battle continues, although it is clear that the British will not be able to achieve the decisive breakthrough that is planned. On the 12th they attack the village of Passchendaele without success. Although Field Marshal Sir Douglas Haig accepts that he cannot achieve his original ambitions of a decisive break-through, he nevertheless is determined to capture the high ground outside Ypres

before the onset of winter. He again makes the village of Passchendaele his main target.

OCTOBER 17

SEA WAR, *NORTH SEA*
A British convoy of 12 merchant ships, which is escorted by two destroyers, *Mary Rose* and *Strongbow*, is moving supplies from

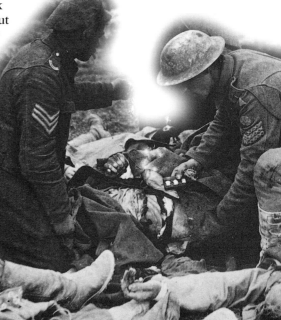

◄ *Italian mechanized transport retreats during the disastrous Battle of Caporetto. The Germans provided specialist assault units to lead the highly-successful Austro-Hungarian offensive.*

crash in enemy territory. This raid marks the end of major Zeppelin raids on Britain. Henceforth, they are used on naval-support duties in the North Sea or to carry out nuisance raids.

OCTOBER 24

WESTERN FRONT, *ITALY*
Austro-Hungarian artillery firing a mixture of high-explosive and gas shells open the Twelfth Battle of the Isonzo, also known as the Battle of Caporetto. In the previous month the Austro-Hungarians have been reinforced by several German divisions and specialist mountain units. Six of the German divisions and nine Austro-Hungarian have been formed into the

new Fourteenth Army, which is commanded by German General Otto von Below. Below's forces, assembled within Austro-Hungarian territory in the area of Tolmino, Caporetto, and Plezza along the Isonzo River, spearhead the offensive. The main target of the Fourteenth Army is General Luigi Capello's Italian Second Army, which has been slowly preparing defensive positions in readiness to meet the expected attack.

The main attack by the Fourteenth Army is backed by the advance of two further Austro-Hungarian armies. The Fifth, in the south opposing the Italian Third Army, is ordered to push along the north Italian Adriatic coast in the direction of Venice. The Third Army, to

▼ *Italian dead, some of the 10,000 killed during the Battle of Caporetto. A further 275,000 were captured and around 20,000 wounded.*

Scandinavia, but is surprised by the *Brummer* and *Bremse*, German light cruisers. Both destroyers and 75 percent of the convoy are sunk.

OCTOBER 19

AIR WAR, *BRITAIN*
German Zeppelin airships conduct what becomes a disastrous raid due to adverse weather and the British anti-aircraft defenses. Three of the 11 Zeppelins committed to the raid are smashed in a violent storm; one is destroyed by ground fire; a fifth drifts out to sea and is never seen again; while the other six fail to reach their targets and are either captured or

◄ *British troops attempt to identify their own and German dead during the Third Battle of Ypres.*

the north of the Fourteenth Army is tasked with heading southwest into Italy, making for the line of the Piave River. It is hoped that elements of this force will deal with an Italian army known as the Carnic Force.

The opening barrage causes panic among many front-line Italian units, whose troops discover that their masks offer no protection against the enemy gas. Advancing through rain and mist, and bypassing points of resistance, the offensive makes rapid progress; by the 25th the attackers are exploiting a 15-mile (24-km) break-through in the Italian line, forcing the Italian commander-in-chief, General Luigi Cadorna, to consider with-drawing to the Tagliamento River.

However, Cadorna is unaware of the true extent of the breakthrough or the strength of the enemy forces he is facing, primarily due to poor commu-nications with his forward units. The order to withdraw to the next defen-sible barrier is finally issued on the 27th. The battered Italian armies are regrouping across the Tagliamento by the end of the month.

OCTOBER 26

POLITICS, *BRAZIL*
Brazil declares war on Germany, the only country in South America to do so. Brazilian merchant ships have been sunk by German submarines on a regular basis.

OCTOBER 26–NOVEMBER 10

WESTERN FRONT, *BELGIUM*
The British again attempt to capture the German-held village of Passchendaele outside Ypres. The Canadian Corps is committed to the

▼ *Disarmed Italian prisoners are hurried into captivity during the Battle of Caporetto, while German troops advance.*

attack, but the rate of advance is painfully slow due to the dreadful ground conditions and the extensive use of mustard gas by the enemy. The village finally falls on November 6, effectively ending the offensive that begun in late July.

 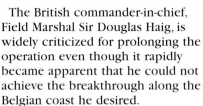
The British commander-in-chief, Field Marshal Sir Douglas Haig, is widely criticized for prolonging the operation even though it rapidly became apparent that he could not achieve the breakthrough along the Belgian coast he desired.

OCTOBER 27

WESTERN FRONT, *ITALY*
During the on-going Battle of Caporetto a young German officer, Erwin Rommel, completes the capture of some 9000 Italian prisoners. For three days Rommel's 250 specialist mountain troops have fought to capture a critical position against heavy odds. For his bravery and leadership Rommel receives Germany's highest award, the Pour le Mérite.

OCTOBER 31

MIDDLE EAST, *PALESTINE*
The British and Commonwealth forces commanded by General Sir Edmund Allenby, some 88,000 men divided between seven infantry divisions and the horse- and camel-mounted Desert Mounted Corps, launch the Third Battle of Gaza.

Allenby has decided on a new plan to break through the Turkish-held Gaza–Beersheba line. Rather than

▲ *British troops move forward at dusk during the final stages of the Third Battle of Ypres.*

▼ *Australian and New Zealand troops of the Desert Mounted Corps advance at the opening of the Third Battle of Gaza.*

By any standards the Third Battle of Ypres has been an awful experience for the British. They have suffered some 310,000 men killed, wounded, or captured to advance a meager five miles (8 km), consuming all of their reserve forces on the Western Front in the process. The French have suffered some 85,000 casualties and the Germans list around 260,000.

▼ *British officers examine an abandoned Turkish field gun and ammunition limber during the Third Battle of Gaza.*

launch frontal attacks against the heavily-entrenched Turks around Gaza on the coast, he opts to use three of his divisions to launch a feint attack against the coastal town, while the bulk of his forces will drive inland against Beersheba to secure its vital water supply and turn the Turkish left flank. The key element is the rapid capture of Beersheba's water – without it Allenby's mounted forces will not progress far in the heat.

▶ *British Foreign Secretary Arthur Balfour (right), who backed the creation of a Jewish state in Palestine but one with the rights of local Arabs protected.*

▼ *Turks captured by the Australian Light Horse at Beersheba during the Third Battle of Gaza in Palestine.*

◀ *Turkish troops rise from their trenches to launch an attack on the British during the fighting in Palestine.*

Allenby is opposed by some 35,000 Turks, chiefly the Eighth Army and elements of the Seventh Army commanded by German General Kress von Kressenstein. Kressenstein also has a small number of German machine-gun, artillery, and technical detachments under his orders. However, his position is somewhat undermined by his long supply lines.

The attack on Beersheba, which will give an alternative name to the battle, lasts throughout the day, but culminates in a daring and successful charge by a brigade of Australian cavalry at dusk. Remarkably, the brigade charges through the Turkish defenses and machine-gun fire, taking Beersheba and its vital wells. The weak Turkish Seventh Army at Beersheba is forced

▲ *German assault troops and their artillery support pass through a recently-captured village in northeastern Italy during the Battle of Caporetto.*

◀ *Italian prisoners captured during the joint German and Austro-Hungarian crossing of the Tagliamento River during the climax of the Battle of Caporetto.*

into headlong retreat, leaving the Turkish left flank exposed to further British advances.

NOVEMBER 2

POLITICS, *BRITAIN*
Foreign Secretary Arthur Balfour writes to Lord Rothschild, the chairman of of the British Zionist Federation, expressing his support for the creation of a Jewish state in Palestine. This letter, known as the "Balfour Declaration," also expresses the need for safeguards to protect "the civil and religious rights of existing non-Jewish communities in Palestine."

WESTERN FRONT, *ITALY*
Capitalizing on the momentum of their advance, the German forces leading the Battle of Caporetto make a crossing of the Tagliamento River under cover of darkness, thereby breaking the recently-formed Italian defensive line.

The Italian commander-in-chief, General Luigi Cadorna, orders his forces to withdraw to the next feasible line of defense, the Piave

▲ German lancers, part of their country's limited manpower commitment to Turkey, patrol the Palestinian countryside.

River. The retreat is completed by the 9th. Remarkably, despite their disorganization, casualties, and continuing enemy pressure, Italian resolve stiffens.

NOVEMBER 3

WESTERN FRONT, *FRANCE*

The first three soldiers of the ever-growing American Expeditionary Force are killed in action.

NOVEMBER 5

POLITICS, *ITALY*

The disastrous Italian defeat at Caporetto sparks a meeting at Rapallo of those nations opposing the Central Powers. Discussions broaden from providing military aid to Italy to include the establishment of a unified command structure. British Prime Minister David Lloyd George suggests creating what becomes known as the Supreme War Council. This will consist of the leaders (or their representatives) of Britain, France, Italy, and the United States.

NOVEMBER 6

MIDDLE EAST, *PALESTINE*

General Sir Edmund Allenby begins to

▼ US troops prepare to disembark from their transport, which has just docked in a French port.

exploit his decisive breakthrough at Beersheba at the close of October; his main aim is to drive a wedge between the retreating Turkish Seventh Army and the Turkish Eighth Army, which is still holding defensive positions around Gaza on the coast. Leading the way is Allenby's Desert Mounted Corps, which is ordered to swing toward Gaza on the coast from its positions around Beersheba to the southeast. However, the Turkish Eighth Army is aware of Allenby's strategy and rapidly withdraws from Gaza along the coast. The Turkish Seventh Army inland retreats toward Jerusalem.

▲ *Turkish field artillery in action during the British advance through Palestine. The weapon is a German-built three-inch (75-mm) design.*

▼ *Dismounted Australian cavalrymen open fire on the Turks during the fighting in Palestine.*

Allenby, eager to maintain the momentum of his advance, orders his various units to pursue the Turks as closely as possible, despite his force's shortage of water.

NOVEMBER 6–7

POLITICS, *RUSSIA*
Bolshevik revolutionaries led by Vladimir Lenin and Leon Trotsky launch a successful attempt to overthrow the Provisional Government headed by Prime Minister Alexander Kerensky in Petrograd. The Bolsheviks will enter into negotiations with the Germans over an armistice.

NOVEMBER 12

WESTERN FRONT, *ITALY*
The Twelfth Battle of Isonzo, better known as the Battle of Caporetto, ends chiefly due to the Germans and Austro-Hungarians having overstretched their supplies. The offensive has been a disaster for the Italians.
Although the Italian commander-in-chief, General Luigi Cadorna, has been able to stabilize his front, his forces have taken a battering and have suffered around 30,000 men killed or wounded. Some 275,000 prisoners

◄ *Russian troops, probably deserters from the front, on the streets of an unidentified town reading propaganda leaflets printed by the Bolsheviks.*

▼ *British field artillery pieces are readied for action against the Turkish forces retreating through Palestine.*

have been captured by the German and Austro-Hungarian forces commanded by German General Otto von Below. In addition, 2500 artillery pieces and huge quantities of stores and other equipment have been lost. The Germans and Austro-Hungarian casualties total some 20,000 men, a remarkably low figure for such a major offensive.

In the space of a few weeks the Italians have been forced back from the Isonzo, where they have fought a series of fruitless battles since 1915, to a line running from just south of the city of Trent along the Piave River, which runs into the Gulf of Venice in the northern Adriatic Sea – leaving the Italians a new front line of some 60 miles (96 km).

◄ *German General Otto von Below of the Fourteenth Army, who led the attack against the Italians during the successful Battle of Caporetto.*

▲ *The German-led offensive in Italy known as the Battle of Caporetto was one of the most successful attacks of the entire war.*

The sweeping German and Austro-Hungarian success has two immediate and important consequences. The chief of the Italian General Staff, General Luigi Cadorna, is replaced by General Armando Diaz, and several French and British divisions under the command of General Sir Herbert Plumer are rushed to bolster the battered Italian units along the Piave.

Remarkably, the disaster of Caporetto transforms the Italian public's view of the war. Previously, the army has fought chiefly outside Italy, on Austro-Hungarian soil; Caporetto has been,

Map:

Tyrol
AUSTRIA-HUNGARY
Bolzano
Carnia
Plezzo
Adige River
Tonale Pass
ITALY
Caporetto
Trentino
Belluno
Tolmino
Trent
Feltre
Udine
Vittorio Veneto
Asiago Plateau
Bainsizza Plateau
Gorizia
Asiago
Mount Grappa
Piave River
Mount Montello
Tagliamento River
Treviso
Vicenza
Isonzo River
Trieste
Venice
Adriatic Sea

······· Front, September 1917
– – – Front, December 1917
——— Front, November 1918

0   20 mi
0   30 km

NOVEMBER 13–15

however, fought almost wholly in Italy. This fact and the scale of the Italian defeat are exploited by several Italian public figures, such as the ardent nationalist poet Gabriele D'Annunzio and soldier-turned-journalist Benito Mussolini. Both issued emotive calls for the invaders to be evicted from Italy. Many ordinary Italians responded to their call to arms.

NOVEMBER 13–15

MIDDLE EAST, *PALESTINE*

British General Sir Edmund Allenby continues his pursuit of the Turkish forces defeated at the recent Battle of Beersheba. The focus of his attack is the Turkish Eighth Army, which has recently abandoned its positions at Gaza and fallen back northward along the Mediterranean coast.

Allenby's troops are able to break through hastily-built Turkish defenses during the Battle of Junction Station – a source of much-needed water – and then turn eastward. However, Turkish reserves led by German General Eric von Falkenhayn slow Allenby's advance on Jerusalem.

NOVEMBER 17

AIR WAR, *AFRICA*

The German Zeppelin *L59*, which is on a 3500-mile (5600-km) supply mission to German East Africa in aid of

▲ *Turkish cavalrymen retreat through Palestine pursued by the British.*

▼ *Italian women dig trenches following the disaster at Caporetto.*

General Paul von Lettow-Vorbeck, is ordered to return to Europe while flying over the Sudan. It is believed, incorrectly, that Lettow-Vorbeck is about to surrender.

NOVEMBER 18

MIDDLE EAST, *MESOPOTAMIA*
The commander of the British and Commonwealth forces in the region, General Sir Frederick Maude, dies after contracting cholera from contaminated milk. He is buried just outside Baghdad. His replacement is named as General Sir William Marshall.

NOVEMBER 20

WESTERN FRONT, *FRANCE*
The British Third Army under General Sir Julian Byng opens the Battle of Cambrai. The main impetus of the

▲ *The funeral of British General Sir Frederick Maude at Baghdad.*

▼ *British tanks on their way to lead the attack at Cambrai.*

▲ *British tanks move forward during the highly-successful opening phase of the Battle of Cambrai. In the left foreground is an abandoned German field gun. However, the offensive stalled as German resistance hardened.*

tank-led attack falls on the section of the Hindenburg Line defended by General Georg von der Maritz's German Second Army. Byng's plan aims to cut through the German positions between the Canal de l'Escaut and the Canal du Nord. Cavalry are to move forward rapidly against Cambrai, while infantry units and tanks take Bourlon Ridge before advancing northeast to Valenciennes.

The battle begins with a short bombardment of the Hindenburg Line by 1000 artillery pieces, which have not been preregistered on their targets. The main attack is spearheaded by 476 tanks, marking the first use of such weapons en masse in the war. The tanks lead six of Byng's 19 divisions in an major advance along five miles (8 km) of the front.

The early attacks are spectacularly successful: the Hindenburg Line is pierced to depths of six–eight miles (9–12 km), except at Flesquières, where stubborn German defenders knock out a number of tanks and the poor coordination between the British infantry and tanks combine to foil the advance.

Despite the outstanding results in the first days of the battle, the British encounter increasing difficulties in maintaining the momentum of their offensive. Many tanks succumb to mechanical failure, become bogged down in ditches, or are smashed by German artillery at close range. The battle concentrates around Bourlon Ridge to the west of Cambrai. The fighting continues into December, with the Germans launching a series of successful counterattacks.

◄ *General Sir Julian Byng, whose British Third Army led the attack at Cambrai.*

▶ *A German light field gun opens fire on an enemy target during the fighting in East Africa.*

NOVEMBER 25

AFRICA, *GERMAN EAST AFRICA*
The outnumbered German General Paul von Lettow-Vorbeck, who is facing several large-scale enemy advances from neighboring colonies, is forced to order a total withdrawal into Portuguese East Africa in the face of overwhelming odds.

However, despite losing one-third of his army, which is surrounded and forced to surrender on the 27th, he continues to fight on, launching highly-successful guerrilla attacks until after the official end of the war in November 1918.

NOVEMBER 30

WESTERN FRONT, *FRANCE*
The German troops engaged against

▼ *German soldiers gather their equipment prior to launching a counterattack on the British at Cambrai.*

DECEMBER 3

British General Sir Julian Byng's British Third Army begin to launch counter-attacks to regain the ground lost on the opening day of the tank-led offensive. Crown Prince Rupprecht of Bavaria, the commander of the threatened sector, has rushed sizeable reinforcements to the aid of General Georg von der Maritz's Second Army, which has borne the brunt of the British onslaught so far.

The German attacks are highly effective chiefly due to three reasons: the use of a short bombardment, the employment of the new stormtrooper units, and the support offered to the advancing units by low-flying aircraft. The British, overextended and lacking immediate reserves, are forced to give up much of their hard-won gains over the following days.

On the same day as the opening of the German counterattack at Cambrai the US 42nd Rainbow Division, so named because it contains men from every state in the nation, arrives in France. The division's chief-of-staff and later commander is General Douglas MacArthur.

DECEMBER 3

POLITICS, *GERMANY/RUSSIA*
German and Russia delegates meet at Brest-Litovsk in former Russian Poland to discuss terms for a final peace (an armistice is already in operation) to the fighting on the Eastern Front. The Russians, led by Bolshevik Leon Trotsky, attempt to stall negotiations. For their part the Germans want a swift conclusion so that they can transfer troops to bolster their forces battling on the Western Front.

WESTERN FRONT, *CAMBRAI*
Although Field Marshal Sir Douglas Haig, the British Expeditionary Force's commander, has rushed reinforcements to Cambrai to prevent the German counterattacks from breaking through the line held by General Sir Julian Byng's Third Army, he decides to withdraw his troops back to roughly the lines they occupied before the beginning of the battle on November 20.

Haig's order effectively ends the fighting by the 5th. Both the British and German forces have suffered roughly equal casualties – about 40,000 men – and the British have captured 11,000 troops to the 9000 taken by the Germans.

However, Cambrai highlights two important points. First, offensives do not have to be preceded by a prolonged artillery bombardment to be successful. Second, the mass use of tanks could achieve a major breakthrough, despite their mechanical unreliability and vulnerability to enemy fire. Both sides will take these lessons to heart in the offensive they are planning to launch during 1918.

DECEMBER 7

POLITICS, *UNITED STATES*
The government declares war on Austria-Hungary.

◄ *US General Douglas MacArthur, one of his country's most prominent generals in World War II, shown here commanding the 42nd Rainbow Division in 1918.*

▲ Turkish cavalrymen pictured in camp during the fighting against the British around Jerusalem.

▼ British tanks captured or abandoned at Cambrai are moved to the rear. Although Germany built its own tanks during the war, chiefly the A7V, it relied on the much more numerous British tanks that had been recovered from various battlefields. The larger A7V was found to have a poorer cross-country performance.

▲ British General Sir Edmund Allenby (foreground) makes his official entry into Jerusalem on December 11.

DECEMBER 9

POLITICS, *ROMANIA*
The authorities agree an armistice with the Central Powers, who have virtually total control of the country.

EASTERN FRONT, *RUSSIA*
Don cossacks revolt against the Bolsheviks, who are taking their land.

MIDDLE EAST, *PALESTINE*
The Turks abandon Jerusalem and British General Sir Edmund Allenby enters the city on the 11th.

DECEMBER 10

POLITICS, *FRANCE*
General Maurice Sarrail, commander of the vast multinational force operating in Greece, is sacked by French Prime Minister Georges Clemenceau, who appoints General Marie Guillaumat.

DECEMBER 30

FAR EAST AND PACIFIC, *JAPAN*
Taking advantage of Russia's instability, Japanese forces occupy the port of Vladivostok, much to the anger of Britain, France, and the United States, who doubt Japan's motives.

1918

This final year of the war the German high command gambled all on winning a clear victory on the Western Front before the arrival of US forces. They came close to victory but were halted. After this defeat Germany's allies gradually sought armistices, its own armed forces began to collapse, and its leaders had to seek an armistice themselves.

security, with disputes to be settled by an international body. The program, although not universally popular with America's allies, will subsequently be the basis on which Germany agrees to an armistice in November.

JANUARY 20

SEA WAR, *AEGEAN*
The former German warships *Breslau* and *Goeben*, which have been under Turkish control since 1914, make a final sortie into the Aegean Sea. Both run into an enemy minefield – the *Breslau* sinks and the *Goeben* is forced aground. Despite intense enemy air attacks, the *Goeben* survives and is towed to safety by the Turks.

▼ British troops, part of the force led by General L.C. Dunsterville, advance through northern Mesopotamia on their way to Baku on the Caspian Sea.

JANUARY 1

POLITICS, *FINLAND*
The Bolshevik government recognizes the independence of this former Russian province, which had declared itself independent the previous month. However, tension mounts between Finland's political groups.

JANUARY 8

POLITICS, *UNITED STATES*
In a far-reaching speech to Congress, President Woodrow Wilson outlines his 14-Point Peace Program. It is designed to prevent destructive wars and at its heart are the principles of national self-determination and collective

▲ German troops and members of the Finnish "White Guard" militia parade in Helsinki, the country's capital.

JANUARY 27

MIDDLE EAST, *MESOPOTAMIA*
A British force led by General L.C. Dunsterville is sent from Baghdad to take over the Russian oil fields at Baku on the Caspian Sea. With Russia in turmoil the Turks and Germans are also eager to grab the resources. "Dunsterforce" reaches Baku in August.

JANUARY 28

POLITICS, *ESTONIA*
The government of this former Russian province, which had declared its independence in November 1917, asks for German aid to deal with Russian Bolsheviks, who are attempting to regain power. The Germans occupy Revel on February 25 and succeed in expelling the Bolsheviks.

POLITICS, *FINLAND*
The country's Social Democrats, backed by their militia known as the "Red Guard," stage a coup and proclaim Finland a socialist workers' republic. The leader of the overthrown government, Pehr Svinhufvud, flees to Vaasa in eastern Finland, whose Russian garrison has been thrown out by General Karl von Mannerheim, the commander of the government's own militia, the "White Guard." Pro-German Svinhufvud calls on Germany for military aid against the "Red Guard."

FEBRUARY 1

POLITICS, *AUSTRIA-HUNGARY*
Austro-Hungarian sailors stage a mutiny at Cattaro, the navy's chief base on the Dalmatian coast.

FEBRUARY 18

POLITICS, *GERMANY/RUSSIA*
The German delegates who have been discussing the terms of a peace treaty with the Bolsheviks at Brest-Litovsk since the armistice agreement of December 1917, recommence hostilities, sending troops farther eastward into the Ukraine and toward Petrograd, the Russian capital. The Germans have become increasingly exasperated by the Bolsheviks'

▼ Germans examine an armored car abandoned by the Bolsheviks during the renewed fighting on the Eastern Front.

KEY MOMENTS

THE 14 POINTS
On January 8 US President Woodrow Wilson gave a speech that had profound consequences not only for World War I but also for the interwar map of Europe and for relations between states throughout the whole century. Wilson, who wished to distance himself from the secrecy that had governed relationships between powers before 1914, laid down principles that, he believed, should govern such relationships after 1918. His speech outlined key ideas that centered on openness in the relationships between countries and the right of self-determination. He hoped to reduce the suspicion between countries and prevent the rivalries that had sparked World War I. Among the 14 Points were:

1) Covenants of peace, openly arrived at, after which there shall be no private international understandings of any kind but diplomacy shall proceed always frankly and in the public view.

2) Absolute freedom of navigation, outside territorial waters, alike in peace and war, except as the seas may be closed by international action for the enforcement of international covenants.

3) The removal, so far as possible, of all economic barriers and the establishment of an equality of trade conditions among all the nations consenting to the peace and associating themselves for its maintenance.

4) Adequate guarantees given and taken that national armaments will be reduced to the lowest point consistent with domestic safety.

5) A free, open-minded, and absolutely impartial adjustment of all colonial claims, based upon a strict observance of the principle that in determining all such questions of sovereignty the interests of the populations must have equal weight with the equitable claims of the government whose title is to be determined.

14) A general association of nations must be formed under specific covenants for the purpose of affording mutual guarantees of political independence and territorial integrity to great and small states alike.

Points 6–13 were related to World War I, including the restoration of Belgian sovereignty, the return of French territory taken by Germany after the Franco-Prussian War (1870–71), and the self-determination of the various ethnic groups comprising what was the Austro-Hungarian Empire, certain parts of Russia, chiefly Poland, and Turkey.

FEBRUARY 24

▶ *German stormtroopers move forward at the opening of Operation Michael, the offensive begun on March 21.*

delaying tactics and are eager to impose an agreement to free their troops on the Eastern Front for service on the Western Front. The Bolsheviks do not have the forces or resources to block the renewed onslaught.

FEBRUARY 24

MIDDLE EAST, *ARMENIA*
Taking advantage of the collapse of the Russian Army in the wake of the 1917 Russian Revolution, Turkish forces reoccupy parts of Armenia they have lost to the Russians. However, they are most interested in securing the Russian oil-producing facilities at Baku on the Caspian Sea.

MARCH 3

POLITICS, *RUSSIA*
After weeks of prevarication the Bolshevik revolutionaries, who have a tenuous hold on the country, are forced to sign a stern peace treaty with the Germans at Brest-Litovsk. They are compelled to give up control of the Ukraine, Finland, the Baltic Provinces (Estonia, Latvia, and Lithuania), the Caucasus, Poland, and those areas of Russia controlled by the "White" Russians who are opposed to the Bolsheviks. German troops continue to occupy the Ukraine as its grain is vital to prevent wholesale starvation in Germany.

MARCH 21

WESTERN FRONT, *FRANCE*
General Erich Ludendorff has planned a knock-out blow on the Western Front. He recognizes that, with the imminent arrival of scores of thousands of US troops in France, Germany is likely to lose the war. However, Ludendorff plans to strike first. He transfers some 70 divisions of troops from the Eastern Front, where the turmoil following the Russian Revolution has effectively ended Russian involvement in the war. In

the short term, therefore, Germany has a clear numerical advantage over the British and French.

Ludendorff's plan is to exploit the differences between Britain's and France's strategies for facing any major German offensive. He believes the French will give priority to the defense of Paris, while the British are more concerned with defending the ports along the north French coast through which their supplies and troops flow. Ludendorff aims to attack at the juncture between the French and British forces in northeast France.

To this end he has three armies – the Seventeenth under General Otto von Below, the Second led by General Georg von der Marwitz, and General Oskar von Hutier's Eighteenth – prepare for the offensive. These are to advance along a 50-mile (80-km) front from Arras to St. Quentin and La Fère. This zone is defended by the British Third Army under General Sir Julian Byng and General Sir Hubert Gough's Fifth Army.

Ludendorff has 63 divisions, many led by elite stormtrooper units, earmarked for the attack, while the British can muster just 26. The offensive is code-named Operation Michael but is also known as the *Kaiserschlacht* ("Kaiser's Battle").

◀ *German officials greet the Russian Bolshevik delegates attending the peace negotiations at Brest-Litovsk.*

▲ British and French troops man hastily-prepared defenses during the opening phase of Operation Michael.

Operation Michael begins with a sudden five-hour bombardment on the British by 6000 artillery pieces. They fire both gas and high-explosive shells. Under cover of thick fog the Germans attack, with the specially-trained stormtrooper units leading the way. The surprise and shock of the onslaught overwhelms the thinly-spread British.

Gough's Fifth Army collapses in confusion, exposing the right flank of Byng's Third Army. However, Byng's forces, which are holding a narrower front than those of Gough, withdraw across the Somme River in good order. The attackers here, drawn from the German Seventeenth and Second Armies, make significantly less gains.

MARCH 23

WESTERN FRONT, *PARIS*
The Germans begin an intermittent bombardment of Paris with long-range eight-inch (21-cm) artillery pieces, which become known as the "Paris

Guns." There are seven of them and they can strike the French capital from ranges of 50 miles (80 km). The bombardment, which has little military value, continues until August 9. The "Paris Guns" fire a total of 367 shells, which kill 256 Parisians and wound 620. The guns are withdrawn in August as the German forces on the Western Front are forced to retreat.

MARCH 25

WESTERN FRONT, *FRANCE*
General Georg von der Marwitz's German Second Army breaks through the juncture of the British Third and Fifth Armies during the continuing Operation Michael. It appears to General Eric Ludendorff, the deputy chief of the German General Staff, that the British are on the point of collapse, so he issues new orders to

▼ One of the German "Paris Guns" undergoes test firing. They were designed by Krupp.

▲ The territory gained by the Germans during their series of offensives on the Western Front in the first half of 1918.

his commanders. He orders Marwitz to make for Amiens, while General Oskar von Hutier is directed to strike at Paris with his Eighteenth Army. General Otto von Below's Seventeenth Army is to continue to make for the ports along the coast of northern France.

The British commander-in-chief, Field Marshal Sir Douglas Haig, is rushing British troops to plug the gap in his line, but his French opposite number, Marshal Henri-Philippe Pétain is, as Ludendorff suspects, more concerned with protecting Paris, so sends few troops to aid the hard-pressed British.

MARCH 26

POLITICS, *FRANCE*
General Ferdinand Foch is made the coordinator of all the British, French, and American forces on the Western

MARCH 27

Front following a meeting of the joint Supreme War Council. One of Foch's key supporters is Field Marshal Sir Douglas Haig, commander of the British Expeditionary Force.

Foch's chief concern is to stop the ongoing German offensive, Operation Michael, which has torn a hole in the British line in northern France. French reinforcements now flood into the threatened sector south of the Somme River, where they and British forces are placed under the command of France's General Marie Fayolle.

WESTERN FRONT, *FRANCE*
General Sir Julian Byng's British Third Army fighting north of the Somme River stops the German advance in part due to effective air support. The Germans attempt to relaunch their attack in this sector two days later, opening Operation Mars, which is aimed at Arras, but it fails. The defeat of Operation Mars signals the end of the German effort north of the Somme and the fighting now concentrates south of the river.

MARCH 27

WESTERN FRONT, *FRANCE*
German troops advancing south of the Somme River capture Montdidier. The town is some 40 miles (64 km) from their start point of March 21 and its fall leaves the German forces within striking distance of Amiens, their chief objective. However, the Germans are exhausted and are facing increasing

numbers of fresh British and French troops. The German attack is finally halted at the village of Villers-Bretonneux, some 10 miles (16 km) to the east of Amiens.

MARCH 29

AIR WAR, *WESTERN FRONT*
US pilot Edward Rickenbacker scores his first air victory. By the end of the war he will be acknowledged as his country's top ace with 26 kills.

▲ *US fighter ace Edward Rickenbacker, a renowned racing driver, was his country's top-scoring pilot of the war. Four of his 26 victories were against enemy balloons.*

APRIL 1

AIR WAR, *WESTERN FRONT*
The British Royal Air Force is created by the amalgamation of the Royal Flying Corps and the Royal Naval Air Service.

APRIL 3

POLITICS, *FINLAND*
Answering a call for military aid from the recently-ousted president, Pehr Svinhufvud, the German Baltic Division commanded by General Rüdiger von der Goltz arrives to aid the fight against the new pro-Bolshevik government and its militia, the "Red Guard."

APRIL 5

WESTERN FRONT, *FRANCE*
General Erich Ludendorff, the deputy chief of the German General Staff and instigator of Operation Michael, calls a halt to the offensive as it has become clear that he will not achieve a decisive victory along the Somme River. His forces have advanced some 40 miles (64 km) and inflicted around 240,000 casualties on the British and

◄ *German troops man an armored train during the fighting between rival political factions in Finland.*

Western Front. Operation Georgette is directed at the British General Sir Herbert Plumer's Second Army and General Sir Henry Horne's British First Army, which are separated by the Lys River. Committed to the attack are General Sixt von Arnim's Fourth Army and General Ferdinand von Quast's Sixth Army. The offensive is to take place on a narrow front in the direction of the English Channel ports through which the British receive their supplies and reinforcements.

Following a three-day artillery bombardment, the attack begins on the morning of the 9th. The German Sixth Army advances from Neuve-Chapelle on a 12-mile (19-km) front against the left wing of Horne's First Army. Two divisions of Portuguese troops under Horne's command reel under the assault and are forced back some five miles (8 km).

The next day four divisions of General Sixt von Arnim's Fourth Army strike against elements of Plumer's Second Army, which is forced to retreat beyond Messines and Wytschaete.

APRIL 12

WESTERN FRONT, *FRANCE/BELGIUM*
German forces attacking along the Lys River in the direction of the north

French. German losses are equally severe, particularly among the stormtrooper units that spearheaded the onslaught. However, Ludendorff now switches his offensive to another sector of the Western Front.

APRIL 9–10

WESTERN FRONT, *FRANCE/BELGIUM*
General Erich Ludendorff opens the second of a series of attacks on the

▼ *British troops take up position behind a railroad embankment during the fighting along the Lys River.*

MARSHAL FERDINAND FOCH

Ferdinand Foch (1851–1929) enlisted in the French Army in 1870 but did not see active service until 1914, when he played a significant role in the defeat of the German invasion of France. In the intervening 44 years he was a professor of strategy and tactics, and later commandant of the country's *Ecole de Guerre* ("School of War"). Both his lectures and writings emphasized the need for a general to gain psychological dominance over his opposite number and then to act offensively.

Despite a number of commands between 1914 and 1916, Foch was next tasked with a number of administrative roles, including that of Marshal Henri-Philippe Pétain's chief of staff in May 1917. Foch returned to action later the same year, when he coordinated the flow of Anglo-French reinforcements to Italy, which had suffered a catastrophic defeat at the Battle of Caporetto. He then joined the Supreme War Council, the body coordinating action against the Central Powers. During Germany's spring 1918 offensive on the Western Front the British suggested that Foch coordinate all the forces opposing the attack, a position that was later extended to other theaters. A thoughtful figure, renowned as an organizer and diplomat, he was able to overcome national self-interest to plan united action against the Germans.

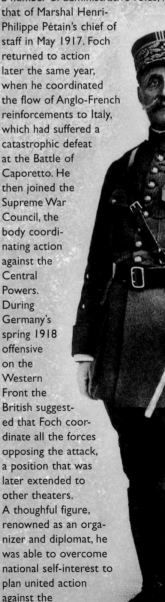

French coast have created a break in the British line some 30 miles (48 km) wide and are closing in on one of their early objectives, the village of Hazebrouck, southwest of Ypres.

The British commander-in-chief, Field Marshal Sir Douglas Haig, issues an order prohibiting any further retreat: "With our backs to the wall and believing in the justice of our cause, each one must fight on to the end." The call to arms works and British resistance hardens.

▼ *French artillerymen go into action with a train-mounted naval gun during the fighting to halt the German offensive along the Lys River.*

APRIL 14

POLITICS, *FRANCE*
French General Ferdinand Foch is officially promoted to the position of commander-in-chief of all those forces of whatever nationality opposing Germany on the Western Front. In June this will be extended to include the Italian theater.

APRIL 17

WESTERN FRONT,
FRANCE/BELGIUM
British and recently-arrived French troops fighting around Ypres

▲ *Open warfare breaks out on the Western Front for the first time since 1914 – German howitzers advance.*

halt the German drive along the Lys River. Although there will be a series of attacks and counterattacks until the end of the month, the German attempt to reach the ports of northern France has failed. Both sides have lost around 100,000 troops in the fighting. However, General Erich Ludendorff, the deputy chief of the German General Staff, begins laying plans for a third offensive.

APRIL 21

AIR WAR, *WESTERN FRONT*
Baron Manfred von Richthofen, the leading ace of the war with 80 confirmed victories, is shot down and killed during a dogfight. He is buried with full military honors by the British. Richthofen's command is taken over by German ace (22 victories) Hermann Goering.

APRIL 23

WESTERN FRONT, *BELGIUM*
The British launch a surprise amphibious assault to curtail attacks by German submarines and destroyers operating in the English Channel from Ostend and Zeebrugge. The operation is masterminded by Vice Admiral Sir

▶ *The funeral service of German fighter ace Baron Manfred von Richthofen.*

Roger Keyes; his plan is to sink old warships across the canals that the enemy craft use to reach open water. In an operation that involves more than 70 vessels, the British concentrate their forces against Zeebrugge.

The attack on Zeebrugge begins with British naval infantry landing from the cruiser *Vindictive* on the harbor's sea-walls, and the destruction of an old submarine packed with explosives, the latter to isolate the German defenders of the sea-wall from the land.

As this action continues, three block-ships, *Thetis*, *Intrepid*, and *Iphigenia*, sail into Zeebrugge's inner harbor.

They are supposed to block the canal. *Thetis* grounds in the inner harbor, but *Intrepid* and *Iphigenia* reach their target only to be sunk in the incorrect position. The smaller attack on Ostend

is even less successful – German raiders are still able to sail. A raid on Zeebrugge on May 9 also fails.

APRIL 25

AIR WAR, WESTERN FRONT
Pilot Willy Coppens scores his first air victory, downing a German fighter. Belgium's leading ace of the war with 37 victories, he will become renowned for destroying observation balloons.

APRIL 28–29

POLITICS, *FINLAND*
"White Guard" forces loyal to the former president, Pehr Svinhufvud, and commanded by General Karl von

▼ *The aftermath of the British raid on Zeebrugge, Belgium, a base for German submarines and destroyers.*

MAY 7

▶ *German stormtroopers cross a makeshift bridge during the drive against the French-held Chemin des Dames.*

Mannerheim win a decisive victory at Viborg over the "Red Guard" militia of the pro-Bolshevik government.

MAY 7

POLITICS, *ROMANIA*

Having been comprehensibly defeated in 1917 and forced to sign an armistice in December, Romania, which declared war on the Central Powers in August 1916, surrenders, signing the Treaty of Bucharest. Since the invasion the Romanian Army has suffered losses of some 400,000 troops and has had to retreat from some 80 percent of its territory.

However, the Romanian monarch, King Ferdinand, does not sign the document, which allows him to claim that his country never surrendered. This will permit Romania to claim full recompense for its efforts following the defeat of the Central Powers.

MAY 19

AIR WAR, *WESTERN FRONT*

Raoul Lufbery, one of the top-scoring US fighter pilots of the war with 17 victories, is killed during air combat. He had served with other American volunteers in the French *Escadrille Lafayette* (originally the *Escadrille Américaine* and credited with 38 air victories) before the United States' entry into the war. Lufbery was the commander of the famed 94th "Hat in the Ring" Aero Squadron at the time of his death. The squadron's nickname was derived from its emblem.

▼ *US troops supported by French-built Schneider tanks advance during the Battle of Cantigny, May 28.*

MAY 27

WESTERN FRONT, *FRANCE*

General Erich Ludendorff, the deputy chief of the German General Staff, opens his third offensive on the Western Front in 1918. It is a diversionary attack against the French forces holding the Chemin des Dames section of the Aisne River. Ludendorff's aim is to prevent the French from sending reinforcements to the aid of the British in northern France, where he is planning to attack again.

The offensive is led by General Max von Boehn's Seventh Army and the First Army under General Bruno von Mudra, a total of 44 divisions. The object of their advances, code-named Blücher and Yorck, is General Denis Duchêne's French Sixth Army, which consists of 12 divisions, including three British.

The German onslaught is heralded by a bombardment from 4600 artillery pieces, which is followed by an attack by seven divisions on a front of 10 miles (16 km). The Germans immediately capture the Chemin des Dames and advance on the Aisne River,

taking several intact bridges. By the end of the day the Germans have advanced some 10 miles (16 km).

Although the offensive is intended to be limited in scope, its early successes convince the German high command to press forward as Paris is just 80 miles (128 km) distant. However, the French are being sent reinforcements

by the commander of the American Expeditionary Force, General John Pershing. They are General Omar Bundy's 2nd Division and the 3rd Division under General J.T. Dickman. These will go into action on the 30th, by which stage the Germans are menacing the Marne River.

MAY 28

WESTERN FRONT, *FRANCE*
US forces undertake their first attack of the war on the second day of the German offensive along the Aisne River. However, the fighting centers on the village of Cantigny to the east of Montdidier on the Somme River sector to the north. Elements of the US 1st

▲ *Tangible proof of the United States' commitment to the Western Front – American troops march through the center of a French town.*

◀ *US and French troops rush ammunition supplies to the front during the fighting along the Aisne River at the height of the German offensives code-named Blücher and Yorck.*

Division under General Robert Lee Bullard are pitched against the German Eighteenth Army led by General Oskar von Hutier. Bullard's troops capture Cantigny, taking 200 prisoners, on the 28th and block a series of German counterattacks over the following days. American losses total some 1600 men, of whom 199 are killed.

JUNE 2–4

WESTERN FRONT, *FRANCE*
The US 3rd Division under General J.T. Dickman goes into action against the German troops threatening Château-Thierry on the Marne River. The division is able to prevent the German assault troops, who are part of the continuing operations code-named Blücher and Yorck, from crossing the Marne at Château-Thierry and then counterattacks with French support, forcing the Germans back across the Marne at Jaulgonne.

JUNE 4

WESTERN FRONT, *FRANCE*
General Erich Ludendorff calls off his twin offensives code-named

Blücher and Yorck, which began on May 27. Although his assault units have advance to a maximum depth of 20 miles (32 km) over a distance of 30 miles (48 km), they have run out of steam. He is also facing increasingly strong counterattacks from French and US forces.

German losses total some 125,000 men, a figure matched by those forces opposing the attacks. However, Ludendorff is already planning what will be his fourth offensive on the Western Front in 1918.

JUNE 6

WESTERN FRONT, *FRANCE*
As part of the ongoing counterattacks against the German forces holding their recently-won gains along the Marne River, the US 2nd Division under General Omar Bundy attacks at Belleau Wood, a little to the west of Château-Thierry. The division's US Marine Brigade and 3rd Infantry Brigade lead the way. Bundy's troops are facing the equivalent of four German divisions, yet the outnumbered US forces launch a succession

JUNE 9

▼ *The Austro-Hungarian battleship* Szent Istvan *keels over to starboard following a successful Italian attack.*

of attacks over the following weeks. After three weeks of fighting the wood is cleared. Bundy's casualties reach 1800 men killed and 7000 wounded.

JUNE 9

SEA WAR, *ADRIATIC*

An Austro-Hungarian attempt to break the enemy blockade of the Adriatic ends in failure with the dreadnought battleship *Szent Istvan* being sunk off the Dalmatian coast. It falls victim to Italian warships commanded by Commander Luigi Rizzo, who has already been credited with the sinking of the Austro-Hungarian battleship *Wien* in Trieste harbor during December 1917.

▼ *A badly-wounded French casualty is evacuated from a front-line trench during the German offensive along the Oise River.*

JUNE 9–13

WESTERN FRONT, *FRANCE*

Under orders from General Erich Ludendorff, the deputy chief of the German General Staff, General Oskar von Hutier's Eighteenth Army launches the fourth in a series of offensives. Ludendorff is aiming to unite two salients carved out in previous attacks in the Amiens and Aisne-Marne sectors. Hutier is to attack westward along the Matz River, a tributary of the Oise River, in the direction of Noyon and Montdidier. However, the commander of the French Third Army, General Georges

▲ *A German eight-inch (21-cm) howitzer is readied for action during Operation Gneisenau, June 1918.*

Humbert, has been forewarned by deserters of the German attack and organized his defenses accordingly. He initiates an artillery bombardment on the enemy assault troops shortly before their onslaught.

However, this is unable to prevent the Germans gaining some five miles (8 km) on the first day of their attack, which is code-named Gneisenau. French resistance intensifies over the following days and the attempted link-up between Hutier's troops and the German Seventh Army under General Max von Boehn, which began an attack from Soissons on the 10th, fails.

Meanwhile, French General Charles Mangin has organized a counter-attacking force of three French and two US divisions. These strike the Eighteenth Army on the 12th, forcing Ludendorff to call off the operation the following day.

French and American casualties number some 35,000 men, while German losses are estimated to be considerably higher. Ludendorff, increasingly desperate to achieve a breakthrough, plans a fifth offensive elsewhere on the Western Front.

JUNE 13

WESTERN FRONT, *ITALY*
The Austro-Hungarians launch a diversionary attack against the Tonale Pass in northern Italy to mask their forthcoming offensive against the Italians along the Piave River.

JUNE 15–22

WESTERN FRONT, *ITALY*
The Austro-Hungarians, now fighting alone against Italy following the withdrawal of German forces to the Western Front, launch what becomes known as the Battle of the Piave River. Some 58 divisions are committed to a huge pincer attack across much of northern Italy. General Franz Conrad von Hötzendorf, who is operating in the Trentino region, is ordered to take

▶ Italian troops holding the Piave River load an artillery piece protected by a sandbagged emplacement.

Verona, while General Borojevic von Bojna is to fan out across the Piave River, making for the Adige River and the city of Padua.

However, the attacks are far from successful. In the north Hötzendorf's Tenth and Eleventh Armies are blocked on the second day of the advance and then vigorously counterattacked by the Italian Fourth and Sixth Armies, which contain several British and

▲ *French prisoners are escorted away from the fighting along the Aisne River during Operation Gneisenau.*

French units. The Austro-Hungarians are forced to retreat, having suffered 40,000 casualties.

To the east the Austro-Hungarians attack across the Piave on a wide front. Their Fifth and Sixth Armies gain three miles (4 km) on a 15-mile

(24-km) front before running up against the defenses of the Italian Third and Eighth Armies. The fighting in this sector continues over several days, with the Austro-Hungarians making some gains before a counter-attack on the 18th forces them back.

The Austro-Hungarian offensive begins to falter, partly due to the worsening weather and Italian air attacks, which weaken their lines of communication and undermines the flow of supplies. By the 22nd the Austro-Hungarians, who are in disarray, are forced back across the Piave. Their casualties, which include 24,000 prisoners, total 150,000 men. However, the chief of the Italian General Staff, General Armando Diaz, refrains from pursuing the defeated enemy and will spend until October building up his forces for a decisive offensive.

JUNE 23

POLITICS, *RUSSIA*
A joint Anglo-French force occupies the north Russian port of Murmansk to aid those forces – "White" Russians – opposed to the Bolshevik government. Similar occupations follow: Archangel and Vladivostok are both occupied in August, the latter by a contingent of US troops.

The two US regiments committed at Vladivostok are commanded by General William Graves. Unlike his allies in the north he is under strict orders not to interfere in internal Russian affairs. His roles are to prevent the Japanese, who have garrisoned Vladivostok since December 1919, from taking the port over permanently,

▲ *US troops keep watch over a section of the Trans-Siberian Railroad during their occupation of Vladivostok.*

▼ *General Max von Boehn, the commander of the German Seventh Army during 1918.*

and to aid in the repatriation of a 100,000-strong group of Austro-Hungarian prisoners later known as the Czech Legion.

US troops guard part of the Trans-Siberian Railroad to facilitate the possible evacuation of the Czech Legion, but they become involved in clashes with Bolshevik and anti-Bolshevik forces. American forces are destined to remain in the region until April 1920.

JULY 9

AIR WAR, *WESTERN FRONT*
One of Britain's top aces, James McCudden, is killed when his fighter crashes during a routine take-off.

JULY 11

POLITICS, *LITHUANIA*
German Prince Wilhelm of Urach accepts the crown and takes the name King Mindove II. The Germans have been occupying the former Russian province since 1915 and continue to exert influence through the Lithuanian Taryba, council of state.

JULY 15–17

WESTERN FRONT, *FRANCE*
German forces open their fifth offensive of 1918. The deputy chief of the General Staff, General Erich Ludendorff, is planning another diversionary attack, this time in Champagne, along the line of the Marne River, to draw his opponents' reserves away from northern France, where he still intends to cut through the British and seize ports along the English Channel. The attacks involves

▶ *Germans cross a bridge destroyed by the French during the fighting along the Aisne and Marne Rivers.*

three German armies: General Max von Boehn's Seventh Army, which is to strike across the Marne and then swing east toward Epernay, where it is intended to link up with General Bruno von Mudra's First Army advancing either side of Reims. To the east of Reims General Karl von Einem's Third Army is under orders to strike for Châlons-sur-Marne.

The French, through a combination of aerial reconnaissance and talkative German deserters, are aware of the offensive and pre-empt it with a bombardment of their own. The German Third Army makes little progress against General Henri Gouraud's First Army, being halted before noon on the 15th. Henceforth, the Germans concentrate their efforts to the west of Reims.

The German Seventh Army, with support from the Ninth Army under General Eben, attack on a 20-mile (32-km) front and cut through General Jean Degoutte's French Sixth Army to reach the Marne River between Château-Thierry and Epernay. However, attacks by the French Ninth Army under General M.A.H. de Mitry, supported by British

and US forces, prevent the Germans from exploiting their bridgeheads over the Marne. By the 17th Ludendorff accepts that his offensive has been stopped in its tracks.

Since the opening of his first offensive, Operation Michael, in March, his forces have suffered 500,000 virtually irreplaceable casualties. In contrast, US troops are arriving at a rate of 300,000 per month. Ludendorff, short of troops, plans a measured withdrawal from the salient he has created running south of

Soissons and Reims to shorten his line. However, the opposing commanders are intending to launch a counter-offensive before he can complete this withdrawal.

JULY 16–17

POLITICS, *RUSSIA*
Several members of the Russian royal family, including Czar Nicholas II and the czarina, are murdered by the Bolsheviks at Ekaterinburg, Siberia,

▼ *US troops open fire on a German sniper holed up in a ruined French village close to the Marne River.*

JULY 18

▲ *The room in the town of Ekaterinburg, Siberia, where the Russian royal family was murdered by the Bolsheviks.*

where they have lived in internal exile since late 1917.

JULY 18

WESTERN FRONT, *FRANCE*
Various French, British, and US forces launch a counterattack against the German forces in the salient they hold between Soissons and Reims in Champagne. The fighting becomes known as the Second Battle of the Marne. The attack is led by three French armies – the Tenth under General Charles Mangin; the Sixth under General Jean Degoutte; and General Henri Berthelot's Fifth. Support is offered by the French Ninth Army under General M.A.H. de Mitry.

The main attack involves the French Tenth Army and is spearheaded by the US 1st and 2nd Divisions, which take 8000 prisoners and 145 artillery pieces for the loss of 5000 casualties. Elsewhere, General Hunter Liggett's US I Corps fights alongside the French Sixth Army, which advances into the salient from the west along the Ourcq River. Three further US divisions from General Bullard's III Corps are attached to the French Ninth Army under General M.A.H. de Mitry, which is driving into the salient from the south close to Château-Thierry. The German defenders of the salient begin

to collapse under these converging attacks and Ludendorff has to contemplate an urgent withdrawal.

JULY 20

WESTERN FRONT, *FRANCE*
General Erich Ludendorff, deputy chief of the German General Staff, calls off his proposed attack

against the British in northern France due to the deteriorating situation in the Second Battle of the Marne.

JULY 26

EASTERN FRONT, *RUSSIA*
A group of former Austro-Hungarian prisoners of war known as the Czech Legion occupy Ekaterinburg. They had been expecting to be repatriated but the plan has been blocked by the Bolsheviks. The troops of the Czech Legion respond by taking arms from Bolshevik units in order to force their way back to their homeland. They will, however, become embroiled in the Russian Civil War, fighting with anti-Bolshevik forces.

170

▲ *Men of the Czech Legion, former prisoners of war fighting against the Bolsheviks, operate an armored train in Russia.*

AIR WAR, *WESTERN FRONT*

Britain's top fighter pilot, Edward Mannock, is shot down and killed by German ground fire. He has been credited with 73 victories in air combat.

AUGUST 2–6

WESTERN FRONT, *FRANCE*

As part of the continuing Second Battle of the Marne the Germans are forced to abandon Soissons and over the next 24 hours fall back to the line of the Aisne and Vesle Rivers, effectively abandoning the salient they have recently captured between Soissons and Reims. The Second Battle of the Marne ends on the 6th. It has been a disaster for the German

▲ *German prisoners captured by the French during the fighting of August 1918 await an escort to the rear.*

forces, who have sustained losses totaling 168,000 men.

Following a series of offensives since March, the Germans no longer

have the resources to launch attacks. They have also suffered huge casualties among their best-trained troops – the stormtrooper units – and those who have survived are suffering from increasingly poor morale.

AUGUST 4

AIR WAR, *WESTERN FRONT*

America's second highest-scoring ace, Frank Luke, begins his short but distinguished career. He downs 14 observation balloons and four aircraft in a few weeks. However, he is forced down behind German lines in late September and, refusing to surrender, is shot.

AUGUST 6

POLITICS, *FRANCE*

In recognition for his outstanding performance in marshaling the various national forces under his overall command during the recent fighting along the Marne River, France's General Ferdinand Foch is promoted to the rank of marshal. Foch is contemplating a major Anglo-French offensive to the east of Amiens.

AUGUST 8–12

WESTERN FRONT, *FRANCE*

Field Marshal Sir Douglas Haig's British Expeditionary Force spearheads what becomes known as the Amiens

◄ *Australian troops occupy a recently-captured German position during the Amiens Offensive.*

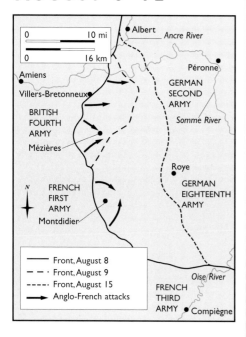

Front, August 8
Front, August 9
Front, August 15
Anglo-French attacks

Albert
Ancre River
Péronne
GERMAN SECOND ARMY
Somme River
Amiens
Villers-Bretonneux
BRITISH FOURTH ARMY
Mézières
Roye
GERMAN EIGHTEENTH ARMY
FRENCH FIRST ARMY
Montdidier
Oise River
FRENCH THIRD ARMY
Compiègne

▲ The British-led offensive at Amiens heralded a series of attacks that smashed the German forces on the Western Front.

Offensive. The attack has been planned to clear parts of the railroad running from Amiens to Paris that have been held by the Germans since their Operation Michael in March.

The offensive is led by General Sir Henry Rawlinson's British Fourth Army, which stages a methodical

▲ Germans taken prisoner on the first day of the Amiens Offensive, a day termed the "Black Day of the German Army," march into captivity.

▼ US troops with French-built tanks move up to the front in the Meuse–Argonne sector of the Western Front.

advance along a 15-mile (24-km) front. The attack is preceded by a short bombardment and more than 400 tanks lead the way forward for the 11 British divisions earmarked for the first phase of the onslaught. Support is offered by the left wing of General Eugène Debeney's French First Army. The German defenses are manned by General Georg von der Maritz's Second Army and the Eighteenth Army under General Oskar von Hutier. The two generals have 14 divisions in the front line and nine in reserve. The Anglo-French attack is overwhelmingly successful with the Germans being forced back some 10 miles (16 km).

There are also more worrying signs for the future of the German Army: some front-line units have simply fled the fighting without putting up much resistance. Others, some 15,000, have quickly surrendered. When news of this reaches General Erich Ludendorff, the deputy chief of the General Staff, he calls August 8 the "Black Day of the German Army." Matters do not improve. The following day many more German troops are made prisoner.

On August 10 the focus of the Amiens Offensive shifts to the south of the German-held salient. Here, General Georges Humbert's French Third Army moves toward Montdidier, forcing the Germans to abandon the town and thus permitting the reopening of the Amiens to Paris railroad.

The first stage of the offensive is brought to a close in the face of increasing German resistance on the 12th. However, there is no disguising the scale of their defeat. German losses are 40,000 men killed or wounded and 33,000 taken prisoner. Anglo-French losses total some 46,000 troops.

AUGUST 21

WESTERN FRONT, *FRANCE*
General Sir Julian Byng's British Third Army opens the second phase of the Amiens Offensive, which began on August 8. Over the following days General Sir Henry Horne's British First Army and the French Tenth and Third Armies join in the attack. Ludendorff, who does not have the reserves to deal with these successive attacks, orders his forces to pull back from the salient to the east of Amiens and the Lys salient to the north. In effect, this is a general retreat.

AUGUST 30

WESTERN FRONT, *FRANCE*
The First Army of the General John Pershing's American Expeditionary Force moves into position around the German-held St. Mihiel salient to the south of Verdun along the Meuse River. Together with the French II Colonial Corps, the First Army will launch an attack on the position in mid-September.

▼ *The opening of the attack on St. Mihiel – three US infantrymen advance by one of their wounded colleagues.*

▲ *US gunners deploy German artillery pieces against their former owners during the attack on St. Mihiel.*

AUGUST 30–SEPTEMBER 2

WESTERN FRONT, *FRANCE*
The German withdrawal from the salient east of Amiens is threatened by repeated attacks by Anglo-French forces. Australian and New Zealand troops force their way across the Somme River, capturing Péronne and Mont St. Quentin. The subsequent capture of Quéant by the Canadian Corps on September 2 forces the Germans to consider withdrawing to the Hindenburg Line, from where they launched their spring offensive during the previous March.

SEPTEMBER 3–10

WESTERN FRONT, *FRANCE*
Closely pursued by Anglo-French forces, the German complete their withdrawal from Amiens and re-occupy the Hindenburg Line. The British are unable to continue their attacks due to a lack of reserves and the Amiens Offensive is brought to a close. The British and French have suffered some 42,000 casualties, but the Germans have sustained more than 100,000 losses, including 30,000 prisoners. General Erich Ludendorff, the chief of the German General Staff, becomes convinced that Germany can no longer win the war.

SEPTEMBER 8

WESTERN FRONT, *FRANCE*
General Erich Ludendorff, who is expecting a major US–French attack, begins to withdraw German forces from the St. Mihiel salient to the southeast of Verdun.

SEPTEMBER 12–16

WESTERN FRONT, *FRANCE*
The American Expeditionary Corps' First Army and the French II Colonial Corps launch an attack on the salient at St. Mihiel to the south of Verdun. It has been held continuously by the Germans since 1914. The advance is led by the First Army's I and IV Corps, which advance into the southern face of the salient, and V Corps, which

SEPTEMBER 14

moves against its west face. The French II Colonial Corps is positioned between the US forces.

The attack begins in thick fog and is supported by 600 aircraft commanded by US Colonel William Mitchell, a staunch advocate of the value of air power. The attackers are facing nine German divisions in the front line and a further five held in reserve. However, German resistance collapses on the first day with the US attacks from the south and west linking up at the village of Hattonchâtel. By the 16th the entire salient has been reduced.

The US troops capture some 15,000 German prisoners and 250 guns at a cost of 7000 casualties. Although General John Pershing, the commander of the American Expeditionary Force, could have continued the offensive, he has begun to transfer his forces away from St. Mihiel in preparation for the forthcoming offensive in the Meuse–Argonne sector of the Western Front.

SEPTEMBER 14

EASTERN FRONT, *RUSSIA*
Turkish forces occupy Baku, an important oil-producing center in the Caucasus, forcing a British force commanded by General L.C. Dunsterville to withdraw.

▼ *Oil-production platforms at Baku in Russia, which was targeted for capture by Britain, Germany, and Turkey.*

SEPTEMBER 15

BALKANS, *GREECE*
France's General Franchet d'Esperey, who has been in overall command in the theater since July, launches his large multinational force known as the "Allied Army of the Orient" against the Bulgarians.

The attack, which becomes known as the Battle of the Vardar River, is spearheaded by the Serbian First and Second Armies. The Bulgarian forces are split on the 25th and Skopje falls on the 29th. Bulgarian forces begin to collapse under the pressure.

▲ *Serbian troops advance against the disintegrating Bulgarians, who will be forced into headlong retreat.*

SEPTEMBER 19–21

MIDDLE EAST, *PALESTINE*
British General Sir Edmund Allenby opens what becomes known as the Battle of Megiddo against the Turkish forces in Palestine. The Turks have three armies, the Eighth, Seventh, and Fourth, commanded by German General Liman von Sanders. His 44,000 men are holding a long line stretching inland from just north of Jaffa on the Mediterranean coast to the valley of the Jordan River. However, they are demoralized and short of supplies, chiefly because Arab forces under British liaison officer T.E. Lawrence have been disrupting the Hejaz railroad along which their supplies flow. Allenby commands 69,000 troops.

Allenby has launched diversionary probes against the Turkish forces in the Jordan Valley, but actually intends to strike along the coast. To this end, real troops concentrations and supply dumps have been camouflaged in this sector, while nearer the valley dummy dumps and camps have been constructed.

Allenby intends his forces on the coast (some 35,000 men and 350 artillery pieces) to push through the Turkish defenders (8000 men and 130 artillery pieces) and then swing eastward, thereby cutting the northward line of retreat of the Turkish Seventh and Eighth Armies.

▶ *British cavalrymen, part of Sir Edmund Allenby's Desert Mounted Corps, pursue the Turks retreating through Palestine.*

The British offensive begins at 0430 hours, with Allenby's artillery opening fire along a 65-mile (104-km) front. This is followed by an attack along the Mediterranean coast, which quickly breaks through the overstretched Turkish line. This gap is exploited by Allenby's Desert Mounted Corps, which races northward in the direction of Megiddo and then swings eastward for the Jordan River. British aircraft bomb railroad lines and Turkish headquarters, effectively destroying their communications system. The Desert Mounted Corps covers 70 miles (112 km) in three days to secure its objectives.

Jerad Pasha's Turkish Seventh Army is virtually destroyed in the enveloping attack and Mustafa Kemal's Eighth Army attempts to escape eastward. Both are harried by British ground-attack aircraft. The retreat turns into a route and some 25,000 Turkish prisoners are captured. The Turkish Fourth Army, positioned around the Jordan Valley, stages a withdrawal northward in the direction of Damascus, but there is no hiding the scale of Allenby's victory. There is no longer any significant Turkish force available to oppose his advance northward toward Damascus and beyond.

SEPTEMBER 26–OCTOBER 3

WESTERN FRONT, *FRANCE*
The First Army of General John Pershing's American Expeditionary Force launches what becomes known as the Meuse–Argonne Offensive to the north of Verdun. It is one of several attacks planned by France's Marshal Ferdinand Foch to drive the Germans from the defenses of the Hindenburg Line and precipitate their surrender.

Pershing's First Army, some one million men split between three corps, is holding a front of some 17 miles (27 km) from Forges on the Meuse River into the Argonne Forest. To the left of the First Army is General H.J.E. Gouraud's French Fourth Army. The US forces are opposed by General Max von Gallwitz's Army Group, while the French are facing Crown Prince Frederick William's Army Group. The US and French deploy 37 divisions, while German forces

▼ *US infantrymen and French officers take a break during the fighting amid the remains of an Argonne wood.*

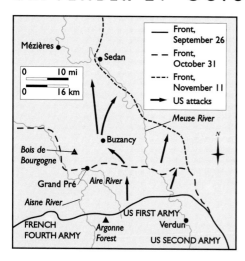

▲ The joint US and French offensive directed toward Sedan from north of Verdun along the Meuse River.

comprise 24 divisions. The Germans hold three strongly-fortified defensive lines in difficult terrain.

The attack begins at 0525 hours and the US forces make rapid gains, advancing some 10 miles (16 km) in the first five days of the offensive. French progress is somewhat less. The Germans rush reinforcements to the sector and slow the pace of the advance, although by the end of the first phase of the battle, on October 3, two of the three German defensive lines have been taken.

▼ Indian lancers and their British officers pose for the camera during a break in their pursuit of the Turks in Palestine.

SEPTEMBER 27–OCTOBER 4

WESTERN FRONT, *FRANCE*
Elements of Field Marshal Sir Douglas Haig's British Expeditionary Force and French units initiate part of French Marshal Ferdinand Foch's plan to crush the German forces on the Western Front. The aim is to attack toward Cambrai and St. Quentin with 41 divisions and break through the Hindenburg Line.

The offensive is led by the British First Army under General Sir Henry Horne and General Sir Julian Byng's Third Army, which break through the German positions, cross the Canal du Nord and advance to with three miles (5 km) of Cambrai on the first day.

▲ Canadian troops and German prisoners watch the continuing fighting around the Canal du Nord.

Elements of the Third Army finally occupy the town's western suburbs on the 30th.

On the 28th the Group of Armies of Flanders under Belgium's King Albert also joins in the general offensive, attacking from around Ypres against Crown Prince Rupprecht of Bavaria's Army Corps. Albert's British, French, and Belgian units quickly evict the Germans from the high ground around Ypres and begin advancing along the low-lying coast, although their progress is slowed by the waterlogged conditions.

On the 29th General Sir Henry Rawlinson's British Fourth Army joins in the attack, supported by General Eugene Debeney's French First Army and several US divisions. Under

▶ *Medical staff evacuate two wounded British soldiers by horse litter during the final push through Palestine.*

increasing pressure General Max von Boehn's Germany Army Group is forced to complete the abandonment of the Hindenburg Line on October 4. This precipitates the retreat of other German forces, which form a hasty defensive line along the Selle River, some 10 miles (16 km) from their original positions.

SEPTEMBER 30

POLITICS, *BULGARIA*
Following the collapse of its forces in the Balkans, the government agrees to an armistice, the first of the Central Powers to do so.

OCTOBER 1

MIDDLE EAST, *SYRIA*
Capitalizing on their recent overwhelming victory against the Turks at the Battle of Megiddo in September, forces commanded by British General Sir Edmund Allenby enter the capital Damascus, taking 20,000 Turkish prisoners. They are led by the Australian Third Light Horse.

Their arrival has been preceded by Arab guerrilla forces. The Arabs, despite British worries, take charge of the running of Damascus. A day later Beirut is captured and Aleppo, some 200 miles (320 km) to the north, falls on the 25th.

OCTOBER 5

MIDDLE EAST, *LEBANON*
French naval forces occupy Beirut as a base for expanding their influence in the Middle East. It has been agreed that France will take over the former Turkish

province of Syria at the end of the war. However, this secret Anglo-French understanding will be disputed by the leaders of the Arab forces that have been waging a guerrilla war against the Turks.

OCTOBER 6

POLITICS, *GERMANY*
The German chancellor, Prince Max of Baden, contacts US President Woodrow

Wilson and requests an armistice based on Wilson's 14 Points outlined the previous January. However, it is made clear that there will be no negotiations until the removal of the country's military leadership.

OCTOBER 14

POLITICS, *TURKEY*
The Committee of Union and Progress, its members better known as the "Young Turks," resigns as the country's military situation worsens. The Young Turks are a nationalistic group dedicated to reviving Turkey's position as the region's leading power and have held effective power since 1908. A new government headed by Ahmed Izzet Pasha seeks an armistice.

OCTOBER 14–31

WESTERN FRONT, *FRANCE*
The second phase of the US and French Meuse–Argonne Offensive begins on the 14th, following a period of reorganization in which the US forces involved in the battle have been divided between two new armies: the First under General Hunter Liggett and

◀ *American artillerymen pound German positions with their six-inch (155-mm) howitzers, Meuse–Argonne.*

▲ *Italian troops take charge of an abandoned Austro-Hungarian position during the Battle of Vittorio Veneto.*

◄ *Growing evidence of the collapse of German morale on the Western Front – prisoners captured by the British.*

the fighting, which dies down at the end of the month, but Pershing"s troops have broken through the German third and final line of defense. The Meuse–Argonne Offensive is to be renewed at the beginning of November after a period of rest and reinforcement.

OCTOBER 17–31

WESTERN FRONT, *FRANCE*
British force cut through the German defenders holding the line of the Selle River, taking 20,000 prisoners. By the end of the month they have pushed the Germans back behind the Scheldt River on a 20-mile (32-km) front. To maintain the pressure on the retreating Germans, the Group of Armies of Flanders under Belgium's King Albert also continues to attack from around Ypres.

OCTOBER 23

WESTERN FRONT, *ITALY*
The Italian commander-in-chief, General Armando Diaz, launches an offensive against the Austro-Hungarian forces in northern Italy from his line along the Piave River. His aim is to use

the Second commanded by General Robert Lee Bullard. General John Pershing has overall command of the two armies.

Liggett's First Army advances northward at a steady pace in the face of intense German resistance, while

Bullard's Second Army moves to the northeast between the Meuse and Moselle Rivers. The Germans are forced to rush reinforcements from other threatened sectors of the Western Front to counter the French and Americans. All suffer heavy losses in

his Fourth Army to penetrate the center of the Austro-Hungarian line in the vicinity of Mount Grappa, while the Eighth Army, supported by the mainly Anglo-French Tenth and Twelfth Armies, is to make for the town of Vittorio Veneto.

The Italian forces committed to what becomes known as the Battle of Vittorio Veneto consist of 57 divisions, including three British and two French, backed by 7700 artillery pieces. The Austro-Hungarians, whose morale is already badly shaken, deploy 52 divisions and 6030 artillery pieces.

The Austro-Hungarians are able to block the advance from Mount Grappa by the Italian Fourth Army, but the key part of the battle is around Vittorio Veneto. Initially, the battle goes well

▲ *Turkish cavalrymen pull back in the face of the British drive from Baghdad toward Mosul.*

for the Austro-Hungarian Sixth Army, which blocks the advance of the Italian Eighth Army as it tries to cross the Piave River. However, the Twelfth Army, commanded by French General Jean Graziani, gains a foothold on the Austro-Hungarian side of the Piave, as does British General Earl of Cavan's Tenth Army. By October 28 both bridgeheads are secure and the Anglo-French forces are exploiting their successes.

MIDDLE EAST, *MESOPOTAMIA*
Taking advantage of what is seen as Turkey's imminent collapse, British forces under General A.S. Cobbe

advance from Baghdad with the intention of seizing the oil fields around Mosul to the north. They are opposed by General Ismael Hakki's Turkish Tigris Group. The Turks retreat slowly and make a stand at Sharqat. After a two-day battle on October 28–29, Hakki is forced to surrender his 11,300 troops and 51 artillery pieces. Cobbe continues his march on Mosul.

OCTOBER 26

POLITICS, *GERMANY*
General Erich Ludendorff is replaced as deputy chief of the General Staff by General Wilhelm Groener. Ludendorff

▼ *A lone British soldier stands watch over a batch of Austro-Hungarian prisoners taken at Vittorio Veneto.*

has recently quarreled with his superior Field Marshal Paul von Hindenburg and has suggested that Germany seeks an armistice. It is clear that Groener shares Ludendorff's views.

OCTOBER 27

AIR WAR, *WESTERN FRONT*

Canadian pilot William Barker survives a crash-landing after inadvertently running into a flight of 60 German aircraft. Although totally outnumbered, he survives a one-sided battle lasting 40 minutes in which his Sopwith Snipe fighter is hit by enemy bullets some 300 times before being forced down. Barker has, however, downed three enemy aircraft during the encounter, taking his tally of air victories to 52.

OCTOBER 29

POLITICS, *GERMANY*

Sailors of the German High Seas Fleet mutiny at Kiel's naval base following suggestions by their newly-appointed commander, Admiral Franz von Hipper, that the navy should make one last "death ride" against the British Home

▲ *Wounded Italians receive front-line medical aid at the height of the Battle of Vittorio Veneto.*

▼ *US troops fight their way through the remains of a wood during their ongoing offensive in the Meuse–Argonne region. The fighting was intense and cost the American Expeditionary Force some 117,000 men killed or wounded.*

Fleet. Some 40,000 naval personnel are involved in the mutiny and they take over Kiel itself on November 4. Their actions sparks risings across Germany, prompting the government to sue for peace before there is a revolution.

OCTOBER 30

POLITICS, *TURKEY*

The government agrees to an armistice following negotiations on the Greek island of Mudros. Under its terms hostilities end, Constantinople is to be controlled by the victorious powers, and all Turkish forces must withdraw from the Trans-Caucasus region.

WESTERN FRONT, *ITALY*

In the ongoing Battle of Vittorio Veneto, the British, French, and Italian drive against the Austro-Hungarians continues. They are able to capture Vittorio Veneto, effectively dividing the Austro-Hungarian forces in northern Italy. After a week of fighting the offensive has penetrated to a maximum depth of 15 miles (24 km) along a front of 35 miles (56 km).

It is clear that the Austro-Hungarian forces are disintegrating. Italian troops reach the line of the Tagliamento River on November 2, while in the Trentino British and French forces are heading rapidly for Trent. The fighting officially ends on November 3. The Austro-Hungarians have had some 300,000 troops taken prisoner, while Italian casualties total just 38,000 men.

NOVEMBER 1

WESTERN FRONT, *FRANCE*

The third and final stage of the US-led Meuse–Argonne Offensive opens. The US First Army commanded by General Hunter Liggett resumes its northward

▲ *German troops are forced to pull back from the Western Front in the face of a series of large enemy offensives.*

advance and punches a way through the German defenses at Buzancy, thereby allowing the French Fourth Army to make a major crossing of the Aisne River.

German resistance is collapsing and the US forces move rapidly along the valley of the Meuse River in the direction of Sedan, which falls on the 6th. Although there is later progress in the offensive, it ends on the 11th with the signing of the armistice. The Meuse–Argonne

Offensive has been successful, but at a high cost – some 117,000 US troops have been posted as casualties since its opening on September 26.

MIDDLE EAST, *MESOPOTAMIA*
British cavalry units, part of General A.S. Cobbe's force advancing northward from Baghdad, arrive outside Mosul, center of the region's oil fields. Although an armistice has been agreed with Turkey, Cobbe is ordered to march into Mosul, which still has a Turkish garrison. The garrison's commander, Halil Pasha, finally agrees to abandon the town to the British during the middle of the month. The occupation of Mosul signals the end of the campaign.

SEA WAR, *ADRIATIC*
The flagship of the Austro-Hungarian fleet, the dreadnought battleship *Viribus Unitis*, is sunk during an Italian attack.

NOVEMBER 2

POLITICS, *LITHUANIA*
The Lithuanian Taryba, council of state, repeals the German-sponsored appointment of Prince Wilhelm of Urach as monarch and announces the establishment of an independent republic. However, Bolshevik forces are preparing to take back this former Russian province.

NOVEMBER 3

POLITICS, *AUSTRIA-HUNGARY*
Following the recent catastrophic defeat at Vittorio Veneto, the authorities seek an armistice on the same day that an enemy naval expedition captures the port of Trieste in the north Adriatic.

The armistice is agreed the next day. It will fuel ethnic tensions between the many groups within the Austro-Hungarian Empire, which will break apart over the following months as its various provinces strive to gain their full independence.

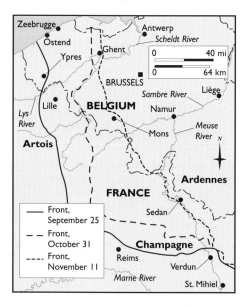

▲ *Between September and the armistice on November 11 the German forces on the Western Front gradually collapsed. Although some troops put up fierce resistance, many – most war-weary – surrendered or headed for home.*

NOVEMBER 7

POLITICS, *GERMANY*
A delegation headed by Matthias Erzberger meets with Marshal Ferdinand Foch to discuss terms for an armistice. Among Foch's demands are that German forces must immediately evacuate all occupied territory and Alsace-Lorraine; surrender substantial

amounts of military supplies (including 5000 artillery pieces and 25,000 machine guns); evacuate German territory west of the Rhine River; allow three zones on the east bank of the Rhine to be occupied; surrender all of its submarines; and intern all other warships at ports indicated by the victors. The discussions, which last four days, take place in a rail carriage at Compiègne, northeast of Paris.

NOVEMBER 8

WESTERN FRONT, *FRANCE*
Forces under the command of Britain's Field Marshal Sir Douglas Haig complete the crossing of the Scheldt River in the face of crumbling German resistance and are close to occupying Ghent and Mons.

NOVEMBER 9

POLITICS, *GERMANY*
It is announced that Kaiser Wilhelm II has abdicated. He goes into exile in the Netherlands the next day. The victorious powers request halfheartedly that he be tried as a war criminal. A member of the chancellor's cabinet, Philipp Scheidemann, announces the creation of a republic. A new government and chancellor, Friedrich Ebert,

▼ *Germany's Kaiser Wilhelm II (third from right) and his staff head for exile in the Netherlands after his abdication.*

are appointed the next day. However, Germany is politically unstable, with various left- and rightwing political factions vying for control.

NOVEMBER 11

POLITICS, *EUROPE*
The armistice on the Western Front, negotiated over four days at Compiègne, comes into force at 1100 hours. It had been finalized just six hours earlier.
POLITICS, *AUSTRIA-HUNGARY*
Emperor Karl renounces his position as head of state, a move that prompts the creation of the separate Republics of Austria and Hungary the next day. These political upheavals spell the end of the multi-ethnic Austro-Hungarian Empire as its other various national groups will also clamor for autonomy.
POLITICS, *POLAND*
German troops are expelled from the former Russian province, whose independence has been recognized by Russia since March 1917. The commander-in-chief of the Polish forces who had fought for the Germans and Austro-Hungarians during World War I, Józef Pilsudski, becomes leader of independent Poland. His

▶ *People take to the streets of Paris to celebrate the signing of the armistice.*

most urgent task is to build up Poland's armed forces as large parts of the country are claimed by several of its neighbours, not least Russia.

Within days of coming to power he will be faced with an attack by Ukrainian forces, which invade, capture Lvov, and proclaim the establishment of the West Ukrainian Republic. It will take six months of fighting for Pilsudski to re-establish Polish authority over the region.

POLITICS, *TURKEY*
The recently-appointed government of Ahmed Isset Pasha falls.

NOVEMBER 12

SEA WAR, *MEDITERRANEAN*
Several allied vessels sail through the Turkish-controlled Dardanelles and anchor at Constantinople, the capital, the following day. Their presence reflects one of the clauses of the armistice agreed on the Greek island of Mudros on October 30.

NOVEMBER 13

POLITICS, *GERMANY*
Against a background of growing domestic political unrest, Bavaria's regent, Prince Otto, abdicates. Other monarchs of the states that make up Germany follow:

King Friedrich August III of Saxony on the same day and King Wilhelm II of Württemberg on the 30th.

NOVEMBER 14

POLITICS, *CZECHOSLOVAKIA*
Czechoslovakia, formerly part of the collapsing Austro-Hungarian Empire,

▲ *Marshal Jósef Pilsudski (seated) became independent Poland's first head of state.*

becomes an independent republic. The new state's first president is named as Tomás Masaryk.

NOVEMBER 15

POLITICS, *RUSSIA*
German troops leave the Ukraine, where they had been supporting the anti-Bolshevik "White" Russian General Pavel Skoropadski. However, Skoropadski is soon overthrown by Ukrainian socialists led by General Simon Petlyura. There is growing resistance to the Bolshevik revolutionaries, which is supported by Britain, France, and the United States.

NOVEMBER 16

POLITICS, *HUNGARY*
Count Mihály Károlyi becomes the first president of the newly-independent republic.

NOVEMBER 17

POLITICS, *GERMANY*
Under the terms of the recently-agreed armistice, German forces begin to leave those parts of France and Belgium that they still occupy.

EASTERN FRONT, *RUSSIA*
Turkish troops are forced to abandon the oil-producing center of Baku on the Caspian Sea following the arrival

NOVEMBER 18

Russia." He joins forces with the Czech Legion and enters eastern Russia to confront the Bolsheviks.

NOVEMBER 21

SEA WAR, *NORTH SEA*
British Admiral Sir David Beatty accepts the surrender of the German High Seas Fleet. His message is unambiguous: "The German flag will be hauled down at sunset and will not be hoisted again without permission." The fleet will later move to anchorages at Scapa Flow in the Orkneys off the coast of northern Scotland.

NOVEMBER 25

AFRICA, *NORTHERN RHODESIA*
Colonel Paul von Lettow-Vorbeck finally surrenders at Abercorn, having belatedly been informed of the end of the war in Europe. His troops, who have waged an outstanding guerrilla war against vastly superior forces (some 130,000 men), consist at the end of 175 Europeans and 3000 askaris.

of a British naval force. They had taken Baku from the British during the previous September.

NOVEMBER 18

POLITICS, *RUSSIA*
A leader of anti-Bolshevik forces, Admiral Alexander Kolchak, a former commander of Russia's Black Sea Fleet, seizes control in Omsk, Siberia, and proclaims himself "Supreme Ruler of

NOVEMBER 26

POLITICS, *MONTENEGRO*
The assembly of the country, which has recently been liberated by the Serbians, announces that King Nicholas has been deposed and that it will unite with Serbia.

DECEMBER 1

POLITICS, *GERMANY*
British, French, and US forces move into

the German Rhineland in accordance with the armistice agreement made on November 11.

POLITICS, *SERBIA*

The Serbian authorities, with the support of Montenegro and the former Austro-Hungarian provinces of Croatia and Slovenia, announce a political union. It will lead to the formation of the Federal Republic of Yugoslavia.

DECEMBER 9

POLITICS, *GERMANY*

Various parts of the German Rhineland are occupied: the British establish themselves at Cologne; the French at Mainz; and the Americans at Koblenz.

DECEMBER 12

POLITICS, *FINLAND*

General Karl von Mannerheim replaces

Pehr Svinhufvud as head of the provisional government. However, skirmishes between Mannerheim's forces and the pro-Bolshevik "Red Guard" continue.

DECEMBER 13

POLITICS, *UNITED STATES*

In a landmark event Woodrow Wilson arrives in France, becoming the first US President to travel outside the United States. He will also visit Britain and Italy, before playing a key role in the negotiations that will lead to the peace treaties that end World War I. He plans that the settlements should adhere to his 14-Point Peace Program.

DECEMBER 18

POLITICS, *FRANCE*

French troops occupy Odessa on the Black Sea, so that supplies can be sent to Ukrainians opposing the Bolshevik government, which is striving to consolidate its influence throughout Russia amid growing resistance.

◀ *Warships of the German High Seas Fleet at anchor in Scapa Flow as part of the armistice terms.*

COUNTING THE COST

When World War I ended the scale of destruction and the loss of life was unparalleled in human history. Unlike previous wars, the fighting had been conducted, to a lesser or greater degree, almost constantly. From August 1914 until November 1918 rarely a day went by when there was no military activity.

Equally, the ferocity of the fighting, chiefly due to the nature of the predominantly trench-bound war and the destructive weapons employed by the warring nations, was previously unknown. It should be noted that all of the following figures for casualties are roughly-accurate estimates.

Out of the 65 million troops mobilized by all of the combatant nations, some eight million were killed and a further 21 million wounded. With regard to the Central Powers, the figures were: Germany, 11 million mobilized and 1.8 million dead; Austria-Hungary, 7.8 million and 922,000; Turkey, 2.8 million and 325,000; and Bulgaria, 1.2 million and 76,000.

The figures for those opposing the Central Powers were: France, 8.4 million mobilized and 1.36 million dead; the British Empire, 8.9 million and 908,000; Russia, 12 million and 1.7 million; Italy, 5.6 million and 462,000; the United States, 4.3 million and 50,000; Belgium, 267,000 and 14,000; Serbia, 707,000 and 45,000; Montenegro, 50,000 and 3000; Romania, 750,000 and 335,000; Greece, 230,000 and 5000; Portugal, 100,000 and 7000; and Japan, 800,000 and 300.

The loss of life in combat was mirrored in civilian casualties on an also unparalleled scale. Some 6.6 million died, chiefly in Russia and Turkey, which accounted for roughly two-thirds of the total. In the case of Turkey many of its 2.1 million civilian casualties were ethnic Armenians killed in Turkey by Turkish forces in their campaign of genocide against the Christian minority.

The fighting left both physical and mental scars on those who survived. Many ordinary soldiers suffered deep psychological trauma, what was termed "shell shock." Soldiers in 1914–18 had to face the threat of death or mutilation like warriors of earlier times. However, unlike their ancestors who might be in physical danger for a few hours at a time during a series of infrequent and usually brief battles, World War I soldiers faced a greater variety of dangers 24 hours a day for weeks – if not months – at a time.

AFTERMATH

The end of World War I marked a dramatic transformation of the world political order, although this was not immediately recognized by many of those in power. Three Europe-based empires, those of Austria-Hungary, Germany, and Russia, had collapsed, and their prewar rivals, Britain and France, were deeply scarred by the war and greatly impoverished. Equally, Turkey, the former leading power in the southern Balkans and Middle East, was a shadow of its former self. The country was weakened by unrest and much of it was under Greek occupation that flared into bitter war between 1920–22.

There were new players on the international stage, principally the United States, which was – tentatively and not without domestic disquiet – being thrust into a worldwide role, chiefly in the Pacific but also in Europe, and recently-modernized, expansionist Japan, which coveted an empire across the Pacific and in China.

CONTINUED FIGHTING

The armistice signed on 11 November 1918 ended World War I, but it did not bring peace to Europe. Almost immediately, fighting broke out in the former provinces of both Russia and Austria-Hungary. Some of the conflicts revolved around the territorial demands of the newly-independent states of Eastern Europe.

For example, the recently-formed state of Poland claimed Russian lands to the east of the Bug River, where there was a large Polish population. Poland launched a pre-emptive strike against Bolshevik Russia in April 1920 and was victorious. The Bolsheviks agreed Poland's territorial claims, but did not view the matter as settled for all time. Equally, the Bolsheviks believed in exporting revolution to other European countries and had an agenda for taking back all of those territories they had been forced to give up following the German-imposed Treaty of Brest-Litovsk in 1918.

Other immediate postwar disputes in Eastern Europe were internal, involving left- and rightwing factions within individual countries. Generally, the leftwing groups were supported by or followers of the revolutionary Bolsheviks in Russia, while some rightwing groups enjoyed a degree of support from the victors of World

▼ *A British tank in Cologne in 1919. To many Germans the occupation was a gross humiliation.*

▲ The victorious statesmen who defined the terms of the peace treaties that concluded World War I. From left to right: Italian Prime Minister Vittorio Orlando, British Prime Minister David Lloyd George, the prime minister of France, Georges Clemenceau, and US President Woodrow Wilson.

War I. Many of the newly-independent countries of Eastern Europe were also rent by ethnic divisions, despite the intentions of the peacemakers to establish nation-states. For example, parts of Austria, Czechoslovakia, and Poland contained large numbers of ethnic Germans. The ethnically-diverse Balkans, including Hungary and Romania, was an almost intractable problem. States were created, essentially conforming to the provinces of the defunct Austro-Hungarian Empire, but they were far from the ethnically-cohesive nations envisaged by US President Woodrow Wilson's 14-Point Peace Program, on which the settlements were based.

A NEW POLITICAL GEOGRAPHY
The peace treaties concluding World War I had, in reality, created a patch-work of small, weak, and internally-divided states across Eastern Europe and the Balkans. The intention had been to prevent the creation of a large new power bloc that might embark on wars of aggression by establishing a number of strong, independent, and united states. In retrospect, the peace left Eastern Europe fundamentally unstable. Its states were mutually suspicious and politically unstable. Skilled rightwing politicians were able to exploit this in the 1920s and 1930s by championing aggres-sive nationalism.

Two pointers to the future came in the early 1920s. In Italy a band of national-ists, the "Blackshirts," led by Benito Mussolini stage-managed the so-called "March on Rome" on October 28, 1922. The king

▶ Benito Mussolini, leader of the Italian fascists known as "Blackshirts," who gained power in 1922.

and government were forced to surrender their authority to Mussolini, who instigated a virtual reign of terror to sweep away any political opponents In November 1923 a fringe rightwing group in Germany attempted a similar, if less successful, coup against the Bavarian government in Munich. It failed and the group's leader, Adolf Hitler, was imprisoned.

Elsewhere, the victors of World War I attempted to reverse the outcome of the Russian Revolution, backing the "White" Russians against the Bolsheviks – but to little affect. The Russian Civil War, which lasted from 1918 to 1921, saw the Red Army defeat the divided "White" Russians and secure the dominance of the Bolshevik regime, which looked to control Eastern Europe.

IDEALS AND SELF-INTEREST

While there was ongoing political turmoil in Eastern Europe, the peacemakers gathered in France, chiefly to define the nature of the peace with Germany. They were far for united. US President Woodrow Wilson, whose 14-Point Peace Program formed the basis on which the negotiations would take place, had to tread a fine line. While he was concerned to establish an open

world order that would prevent such bloodletting occurring again, he had also to take into account the demands of the British, French, and Italian delegates, some of whom wanted to extract draconian recompense from Germany, which they considered to be the instigator of the conflict. Nor were the victorious colonial powers going to give their colonies self-determination, a key clause of the 14 Points – they also wanted Germany's overseas possessions divided between them.

The French and British did get their way with regard to recompense and Germany's colonies. The Treaty of Versailles, signed in July 1919 and taking force in 1920, reduced German territory at home and abroad (where colonies became mandated territories run by the victors), limited the postwar German armed forces to a rump designed for nothing more than home defense, implemented extreme reparations, and, most galling of all, forced Germany to accept responsibility for the outbreak of World War I. Nevertheless, some commentators regarded the treaty as being too lenient; Wilson, in fact, fought successfully to prevent the wholesale dismemberment of western Germany.

▲ *Hitler and other leading members of the Nazi Party commemorate the failed Munich coup of 1923.*

▼ *Members of the German rightwing Freikorps bury a comrade killed in fighting against leftwingers.*

However, Germany was reduced to a shadow of its former self. It was smaller, believed itself to be defenseless, was industrially weak, and saddled with an enormous debt for reparations. Worse, the country had turned in on itself, with left-and rightwing factions vying for power, while the German National Assembly based in Weimar, strove with little success to maintain a semblance of order.

The assembly, formed in February 1919, had been born out of the street-fighting of 1918–19, in which rightwing groups of ex-soldiers (Freikorps) successfully battled to prevent leftwing groups from taking control of the country. Among the leftwing casualties of this were Karl Liebknecht and Rosa Luxemburg. Both were murdered by the Freikorps and their bodies dumped in a Berlin canal. The Weimar Republic was generally unpopular with both the Freikorps and the masses, particularly after a mild economic recovery beginning in 1923 was snubbed out by the Great Depression of 1929.

WILSON THWARTED
Wilson did succeed in creating an international body to oversee the conduct of international affairs and to arbitrate on disputes between member states. He also hoped that it would modify the more punitive provisions of Versailles in the future. The League of Nations, which began on January 10,

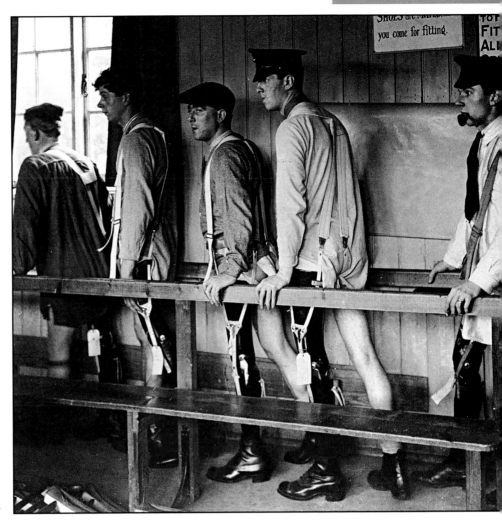

▲ The human cost of World War I, seen here as mutilated ex-servicemen learn to walk again, was matched by deep psychological traumas in many of those who had survived the fighting.

1920, attempted to curtail conflict, but it lacked teeth, not least because few of its leading members were wholly willing to set aside their ambitions in the cause of international amity.

Remarkably, the United States did not join because Wilson was unwilling to accept Senate resolutions limiting the League's power, particularly relating to Article X of its charter, which obliged each member nation to defend all other nations from armed aggression or other threats to its independence. Indeed, Wilson, already exhausted by the Versailles talks, had to return to the United States to popularize his message with the electorate in the face of opposition from some US senators. His whirlwind tour was cut short on September 25, 1919. Shortly thereafter, he suffered a thrombosis that left him debilitated and allowed his political opponents to block ratification.

World War I also had a deep impact on ordinary people, those who had lived through the conflict. Many believed that the world could never survive such a bloodbath again. Most

families had lost loved ones, often in dreadful circumstances. Some believed that such terrible wars should never occur again and carried this conviction with them when they rose to political prominence in the interwar period, believing that discussion and compromise rather than armed might could resolve disputes. Their mistake was to believe that other politicians, who themselves had fought in World War I, shared their views. As events in the 1930s showed, this was not the case.

World War I ended one set of problems, chiefly the frictions between the then world powers. However, the peace treaties that were implemented to prevent such carnage set the stage for World War II, 20 years later. That conflict, involving virtually the same countries, would extract a butcher's bill of approximately 45 million dead.

INDEX

Entries in **bold** refer to major battles or offensives; page numbers in *italics* refer to picture captions.

ACKNOWLEDGMENTS

Robert Hunt Library, pages: 1, 2–3, 4–5, 6, 7(top and bottom), 8, 9, 10(both),
12(top right and bottom), 13(bottom), 14–15, 18(bottom), 21, 22(top left and
right), 23, 24(top), 26–27, 28(bottom), 31(top and center), 33(top), 38–39(top),
40(bottom), 42–43(top), 46–47(bottom), 49(bottom), 50(bottom), 52(top),
55(top), 58–59(bottom), 62(top left), 64(top), 65(top), 66–67(top), 68(top),
69(center left), 74–75(top), 82, 83(center), 84(bottom), 86(both), 88(bottom),
90(bottom), 93(center and bottom), 94(bottom), 98–99(center), 100–01(bottom),
118(bottom), 119(bottom), 121(top and bottom), 122(top), 124(top and bottom
left), 126(top), 128–29, 131(top), 135(top), 136((top and bottom), 140–41(top and
bottom), 146(bottom), 148(top), 153(bottom), 154–56(top), 170–71(top),
184–85(bottom), 186–189(all).
Robert Hunt Library/Australian War Memorial, pages: 36(top), 144(bottom),
147(bottom).
Robert Hunt Library/Bapty, pages: 11(top), 46–47(top), 70(top), 150–51(top).
Robert Hunt Library/Bayerische Hauptstaatsarchiv, Munich, pages:
22–23(bottom), 39 (bottom), 101(top), 106(both), 128(bottom), 158(top).
Robert Hunt Library/Bibliotheque Nationale, Paris, pages: 20(top), 60(bottom),
73(bottom).
Robert Hunt Library/Bundesarchiv, pages: 7(center), 11(bottom), 51(top),
71(top), 83(top and bottom right), 139(bottom), 149(top), 153(top), 156–57(top),
159(bottom), 184(top), 184–85(top).
Robert Hunt Library/CAR, Warsaw, page: 183(top).
Robert Hunt Library/Central News, page: 19(bottom).
Robert Hunt Library/ECPA, pages: 87(bottom), 88(top), 118–19(top),
130–31(bottom), 138–39(bottom), 164–65(bottom), 166(bottom), 167(both),
171(top).
Robert Hunt Library/Faruk Kenc, page: 48(bottom).
Robert Hunt Library/Heeresgeschichtliches Museum, Vienna, pages:
102–03(top).
Robert Hunt Library/Imperial War Museum, London, pages: 12(top left),
13(top), 14(top left), 22–23(center), 25, 26(top and bottom), 27(top), 29(bottom),
30(top), 30–31(bottom), 32(top), 32–33(bottom), 34(top), 34–35(bottom), 35(top
and center), 36–37(bottom), 37(top), 38(top), 39(top), 40(top),
40–41(bottom), 41(top), 43(bottom), 44–45(top), 45(bottom), 46(bottom),
47(bottom), 48–49(bottom), 50(top), 51(bottom), 52(top), 52–53(bottom),
54(top), 55(top), 56–57(all five), 58–59(top), 60(top), 61(top), 62(top right),
62–63(bottom), 63(top), 64–65(bottom), 66(bottom), 67(bottom), 68–69(top),

71(bottom), 72–73(top), 74 (center), 74–75(bottom), 75(top), 76–77(all four),
78(top), 79(top), 80–81(all four), 84–85 (top), 85(center), 89(both), 90–91(top),
91(top), 92(top), 93(top), 94(top), 94–95(center), 95(bottom), 96–97(all three),
98(bottom), 99(top), 100(top), 101(bottom), 102(top), 102–03(bottom), 103(top
and center), 104(both), 105(bottom), 107(all three), 108–09(all three), 110(top),
112(bottom), 112–13(all four), 114–15(all three), 116–17(all three),
118–19(bottom), 120(bottom), 120–21(top), 122(bottom), 123(both), 124(bottom
right), 125(top), 126(bottom), 126–27(top), 127(both), 128(top), 129(top),
130(top), 131(bottom), 132–33(all four), 134(bottom), 135(both), 136(top),
139(top), 140(top), 141(bottom), 142–43(all four), 144(top and center), 145(both),
148–49(bottom), 150(bottom), 151(top and bottom), 152(both), 155(top and
bottom), 156(bottom), 157(bottom), 158(both), 161(bottom left), 162–63(all four),
166(center), 168(bottom), 170(top), 170–71(bottom), 172(top), 174–75(all four),
176(top and bottom), 178(left), 178–79(top), 179(bottom), 180(top), 181(top),
182(bottom), 182–83.
Robert Hunt Library/Kriegsarchiv, Vienna, pages: 20(bottom), 24–25, 36(center),
44(bottom), 49(top), 54–56(bottom), 61(bottom), 67(top), 69(bottom),
70(bottom), 78–79(bottom), 83(bottom left), 91(bottom), 95(top), 147(top),
179(top).
Robert Hunt Library/Military Museum, Belgrade, pages: 42–43(bottom).
Robert Hunt Library/Musée de la Guerre, Vincennes, pages: 32(bottom),
87(bottom).
Robert Hunt Library/Museo del Risorgimento, Milan, pages: 72(top), 105(top).
Robert Hunt Library/Museo Storilo Navale, Venice, page: 166(top).
Robert Hunt Library/National Library of Ireland, page: 92(bottom).
Robert Hunt Library/Naval Ministry, Rome, page: 84(top).
Robert Hunt Library/Roger Viollet, pages: 14(bottom), 16–17, 17, 18(top),
19(top).
Robert Hunt Library/US Library of Congress, page: 111(top).
Robert Hunt Library/US National Archives, pages: 72(bottom), 110(bottom),
134–5(top), 135(bottom), 146(top), 154(bottom), 160(bottom), 160–61(top),
161(bottom right), 164(top), 164–65(center), 165(top), 168(top), 169(both),
172(bottom), 172–73(top), 173(top), 177(top), 180–81(bottom).
Robert Hunt Library/US Naval Academy, pages: 176–77(bottom).
Robert Hunt Library/Vereenigde Fotobureaux, Amsterdam, pages: 20–21.
Robert Hunt Library/VHU, Prague, pages: 28–29, 52(bottom), 68–69(bottom),
98(top).